To Stan Quin
My Best Buddy.

Arnold P. Hanson

BEARS, SKUNKS & WILDCATS

Gerald Peter Hansen
Lieutenant Commander, USN (Retired)

JERMAR
PRESS

Jermar Press
Albany, Oregon

ISBN Number 978-0-9705401-2-4
Library of Congress Control Number: 2004118306

Hansen, Gerald Peter
Bears, Skunks & Wildcats

Cover and Text Design: MagicGraphix, West Fork, AR

Distributed to the trade by: Biblio Distribution, Lanham, MD a division of National Book Network, Inc.

JERMAR
❧ PRESS

Jermar Press
1790 N. W. Grandview Drive
Albany, OR 97321-9695 USA
www.jermarpress.com

Cover Photo: USS Pollack SSN-603. Taken upon return from sea trials in 1964. When the photo was taken, the author, who was a chief electronics technician and the leading reactor operator on the ship at the time, was manning the reactor plant control panel and the ship was making full speed on the surface.

DEDICATION

To my grandchildren, who don't know me. Enjoy.

To my children, Anna, Teresa, Susan, Brian and Gary, who were born in the Navy and raised by a part-time father. Please forgive me.

To my wife, Marleeta Fay Basey, who picked up the little pieces and put them back together again. Thank you, Sweetheart, for everything.

Preface

To many, my biography was written once. It was chipped in stone and contained no errors, so there was no reason to write this book. My friend, Doyle, once said, "Give up your past and your keepsakes, Jerry; nobody cares." I had come to the same conclusion, but I still had all those memories and didn't know what to do with them.

My wife, Marty, urged me to write down my stories. She taught me to turn on her laptop and do simple word processing and I started in. My original plan was to write stories the way I told them, but it turns out that writing is not like telling. The results were discouraging and she kept saying, "Show, don't tell."

For a country boy deficient in fifth-grade English, that was a hard nut to crack. Finally, I came up with the idea of placing myself back when the stories occurred, then reporting them as accurately as I could. Well, that method produced an unexpected result: The writing throughout the three parts evolved in parallel with my progress in real life. I didn't plan it that way; it just happened.

I started out believing that if a little was good then a whole bunch was better when it came to details, and I was quite proud of my manuscript at the time. But my wife, who likes "tight writing," made me groom it down. As I did what she asked, admittedly suspicious that she was destroying a work of art, I began to see what she saw, a potentially beautiful garden overgrown with weeds. When she finished with her machete (red pen), we could see neat rows of vegetables, instead of just the weeds.

This book is a series of brief stories that are autobiographical in nature. Part one contains narrative about my early childhood and boy stories from ages eight to sixteen, which explain in part why I am what I am. Part two has stories about my early manhood and sea stories from my navy career as an enlisted man. The sea stories in part three cover my last ten years as a mustang officer in the nuclear submarine force.

I believe this book presents a unique view of a part of the country and a part of the Navy that have not been adequately reported.

The Dark

When we lived on the farm, we could stand on the back porch and see for seventy miles. We could see beyond the Sleeping Ute Mountain to the Ship Rock, way down in New Mexico. At night there wasn't a single light in any direction except what came from the moon and stars. When the sky was overcast, the nights were pitch black and all we could do was imagine what was out there, and nourish our fears.

There are many kinds of fear. Most people know the fear of life-threatening danger and some are afraid of ghosts, but there is another fear that few people experience today, an ancient emotion with a telltale sign. When you feel it, the hair stands up on the back of your neck and a shiver goes down your spine. Fear of the dark is really innate fear of predators—animals that can kill and eat you.

Our only defense against the dark was one kerosene lamp, which normally sat on the kitchen table. When someone needed it in another room, anyone reading or doing homework had to wait in the dark for the light to return; the little kids jumped up and rushed after it. A trip to the outhouse or barnyard after dark was a major expedition requiring at least two people, usually preceded by a lot of whining like "It's dark outside."

The dark created a tradition in our family. Whenever we were out in the gathering darkness and started for the house, one of us kids would yell, "Bears! Skunks! and Wildcats!" and everyone took off running.

"Bears, skunks and wildcats" was our expression for all the evil that lurks in the dark and our way of saying, "Here comes the boogieman!"

Contents

PART ONE
The Boy

CHAPTER ONE
Little Memories

During the fall roundup, just before I turned five, I was watching cowboys dehorn some big steers and realized they were not doing it right. Usually a big steer was put in a squeeze chute so it couldn't move, and a curved steel bar was locked over its nose to hold its head, which allowed the operation to go faster. This time, two cowboys had a steer with long horns down and hogtied. One cowboy was sitting on the steer's shoulder and neck, holding it by the nose and one horn so the steer's head was twisted back into his lap. The second cowboy was holding the other horn in his left hand while trying to cut it off with a meat hacksaw in his right hand. The second cowboy made a few strokes with the saw then the steer suddenly let out a bellow, raised up his shoulders, swung his head around and drove his good horn clear through the first cowboy's foot, from the top down, through the instep, boot and all. Now they had a bawling cowboy to deal with, so Dad sent me back to the house.

During the winter, Dad sometimes took me along when he fed the cattle. He loaded a big sleigh with alfalfa hay, then drove the team and sleigh out into the fields where the cattle were. He started the team in one direction, tied the reins to the front post of the hayrack and set me next to the post to "drive" while he threw hay onto the snow with a pitchfork. He yelled "gee" and "haw" to make the team turn left or right. I loved to ride on the loaded sleigh and marveled at how it could glide so smoothly and quietly through the deep snow. It was like floating on a cloud, a sensation everyone should experience at least once in their lifetime.

When the weather was bad, Dad sneaked out to feed the cattle alone and left me in the house. Mother claims that as soon as I realized he was gone, I would stand by the window and yell, "Gib, you son of a bitch, come back here!"

The first time I got to ride my horse Crimpy was during the summer after I was five when Dad took me with him up to the San Juan Mountains where he was running our cattle. Dad was busy repairing fences, so one of the cowboys volunteered to take me for a ride. I was on Crimpy with Dad's saddle and the cowboy was riding his own horse. My feet didn't reach the stirrups, but I could handle the reins and hold onto the saddle horn.

We rode in a big circle about two miles out through the alpine countryside and then headed back around. A quarter mile from Dad's location, we emerged from a grove of quaking aspen into a grassy meadow. On the far side of the clearing under a big ponderosa pine, we saw a black bear on its haunches, scooping up maggots with both paws from the carcass of a dead cow.

The sight of the bear spooked the horses and they bolted. I managed to hang on, and since they were running in Dad's direction, we let them go. As we neared Dad, the path took a sharp turn to the right, which Crimpy handled all right, but I went flying straight ahead into a small grove of scrub oak. Dad ran over and picked me up, brushed me off and said, "Don't tell your mother, or she won't let you go with me next time."

For better or for worse, I lived close to nature as a boy and the world was revealed to me in raw and vivid terms. I was raised in a large, poor family that scratched out a living in a rugged part of the country, but I was also lucky; it happened to be a big, wild and beautiful country.

I was born in a one-room log cabin with a dirt floor about a mile and a half south of the Long Draw Well near present-day Eastland in San Juan County, Utah. My dad was Gilbert Peter Hansen, a cowboy from Emery, Utah, and my mother was Opal May Mourer, an Okie whose family had left Longdale, Oklahoma, to escape the Dust Bowl. I am the second child and eldest son of seven children. My maternal grandmother attended my birth, but no doctor was present, so it was never recorded. The first official record of my existence was the 1940 Census.

San Juan is the largest county and cut off from the rest of Utah by the Colorado River, which runs down across the southeast corner of the state like the hypotenuse of a right triangle. Within its borders are numerous broad plateaus, a lot of rugged canyon country, the San Juan River and the Blue Mountain. To me, it will always be a special place, my boyhood home and sacred ground that I love.

My fondest memories are of the red Indian paint brush coming out around the sagebrush in early spring and the brilliant mountain bluebirds flying along the fence lines. In summer, I was thrilled by sudden thunderstorms that stabbed the hills with lightning and rumbled through the canyons, shattering the peace of the high desert and leaving the air filled with the pungent aroma of wet sagebrush, juniper and red dirt. In autumn, I was awed by the bright foliage of mountain maple, scrub oak and quaking aspen that frost spread across the slopes of the Blue Mountain. In winter, the new-fallen snow on the piñon and rim rocks at the edge of Montezuma Canyon took my breath away.

I came into the world on a cold and rainy night in November 1932 in the depths of the Great Depression and in an area of the country that remained the Old West. At the time, most people in San Juan County were still in the horse and buggy days and teams of horses probably outnumbered automobiles. Except in towns, few had electricity or indoor plumbing and most adults had an eighth-grade education or less. The countryside was still largely covered with piñon, juniper, scrub oaks, and sagebrush and a lot of the land was not yet cleared for cultivation. Until after the end of World War II, large portions of the western part of the county remained roadless areas marked "unexplored" on maps.

Shortly after the war ended, government rangers started rounding up wild horses in those remote areas and when they went down in Dark Canyon,[1] which is a big, deep canyon running west from the Blue Mountain[2] to the Colorado River, they made an interesting discovery.

The canyon is ringed by high sandstone cliffs that makes it almost totally inaccessible to man or beast, so there is a large and isolated region in the bottom of the canyon. When the rangers explored it, they found about twenty head of horses that had been trapped and roaming there for generations. The mustangs had inbred or reverted back to the point where full-grown members of the herd were only three feet tall. During their sweeps, the rangers also rounded up some unbranded Navajo Indian ponies and sold them at auction. That upset the Navajo Nation, so there was a time around 1947 to 1948 when the white men and the Indians in Southern Utah were shooting at each other with hunting rifles and that may have been the last of the Great Indian Wars.

During the first few years of my life, we lived out east of Monticello in an area called Horsehead. There is a famous "horsehead" on a steep slope near the top of the Blue Mountain just west of Monticello. It is actually a grove of spruce trees growing in a pattern that resembles the head and neck of a black horse with a white forehead, which is most pronounced when there is snow on the mountain. You can't see it from Horsehead, though, which makes me wonder how that area got its name.

---

[1]Now the Dark Canyon Wilderness and Primitive Area.
[2]Some maps call it the Abajo Mountain, but the natives have always called it the Blue Mountain (and have a song about it). Abajo Peak (11,360 feet) is the highest peak in the range.

This is a book about things that I remember and one of my clearest memories is my first. I was on Mother's lap next to my sister Devon while Dad was driving a team and wagon down a dirt road through timber on a cold and windy day. I know it's not much, but I've remembered it a long time, so there must have been a good reason.

In that country when the snow is almost gone, the ground is wet and the sagebrush and juniper are still damp, so the southern breezes pick up an earthy smell that is incredibly fresh and aromatic. An early spring day would have seemed cold and windy after a winter of being cooped up in a log cabin and I was probably feeling the first breath of spring. If that was what happened, it was definitely a nice way to start remembering my life.

I also remember a few things about the time when I was quite young, despite claims that you can't remember anything before about the age of four. Mother baked a peach cobbler one evening and set it on the window sill to cool. The open window didn't have a screen, so I was worried that something might come out of the dark and get the cobbler.

One time Dad had some horses in a corral and was trying to rope one of them. The corral didn't have a gate, so he stationed me in the opening to keep the horses from running out. . . . *I'm just a little boy . . . the horses are wild . . . they might run over me . . .*

When I was about three, we moved to the Montezuma Valley in Colorado, which is just across the state line and northwest of Mesa Verde National Park. We lived on an irrigated farm fifteen miles northwest of Cortez and a couple of miles west of Ariola. I turned four while we lived there and my memories got a little better, but they are still just flashes.

I played with stick horses cut from willow poles and fought a lot with two boys who lived across the canal. One was a year older than I and the other, a year younger. I remember beating up on one of them for pushing Devon into a post hole that Dad had just dug. Aunt Offie claimed that I whipped them both and ran them back across the canal because their stick horses had been eating my stick horses' grass, which sounds like the kind of thing I would have done, but I have no memory of it.

Dad got a puppy dog soon after Devon was born and I think he was a cross between an Australian Shepard and a Spaniel. He was about the size and shape of a big Spaniel with long, reddish-brown fur and a bobbed tail, so Dad named him Bob. Us kids called him Old Bob. Old Bob was a good family dog and a great cattle dog. In rough country where the cattle got up under the rim rocks or in thick scrub oak, Dad called Old Bob to jump up into the saddle where he could see, then showed him the cattle and said, "Sic 'em!" Old Bob jumped down, ran in and chased them out, nipping their heels and even drawing blood sometimes.

On Christmas morning after I turned five, when I saw presents under the tree, I asked Mother where they came from. She said that Santa had brought them, so I asked her how he got in the house. She said he parked his sleigh and reindeer on the roof and came down through the chimney. Well, we had a fireplace and chimney, but I didn't think a bunch of deer could pull a sleigh through the air and land it on the roof, so I went outside and looked up at the roof, which was covered with six inches of snow. There were no sleigh tracks in the snow.

That same year Dad gave me a horse of my own, whom I have already mentioned. He was a black gelding with a white star on his forehead and about the size of a Navajo Indian pony with some Shetland blood and a similar thick, bowed neck. He was born in the winter and while he was a newborn, the tips of his ears froze, which made them slightly crimped at the ends, so Dad named him Crimpy.

We moved to a smaller farm about a mile east of Ariola in the spring of 1938 and in July my first brother was born. Dad named him RA after his own eldest brother, Rual Alford, who used the nickname RA. He was born prematurely at seven months and was tiny. Although the weather was mild, to keep him warm, Mother wrapped him in his blanket and put him in a shoe box, which she set in the oven of the wood stove with the door open and a small fire going.

To catch my fall when I jumped down from somewhere, I used to hold my arms out in front of me, bent at the elbows like a boxer getting ready to fight. One day when we were visiting Aunt Offie, all of our cousins and us kids were out in the corrals playing when my cousin Ray yelled, "Here comes a mad dog!" There had recently been a case of rabies in the area, so everyone started running toward the house.

I ran across the corral, climbed to the top of the gate, jumped down and landed on my elbows. My left arm hit the hard ground and broke just above the elbow. I got sick, so Aunt Offie let me lie on her bed with my clothes on, which was the part I remember best. Normally, even sitting on her bed with your clothes on was strictly forbidden.

Mother and Dad took me to Cortez to get my arm set. The doctor, who was assisted by a nurse, placed me on the operating table, put a mask over my face and started giving me ether. When I breathed it, I kicked out and got the nurse in the stomach, which put her out of commission, so Mother had to help the doctor administer the ether.

When the cast came off, I strengthened my arm by carrying gallon buckets of milk. We had two or three cows that needed milking morning and night, so we had more milk than we could use. The Depression was still on; milk was precious and sold for about thirty cents a gallon when the going wage was a dollar a day, yet we couldn't even give ours away. So I carried it out to the pasture and poured it down prairie dog holes. When my arm got better I started landing my jumps the regular way.

I started school in September 1938 in a four-room yellow schoolhouse located near the highway in Ariola, Colorado. I didn't turn six until November and was not mature enough to start school; others will argue that I wasn't tame enough. In any event, I flunked the first grade. The only thing I remember clearly about this attempt at first grade was the day a big truck came down the highway from the north, missed the dogleg curve by the school and plowed out through the cattails on the west side of the highway. It took them all day to get it out.

By the time I started school, I'd already learned many lessons. Some were right and some were wrong, but they were based on my interpretation of things and I didn't accept anything until I proved it to myself, using my own methods.

But, that is just my opinion. Aunt Offie's evaluation of me went in another direction. She told me on numerous occasions, "You're the meanest little bastard I've ever seen, ornery enough to push little chickens off in the creek." And that was from someone who loved me.

CHAPTER TWO
Slick Rock

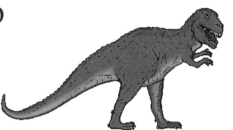

In the autumn of 1938, Dad sold all the cattle and most of the horses. He bought a new 1939 Ford, the model that looked like a black beetle, and we went on a trip that lasted all winter. We first traveled to Emmett, Idaho, to visit Dad's youngest sister Aunt Vivian, Uncle Harry and our cousins. Then we went on to Oregon where Dad tried to get work, but couldn't get a job unless he belonged to a trade union and he couldn't join the union unless he had a job, so I'm not sure how he made a living while we were there.

We spent most of the winter in Hood River, but I don't remember much except that it rained all the time and there were lots of big trees around. I was still making attempts at the first grade, so I went to school some of the time. One day two of my schoolmates were excited because they were going to have ketchup for supper. I had never heard of ketchup, so that afternoon I asked Mother to get some, but she never did. I'm not sure when I actually tasted ketchup for the first time.

In late winter we left Oregon and headed south to visit Uncle RA, who lived in Grass Valley, California. Behind the car, Dad pulled a two-wheeled trailer in which they had stowed Mother's gasoline-motor-driven Maytag washing machine, Dad's saddle, a wooden trunk full of clothes and bedding, plus some other things including fruit canned in glass jars. All the small items were stowed in wooden orange crates with wheat straw as packing material.

As we were driving through the mountains of Southern Oregon, a car pulled alongside and the driver yelled to Dad that the trailer was on fire. Mother and Dad both smoked, so they had probably thrown a cigarette out that flew back and landed in the straw. Dad pulled over, ran back and put out the fire by beating it with his hat and throwing things off the trailer. The fire had only burned for a short time and there was little damage, but it had severed the rope holding Dad's saddle on the load and it was gone.

Dad was devastated. He'd had that saddle made during his cowboy days and it held a lot of sentimental value. We all piled out of the car and were standing alongside the road, dazed by the situation and trying to figure out what to do, when another car pulled over and stopped. A man got out and walked back toward us. He had a big grin on his face and Dad's saddle in his hands. The only damage was a few scratches on the horn where it had landed on the highway.

Later that afternoon we arrived at the California border and were stopped at the Agricultural Inspection Station. They wouldn't let us proceed until we got rid of all the straw in the trailer. Dad pulled over to the side and, under the watchful eye of the fruit inspector, unloaded the trailer and removed all the straw. Again, we were standing around with our stuff spread out while Mother and Dad tried to figure out how to pack everything so it wouldn't break, when a man driving a team of horses with a wagon loaded with straw came up the road from California. Dad talked him into giving us a couple of pitchforks of straw, then we packed everything again and down the road we went, to the chagrin of the fruit inspectors.

We visited with Uncle RA for a while and I thought the area around Grass Valley was very pretty. Devon and I especially liked the big pinecones, which were as big as pineapples, and the manzanita brush. We thought it was a beautiful bush, especially the red limbs, and that it had a neat and exotic name. Mother took home two of the pinecones and kept them on her dresser for many years.

Then we went on down to San Francisco, where we saw the Pacific Ocean and the Golden Gate Bridge. While we were there, Mother bought two seashells that she also kept on her dresser. On many occasions, us kids would hold the seashells up to our ears, listen to the sound of the ocean and remember what it was like at the Cliff House in San Francisco, where we had seen the ocean for the first time.

Finally, we traveled up over Donner's Pass, through Nevada and Utah, and arrived back home in the Montezuma Valley of Colorado in the early spring of 1939.

After we got back from our trip, Dad bought some equipment and started mining for vanadium in the canyons of Western Colorado. Vanadium is an element used to strengthen steel and is found with uranium in ore form in that part of the country. When Dad started mining, there was a market for vanadium ore, but that was before the first nuclear reactor or the first atomic bomb, so the miners were not paid for the uranium at the time.

We first lived in Edgnar, Colorado, according to Devon, who is famous for trying to rewrite history and with whom I have an ongoing battle over these matters. I always thought we moved to Slick Rock first, but in this case, she may be right. I remember very little about Edgnar, but have clear memories of Slick Rock, so I was probably older when we lived there.

Edgnar was a wide place in the road about fifteen miles northwest of Dove Creek, which is now the Pinto Bean Capital of the World. Our house, which was on a big lot, sat back in a grove of piñon trees about a hundred feet from the road on the east side of the highway. We were living there when the government tracked me down for the 1940 Census.

I only remember a few things about Edgnar. Our neighbors to the south lived in a big house on the other side of a small swale that separated our lots. They also had several kids whom we fought with all the time. During one particular fight, even the mothers were involved as we accosted each other across the swale, yelling and throwing rocks. I threw a small stone that hit one of the neighbor girls right on the top of her head and that stopped the fight.

We had to walk about two miles to school and Mother sent me off each day with my lunch packed in a half-gallon lard can. On the way home every afternoon, I fought with the other kids, and by the time I got home, the lid and bail were missing and the lunch bucket was hopelessly dented. One day Mother said, "You'd better start taking it easy; I'm running out of lard buckets."

Probably in late spring of 1940, we moved to Slick Rock, which was located on the west side of the Dolores River about a mile north of the present highway bridge and about twenty-five miles north of Dove Creek. There isn't a town there now, but the old site is fenced off and posted because the area is contaminated with radioactive uranium ore.

We lived in a house located beyond the southern end of town, just north of the present road and just south of a small gully and the point where the old bulldozer road comes down and enters the river bottom. According to Devon, Dad built the house, so it was probably a combination log and frame structure. Anyway, there were lots of mice scratching around at night, and we could even see them run back and forth along a two by four in the wall through a crack above the kitchen counter.

One day Mother told Dad that he had to "do something about those mice," so that night he got the butcher knife, held it at the ready and stationed himself by the crack. When a mouse ran by the hole, Dad tried to stab it. I don't remember how many he got, but he did get some.

During the summer of 1940, I had reached the point where Mother gave up trying to control me and left me to my own devices. That's when my life story really begins. The rest of this book is made up of short stories about what happened to me along the way. Each story has a brief title for reference and all are snapshots of my life. I have included names sparingly and only in those cases where I wanted to give credit or praise. I excluded names to protect the innocent and the guilty. The stories are all true to the best of my memory.

Since they were written from memory, some details might inadvertently be wrong and some conclusions might only be my opinion. For those who find errors, I am sorry. For those who may disagree, here's my advice: Write your own book and tell your side.

Boys

One day during the summer of 1940, when I was between the first and second grades and had just started to run free, another boy and I got some ropes and old bed sheets then headed for a cliff on the west side of the Dolores River about a quarter mile downstream from the town of Slick Rock.

We planned to use the ropes and bed sheets to make parachutes then launch ourselves off the cliff, float down and land in the river. The sheer sandstone cliff went straight down a good eighty feet to the river, which was only about two or three feet deep along there at that time of year. Neither of us could swim, but we figured the water was deep enough to cushion our fall and not deep enough to drown in.

On our way through town, we happened to run into two other boys who had a better idea. They had three or four sticks of dynamite, a handful of blasting caps and about ten feet of fuse. We had a short discussion about which was better, parachuting off a cliff or blowing things up, but since boys love to make noise and break things, there was really no contest. We spent the afternoon busting rocks and splitting trees with dynamite.

We had watched our dads use dynamite in the mines, so we knew how to handle and prepare the dynamite sticks for blasting. We cut them in two with a pocket knife so we could have twice as many good-sized explosions. Next we cut a foot-long length of fuse and inserted it in the female end of a blasting cap, then split the other end to expose the powder for lighting. Finally, we punched a small hole in a half-stick of dynamite and pushed the male end of the cap into it. Then we were ready.

We placed the capped and fused dynamite in the desired location. Then one of us stayed behind while the rest ran and hid in small caves or under rock ledges to watch the explosion. When everyone was ready, the one who stayed behind lit the fuse then ran for cover. The fuse burned at the rate of one foot per minute.

Flash Flood

When we lived in Slick Rock, us kids spent a lot of time playing in the Dolores River bottom, which was dry during late summer, except for some deep pools scattered here and there. The big pools contained fish, some of which were quite large. We cut willow poles, sharpened them into spears, then waded out in the pools and tried to spear the fish.

While wading one day, I heard a noise from upstream that sounded like rocks clicking together. I looked but didn't see anything, so I went back to spear fishing. Suddenly, the sound got louder and I looked again, just as a three-foot wall of muddy water washed around a bend and rushed toward us, tumbling rocks at its base.

I yelled, "Run up the bank!" and we scrambled to high ground just in time. Within seconds, the river bottom filled with rolling, muddy water a hundred feet wide and ten feet deep.

T. Rex

One weekend Uncle Hank, Dad and another man went prospecting for vanadium and I got to tag along. According to my memory, we were prospecting on the east side of the Dolores River somewhere northeast of Slick Rock.

We were walking around a canyon bench near the bottom of a cliff looking for outcroppings of vanadium. The ore, which was usually a dark grey color with blue, yellow and green mixed in, was fairly easy to see because it stood out against the drab sandstone.

As usual, I was running ahead exploring when I ran between two small, bushy juniper trees and straight into something that made me stop suddenly. Two feet on each side of me, things that looked like rock posts curved up out of the ground and back toward each other about a foot above my head. At first, I thought it was some sort of trap or small corral.

I whirled and ran out, then stopped and looked back. After some scrutiny I recognized the shape; I had run into the belly of a dinosaur. The huge petrified skeleton was lying upside down with the backbone still buried and the intact rib cage sticking up in the air. It had become exposed as the earth around it eroded away over the millennia.

The others arrived about that time. We looked it over for a while, marveled at its size, tried to move the ribs and then went back to prospecting. It was interesting, but not earth shattering, because we had seen dinosaur bones before. Uncle Hank told me many years later that a university had dug it up and taken it away.

Dynamite

One Saturday, Dad and two other men were hauling eight boxes of dynamite to the mine and again I got to tag along. Mine safety rules didn't allow miners to carry dynamite and blasting caps in the same vehicle or stow them in the same location, so they couldn't transport the dynamite on regular trips because they always kept the blasting caps in the glove compartment of the pickup. I had a couple of better solutions but wasn't in charge.

Dad and I were in the back of the pickup, sitting on two boxes of the dynamite. As I remember, each box weighed about forty pounds and contained fifty sticks of dynamite. The boxes were roughly fourteen inches long, twelve inches wide, ten inches high and sturdily made from thick wooden panels with mortise joints at the corners.

Dynamite is basically sawdust soaked with nitro-glycerine and wrapped in heavy waxed paper tubes called sticks. The sticks are quite stable and can be handled with little danger. They can be pounded down drill holes, for example. You can even set one on fire and it will just burn like a road flare. On the other hand, nitroglycerine in pure form is extremely unstable and will explode if exposed to a slight jolt.

We had driven about four miles over a rough mining road that was really just a bulldozer track through canyon country when Dad moved one of the boxes to make more room for his legs. He noticed a stain on one of the boxes and quickly pounded on top of the cab. The driver stopped and we all scrambled out. Dad showed the stain to the other guys, then took out his pocket knife and carefully pried open the box. It had apparently been stored too long or allowed to get too warm, so the nitroglycerine had seeped out of the sawdust and formed icicle-like crystals on the edges of some sticks.

We had stopped where the road ran along the top of a cliff, so Dad carried one of the sticks to the edge and threw it over. It landed on the canyon bench, about fifty feet below, and exploded with a loud bang. Then we threw the remaining contents of the stained box over the cliff, one stick at and time, and a good portion of them exploded on impact.

Bonfires

Slick Rock was located down in rugged canyon country carved out by the Dolores River, which runs north from the San Juan Mountains and empties into the Colorado River. I don't believe there was even a road through that country before they started mining for vanadium there, so it was just a remote mining town with a few families, which left very little choice in the entertainment area.

So far I had speared fish and played with dynamite, but someone finally came up with an activity that all the kids loved: bonfires. In the evening, everyone from five to fifteen went out to the edge of town, to a flat canyon bench scattered with juniper and piñon trees and big sandstone rocks that had fallen from the cliffs above, and built big bonfires in a clearing.

After dark, we played hide-and-go-seek. The person who was "It" stood by the fire and counted to a hundred, which was twice as long as needed, while everyone else ran into the darkness and hid amongst the rocks and trees. When the person counting reached a hundred and said, "Ready!" the game began, with the objective of getting back to the fire without being tagged. The first person tagged became It for the next round.

After reaching a hundred, It usually strode around the fire making noises and saying things to frighten the little kids. That ploy usually led to a tense silence, but sooner or later someone made a run for it and got caught about half the time. Meanwhile, a bunch would rush in from the other side, screaming, laughing and yelling as they came.

There was nothing but rugged canyon wilderness in every direction for many miles, making the area outside the ring of firelight a dark and scary place, so the hard part of the game, especially for the little kids, was having the courage to wait in the dark for a good chance to run to the fire. Most games were over in a few minutes, but sometimes all the holdouts were big kids, so the game could go on for a while.

Afterward, we sat around watching the fire, sometimes roasting thin rounds of raw potatoes on willow sticks. They say that time spent gazing at a campfire is added to your life span; perhaps that's why I am so old.

Am I Not

I attended second grade in a classic one-room schoolhouse near Edgnar, Colorado, complete with a stove in the center, a coal bucket and a small scoop shovel. It had about twenty kids in grades one through eight and only one teacher, whose name was Miss Cusman.

One day the teacher presented her latest plan to get everyone to stop saying the word ain't. The first kid who said the forbidden word had to take the coal shovel outside and dig a hole. Everyone would then write the word ain't on a piece of paper, walk by the hole and drop it in. The guilty one would cover the hole with dirt and, as Miss Cusman explained it, the word ain't would be dead, buried and gone forever and we could never use it again.

Well, guess who was the first one to screw up and say ain't? Miss Cusman handed me the coal shovel. I took it outside, but instead of digging, I hid it in some bushes, then ran home and told Mother the teacher was goofy. I knew you couldn't destroy a word, no matter what you did.

A few days later, while I was still on probation, Miss Cusman told us a public health nurse was coming by during the noon hour to give us our smallpox vaccinations. Then she made the fatal mistake of explaining exactly what the nurse planned to do.

Some of us boys were not about to let them do that to us, so when the time came, we bolted into the woods and I ran on home. Mother and Dad took me back and made me get vaccinated, but they had to plead with the Principal to allow me back in school.

CHAPTER THREE
Blanding

Dandelion Greens

In the early spring of 1941, Dad got some new vanadium mines located in a canyon southwest of Blanding, Utah, so we moved to Blanding. We lived in a small frame house on the east side of Main Street about a half block north of the intersection where highway US-191 from Monticello comes into town. Most of the town was spread out south and west from there.

As an independent miner, Dad didn't get paid unless he sold some vanadium ore. He was a good miner, but the mines were only as good as nature made them, so for the first few months in Blanding, he didn't earn very much and we were quite poor.

There was a time during the spring and summer of 1941 when all we had to eat was bread and gravy, three times a day. Mother made a roux from lard and flour, then mixed in water as it cooked to make gravy. She also made homemade bread that was always very good. She kneaded it by pushing her palm into the dough, then folding it over again and again. As I watched one day, she said, "I've been doing this since I was nine years old and when I started I had to stand on a chair to reach the bowl."

Even at eight, I knew that our diet was not very healthful and can remember worrying about it. When the weather warmed up, Mother went out and gathered dandelion leaves and a wild plant she called pigweeds, which is also called lamb's quarters. The steamed plants looked and tasted like spinach and were probably very nutritious. We put salt, pepper and a dash of vinegar on them and they were quite tasty.

The best dandelion leaves come from wet areas, where the plants grow big and fast. Pigweeds grow in ground rich in fertilizer, like that around old corrals and pigpens, which may account for the name. Pigweeds grow in patches of individual plants with stems bearing small oblong leaves that are a nice green color on both sides. We picked them when they were about five inches high.

Whenever I think of this story, I am reminded of one of Mother's country sayings. "Root, hog, or die," she used to say.

Ambushed

Almost all the people living in Blanding, Utah, were members of the Mormon Church. Dad had been raised as a Mormon and Mother had some Baptist experience, but we never went to church. That part of Utah was off the beaten track and few people moved in or out of town, so the town was quite backward and self-centered. The nearest railroad was a hundred miles away and the ocean was about a thousand, but while we lived there, I met grown men who had never seen a train, let alone the ocean. At eight, I had already seen both.

I don't believe Mother had registered us in advance at the grade school in Blanding, so when Devon and I showed up on the first day, we were on our own. I was starting third grade and she was starting fifth, so we went our separate ways. I found my classroom all right and was seated when the teacher came in and started talking to the class. When she spied me, she stopped talking, got up from her desk and brought a piece of paper and pencil to me while the rest of the class sat and watched. "Do you know how to spell your name?"

"Yes, Ma'am."

She handed me the paper and pencil and said, "Print your full name."

I printed my full name, including my middle name written out, then handed it back; I was a Cusman-trained boy.

She looked at it and asked, "Is your name Gerald?" She pronounced it with a "G," like in Gary.

"No, it's Gerald, " I said, pronouncing it with a "J," like in Jerry.

She studied the paper silently as she walked back to her desk. She seemed upset that I printed neatly and spelled my name correctly, which made no sense to me, although I saw later that many in her class couldn't do either.

That was my first encounter with prejudice, but at the time I had never heard the word. An argument can be made that it was religious prejudice—everyone knew I wasn't a Mormon—but to me it felt like something I had faced before: I was the new kid in town and different, that's all.

Although I had never heard of the law of the jungle, I knew that every playground was a jungle. At the time, that part of the country had some rough playground rules, which I knew well, but always before I had dealt with other boys one on one; now it was them against me.

I didn't back down easily, so I had to fight almost every recess and fight my way home every afternoon. As with most things, I didn't seek help from my parents, or the teachers who seemed indifferent to my situation. Fortunately, I could handle most of the boys individually, but when they ganged up, hid in the willows and ambushed me on my way home with sling shots and BB guns, it got pretty bad. I saw boys whom I had never talked to before shooting at me and didn't understand what was happening.

One noon hour, I was crossing the school grounds going to the lunch building when a boy from my class jumped me from behind. He got me down, with his legs locked around my neck, and was choking me; I couldn't breathe and was running out of air fast.

While flailing around, I found a fist-sized rock, grabbed it and busted his head open above the ear. He let go, started spouting blood and screaming. I got up and ran home and could hear him screaming all the way, which was slightly over four blocks from the playground or whatever the hypotenuse of three blocks south and three blocks east would be. I found out later that it took eighteen stitches to close the wound and I was terrified that he might die and I would go to jail.

At school the next day, the teacher told the class that no one was to play with me for two weeks. She never asked for my side of the story. One good thing did come of it; the Mormon boys left me alone after that, almost. The next time they got a chance, they tried to kill me.

Moving Day

One afternoon, soon after I started the third grade, I came home from school and found my family gone and a Mexican[3] family living in our house. They said the house had been empty when they arrived about noon. I walked out to the end of the driveway, looked up and down the street and got a bad feeling.

I had no idea where my family was but I decided it must be somewhere in town, so I made a plan. I would walk south on Main Street, looking up and down each side street as I passed, to the south end of town then go east two blocks then come back north on that street. I planned to repeat that search pattern until I found them or covered the entire town.

I scoured each street for our car as I went, fearing that I wouldn't find them and trying to figure out what I'd do if I didn't. I walked about six blocks to the end of town then turned

---

[3]They were actually Americans of Hispanic decent, who were commonly called Mexicans in that area at that time.

and walked one block east. From there I saw our black Ford parked two blocks farther east on the right side of the road. I had inadvertently gone directly to our new house. It was just getting dark as I walked in the yard. Mother looked up and said, "Oh, there you are," and went back to unpacking.

The next morning Old Bob was missing so Dad and I went back to the old house to look for him. The Mexicans told us they hadn't seen any dogs around. As we talked, I was looking around and noticed they had banked dirt up around the back porch, so I went over to investigate. When I got near the porch, Old Bob, who was trapped underneath, saw or smelled me and started whining. We dug him out and went home.

Honeybees

Our new house in Blanding was located on an acre lot at the extreme southeast corner of town. The street in front was graveled, lined with a row of mulberry trees on our side and continued east as a dirt lane leading out into the country. The house was a three-bedroom, frame-style structure built around 1920 that sat back about fifty feet from the road. It had city water and electricity, but no one had lived there for several years. There was an overgrown orchard on the west side, some corrals and sheds on the south side, and Mother planted a garden on the east side between the house and the corrals.

The kitchen, which was located in the northwest corner of the house, had a couple of outside wallboards loose and some honeybees had built their hive inside. After we moved in, our new neighbor, Mrs. Hoagland from across the street, told us the beehive had been there for many years. She said there must be a lot of honey in it and tried on several occasions to get Dad to raid the hive.

One rainy day that autumn, Dad finally decided it was time. He put cheesecloth over his hat, pulled his shirt collar up and tied the cheesecloth around his neck with string. He put on a pair of gloves and tied down the ends of his shirt sleeves and pant legs. He built a fire and used smoking firebrands to drive the bees out of the hive. Finally, he removed the wallboards and collected the honeycombs in galvanized washtubs. The hive covered the two-by-four-constructed wall, floor to ceiling, for about ten feet.

While Dad was raiding the hive, Mrs. Hoagland, who was a large woman and pleasantly plump, stood by and watched approvingly. She was going to get some of the honey. Meanwhile, the smoke-dazed bees were crawling all over the lawn and Dad told me later, "One of the bees crawled up her leg and got clear up to where things got tight, then it stung her and she ran back across the road yelling and slapping her leg."

We got over three washtubs full of honeycombs and the Hoaglands got their fair share.

Bone Horses

The Hoagland family had a son who was a year or so older than I. His name was Larry and he was a real country boy. He liked to hunt and trap and I remember that he wanted to drive big trucks when he grew up.

One afternoon on my way home from school, I smelled a skunk. The closer I got to home, the stronger the odor became. By the time I walked into our yard, it was overwhelming and when I went in the house, Mother was furious. She told me that Larry had found a dead skunk alongside the road, stayed home from school and skinned it in their backyard. I never found out what happened to Larry, but you could smell skunk all over the neighborhood for weeks.

Larry introduced me to a new game he called "bone horses." He went out in the countryside and gathered small bleached bones from the skeletons of deer, sheep and cattle. He selected a particular bone found in the ankle of all four-footed animals; it may even have been the ankle bone itself. These bones, which varied in length from a half inch to three inches depending on the species and age of the animal, were all shaped the same: one end was larger and had two grooves on its face and the other end was curved like your rear end; the back and sides were rounded and the bottom was flat with two small bone points at each end, like feet.

We played with the bones and pretended the small ones were calves, colts and sheep and the bigger ones were cows or horses. We filed or cut our brands on their sides. We cut willow sticks for posts and pole corrals and used thin copper wire from an old coil to make wire fences. We built complicated ranches, complete with fenced fields, corrals and loading chutes. We moved the bone horses by holding them between our thumb and forefinger then bouncing them along the ground.

The Black

Before our trip to Oregon, Dad had sold most of our horses, except a few he left with someone for safekeeping. While we were traveling and living in Slick Rock and Edgnar, Colorado, the only one I remembered was my horse Crimpy.

One day shortly after we moved into the new house in Blanding, Mother told us that Dad had gone to get Crimpy and Old Smokey. Old Smokey was a big workhorse gelding that Dad had owned since he was a colt. He was an off-white color with blue hairs on his flanks that gave him a smokey tint. I remember him having big brown spots like freckles on his shoulders as well. Dad also brought back some other horses, including a big black workhorse stallion he called The Black. He was about two years old and had some Percheon blood in him.

One day a guy came by with a mare he wanted to breed to our black stallion. I was out in the corrals with Dad and got to stay for the event. When they arrived, Dad had a halter on The Black with the halter rope tied up short to a corral post. The man was riding the mare, so he stopped outside the corral and took the saddle off. When they approached the corral, The Black started to whinny, blow his nose and stomp around.

The man left the bridle on his mare and led her into the corral. Apparently she was in heat and at the top of her cycle. She gave a low whinny, spread her back legs and urinated. Dad loosened the halter rope and let the stallion go. The Black approached the mare, blowing and snorting, took one sniff and mounted her. It was all over in a few seconds. I already knew what it was all about, but I believe that was the first time I saw animals have sex.

One day the next spring while I was still nine, Dad told me to come outside and help him. He took me out to the lane that ran along the east side of our lot toward the fields south of us. There were gates in our corral that opened into the lane, where Dad had The Black down and hogtied.

There was a small fire burning and Dad's branding iron, the type they called a "running iron," was heating in the fire. It was about sixteen inches long with a handle made from a piece of half-inch iron round bar. Welded at one end was an oval head that had been ground out of a piece of solid copper about two by three inches and a quarter inch thick. The whole assembly looked like a flat wooden spatula. It was the kind of branding iron you could use to "draw" any brand you wanted. Dad carried it in a small scabbard under the stirrup of his saddle and I suspect he may have altered a few brands in his time.

Dad had also cut a foot-long piece of wooden two by four in two lengthwise, then whittled notches near one end of each piece. He placed the pieces side by side with the notched ends together, then twisted baling wire around the notches so one end was held together and the other end could be opened to form a V. When closed, the two pieces laid snugly against each other.

Dad wanted me to help him castrate The Black and said, "Cutting horses is a risky business, because it's easy to lose one."

He told me he had never lost a horse and had a special way of doing it that he wanted to teach me.

I'd seen cowboys castrate animals. They slit the scrotum open with a sharp knife, pulled the testes out, cut the cords and threw the testes away or roasted them on the branding-iron fire to eat as rocky mountain oysters. Dad's method was to place the wooden clamp around the neck of the scrotum, between the testes and the horse's crotch then squeeze the narrow scrotum neck containing the cords between the clamp's two sides. Then he ran a red-hot running iron along the clamp side and burned through the scrotum neck and cords, thus cutting, sealing and cauterizing the wound all at the same time.

My job was to hold the clamp tightly closed around the scrotum neck while Dad cut it with the branding iron. The Black grunted a lot and I was right down in the heat and smell of it.

It was all over in a few seconds.

Swimming

During the summer following the third grade, I was out walking in the fields south of Blanding when I came across some boys swimming in a pond. I stopped to talk and they asked if I wanted to go swimming. I told them I didn't know how and some of the older boys said they would teach me, so I took off my clothes and jumped in.

They told me to get on a pole raft, and when I climbed aboard, they pushed it out in the pond. When the raft was about twenty-five feet from the bank, they suddenly pushed me off into water about ten feet deep. Apparently, the Mormon boys viewed this as an opportunity to get even with me for bashing their friend in the head with a rock.

As I fell, I noticed that I was only about ten feet from the dam side of the pond, which is also the deep end. I knew the dam bank curved down sharply underwater, so I held my breath and purposely sank to the bottom. I dug my hands into the mud and clawed my way to the dam, then crawled up the bank and out of the water. I grabbed my clothes and went home. I told Dad about the incident and his advice was to stay away from them.

The next afternoon I went down to another pond where I knew I could be alone. I went around to a shallow side and carefully waded out until the water reached my bottom lip, then turned and faced the bank. I knew all the water between me and the bank was shallow enough to stand up in since I had just waded out there.

I held my breath and dove toward the bank, moving my arms and legs in swimming motions until I sank or reached water too shallow to swim in. I repeated that maneuver over and over, until I found a combination that worked. I discovered that swimming is a lot harder than it looks.

Before too long, I had learned how to stay afloat dog paddling and by the end of the afternoon, I could swim.

The Track

After Dad retrieved the horses, I rode Crimpy whenever I got a chance. I was still too short to bridle him, so I got Mother to do it whenever she would, which wasn't often. I led him up alongside a fence, rock or stump to mount him then rode bareback. I dismounted by jumping down. Sometimes Larry Hoagland rode with me on his horse, but most of the time I went alone.

I always took the lane going east from the front of our house, which was a dirt road with irrigated alfalfa fields and pastures on both sides for a mile or so, then nothing but open country for miles. The open range was covered with juniper, piñon and sagebrush and had several small canyons crossing it on their way into Montezuma Canyon, which is a big canyon that runs south and empties into the San Juan River.

One afternoon while riding the area, I came across a small draw with a big dry wash in the bottom. I knew there was a pool of water from a recent rain about a hundred yards off the trail and decided to give Crimpy a drink.

When I tried to rein him onto the trail to the pool, though, he started snorting, blowing his nose, and moving his ears rapidly. Eventually, I got him headed down the trail, but the closer we got to the pool, the more nervous he became.

When Crimpy finally put his head down for a drink, I leaned over and was gazing down at the water when I saw a huge mountain lion track in the soft mud at the edge of the pool. A trickle of water was still running into the deep track. The hair on the back of my neck stood up. Somebody else had wanted an afternoon drink and was probably still watching us.

Yellow Cake

Sometimes on weekends I went out to the mines with Dad to pick up pieces of high-grade ore from the tailing piles and put them in small canvas bags. On one such trip, Dad and I were going to muck out a new open-pit mine on top of a cliff where he had set off a dynamite charge at quitting time the day before. Dad was driving the Ford and when we arrived, he parked it in a grove of cottonwood trees across a dry wash from the mine.

Down in the shallow mine pit, we found a tree trunk that had been exposed by the blasting. The log was about six feet long and eight inches in diameter. It was still intact, just as it had been millions of years ago when it was buried in the sand. The bark of the log, which geologically speaking was a replacement deposit, had turned into a brownish-red uranium ore and the wood core was now a high-grade uranium ore the miners called yellow cake.[4] It had about the same color and

---

[4]True yellow cake is purified uranium-oxide (U3O8) obtained during the uranium production process.

texture as cornmeal. We cracked open the bark and pried it out in pieces with a pick then scooped the yellow cake out with our bare hands to fill about five or six high-grade ore sacks.

We spent the rest of the day mucking out the pit and then headed back to the car. When we got to the dry wash, we found some water and evidence that there had recently been a lot more: the Ford was half-buried in mud and driftwood debris from a flash flood that had come down the wash during the day. The water level had reached the top of the hood and the engine compartment was full of wet sand. We had to walk out to the highway and hitchhike home.

Dad eventually got the car out and cleaned up, but he was afraid to drive it very far. He didn't know how much damage the sand would cause to the engine, so we now had a big problem. The war was still going on and cars were hard to get.

Fortunately, a man had been trying to get Dad to sell him the Ford, so one day Dad took it over and traded it to him for a green GMC panel truck. I think the panel truck was newer and better suited to our needs, so it was a good deal for us. Dad didn't mention that the Ford had been in a flash flood and when I asked him about it, he grinned and said, "Son, trading cars is like trading horses."

Promises

When I think back to that time in Blanding, I always remember a particular incident. One day Dad told me to take Crimpy and move our horses to a new pasture, a section of fenced rangeland with good grass. Dad normally did jobs like that himself, but he was busy working, so when he told me to do it, I did. Nothing happened for about a month, then a guy riding a horse came by one day and threatened to whip Dad for putting our horses on his property without permission. Dad talked the man out of a fight by saying that I'd put them in the wrong pasture by mistake and that he'd move them right away.

Dad was lying when he blamed me, and although I didn't say anything, that really bothered me.

A lot of other things were happening to the family about that time. There was the move that no one had told me about. Nothing was ever said about it, but I suspect the owner had kicked us out for nonpayment of rent and in the ensuing confusion they had just forgotten about me. We were eating bread and gravy three times a day, and just after we moved, Dad went out one night and stole some chickens so we could have meat. Mother was pregnant with my brother Dean and upset a lot of the time. Now, Dad had brought all the horses to Blanding and we didn't have a place to put them.

At the same time, I was experiencing life in my usual way. I didn't just do things; I plunged into them. I was observant and fascinated with whatever interested me, which was almost everything, and I believe that I saw the world in bolder colors than most. At about nine, I noticed that my behavior was having a bad effect on my life. I had been told that I was an ornery little bastard, but excused myself defiantly. The way I looked at it: you had the name, you might as well play the game. Still, I could see that the way people looked at me was not the way I saw myself and that made me realize that I was not presenting myself honestly, so I started mulling things over.

I had started to think deeply and draw my own conclusions, so it was a time of internal changes as well. I remember realizing that I couldn't rely on my parents for some things, which meant that if I was going to make out, I had to do it myself. This grew into a sense that it was me against the world, which remained with me most of my life and profoundly influenced how I looked at things.

I also realized that what a lot of people accepted as right was obviously wrong, and that presented a real problem. If I just coasted along accepting conventional wisdom, I would be wrong a lot of the time and in my situation, without a safety net, I couldn't afford that. My decisions had to be based on solid thinking and good factual information.

These realizations and the general situation led me to one significant decision and several promises to myself, which represented a turning point in my life.

The decision was to start looking at all problems from at least two points of view. First, I evaluated a situation or problem using conventional wisdom, then I looked for other possible explanations. I pretended to accept the conventional answers while keeping the alternatives in the back of my mind and waited to see which turned out the best. After a while, it became second nature for me to look at all problems this way and that was one of the best evolutions I ever made.

Then one day when I was alone out in the canyons, I made a deal with myself. I promised that I would always admit the truth to myself; that I would always pay my bills; that I would always finish a job; and that I would graduate from high school, no matter what.

CHAPTER FOUR
The Farm

Country Living

About two weeks after I started the fourth grade in Blanding, Dad went broke mining and rented a farm about four and a half miles south of Monticello, Utah, which I always thought of as my boyhood home. My fondest childhood memories are of the time we lived there.

The farm was a half section of land, three hundred and twenty acres, with about two hundred acres of dry land under cultivation, about six acres under irrigation and the rest, hillsides or rocky ground. It was situated on an eastern-sloping plateau that stretches from the base of the Blue Mountain about four miles to the west and ends at the rim of Montezuma Canyon about three miles to the east. We raised winter wheat and pinto beans on the dry land and alfalfa hay on the irrigated land.

The house was located near the center of the property, about a third of a mile from the highway, on the edge of a wooded hillside overlooking a large draw to the south named Bull Hollow. The main fields were on the north half and southeast corner. There were two hayfields, one near the highway and one in Bull Hollow.

The house was a four-room frame structure, probably built around 1910, with a living room in the northwest corner, a kitchen in the northeast corner and two bedrooms in the southern corners. The back door led from the kitchen to a wooden porch with a pole railing on the south and east sides. The house rested on a stone cellar that had a door in the downhill side like a daylight basement. The cellar stones were about eight by eight by sixteen inches and had been cut with precision from sandstone. The same kind of architecture can be seen all over Southern Utah, especially in Bluff. I think the old Mormons must have had some good stonemasons in their group. Years later, after the house was gone, someone dismantled the cellar and took the stones away.

While we lived there, our life was good, but quite primitive. We had no electricity or indoor plumbing. Mother cooked on a wood stove and Dad hauled a fifty-gallon wooden barrel of fresh water from Monticello once a week, which we used for drinking, cooking and washing. By the back door was a small stand with a galvanized bucket of drinking water, a dipper and a wash pan on top. We used the dipper to drink from the bucket and break the layer of ice on top on cold winter mornings. We had no refrigerator or ice box and only one kerosene lamp for light. The toilet was an outhouse and we took a bath in a number three galvanized washtub every Friday night, whether we needed it or not. The girls always got to bathe first. Mother did have her gasoline-motor-driven Maytag washing machine.

Soon after we moved to the farm, Dad got two milk cows, a Jersey and a Holstein, and some pregnant sows. The next spring Mother got a hundred white leghorn chicks and planted a big garden. Until the garden produced the next summer and the chickens got big enough to butcher, we didn't have a lot to eat, especially meat. We lived on pinto beans, potatoes, milk, butter and homemade bread. Sometimes we had rice and raisins with cream and honey for dessert. For breakfast we usually ate oatmeal or farina that Mother toasted in the oven before cooking.

Our menu left a lifelong impression on me. To this day, my favorite meal is a bowl of pinto beans with ham hocks, homemade bread with butter, a tall glass of cold milk and a salad tray with green onions, lettuce, radishes and vine-ripened beefsteak tomatoes. Because the best apricots grow in that country, for dessert I like apricot pie with vanilla ice cream.

Mother made nine loaves of bread each week, from scratch. She called it "light bread," but I don't know why. Once in a while she rolled dough into a pad about fifteen inches in diameter and a quarter inch thick, poured a layer of fresh whole cream over it, sprinkled a cinnamon and sugar mixture on that, rolled it up, cut it into one-inch sections, put the sections in a pan greased with lard and baked the most incredible cinnamon rolls you can imagine. I also love cinnamon rolls.

The garden was planted in an old corral area at the edge of a big field just north of the house and because we had irrigation water, it was the most productive garden with the best-tasting vegetables I have ever seen. By September, we had baskets full of beefsteak tomatoes that weighed over a pound apiece and a lot of huge winter squash. Mother canned about two hundred quarts each of string beans, corn and tomatoes.

We went to the grocery store once a month and altogether bought less than twenty items of dry goods. All the meat, fresh or canned vegetables, milk, butter and eggs came from our animals, the garden or wild game.

During World War II many things were rationed, but the only items that really affected us were shoes and sugar. We were only allowed one pair of leather shoes a year, so we went barefoot in the summer to conserve them for cold weather and school. I got a candy bar when I was about ten and remember arguing with Devon about whether it was the second or third one I'd eaten in my life. Devon and I have been arguing about such things for a long time. Just after World War II ended, when I was about thirteen, Aunt Offie gave me a pack of chewing gum and I didn't know what it was, but Devon did.

My Teacher

My fourth-grade teacher was Miss Washburn. She was a beautiful blonde about twenty-three who was probably on her first year of teaching. I was not yet into pretty girls, so to me she was just another teacher.

During the last period one afternoon, she told us to read the next chapter in our readers to ourselves. It was a good adventure story that I had already read at least twice, so I was left with nothing to do, which was never a good situation. Everything got quiet as the other kids opened their books and started reading. Miss Washburn was sitting at her desk, busily correcting arithmetic papers.

I sat there for a while, looking out the window. I considered reading another story farther along in the book, but it was a nice sunny afternoon and I really wanted to go outside. I decided to let out a quick, sharp yelp, pretend it wasn't me and see what happened. Well, Norma Barton, who had long braids and sat in front of me, squealed.

Miss Washburn pointed to the door and said, "Gerald! Go see the Principal!"

As I went out the door, I gave her the finger. Fortunately, the Principal wasn't in, so I sneaked by his office, and went down to the playground where I started playing marbles with the third graders, who got out early. My school books and homework were still in my desk in the classroom, so I stayed on the playground until it was late then sneaked back up to get them. When I opened the classroom door, I found Miss Washburn at her desk with her head in her arms, crying. I walked up slowly and asked what was wrong. She raised her head, tears in her eyes, and said, "It's so hard to teach when mean boys disrupt the class."

Well, that did it. One thing led to another and pretty soon we were both crying. I promised her that I would never disrupt class again and if anyone else did, they would have to answer to me. I kept my promise and for the rest of the year nobody fooled with my teacher.

Model 37

Late in our first summer on the farm, Dad let a man go hunting for sage grouse on our property. After he'd hunted for several hours without success and was saying goodby, I noticed a .22 rifle on the back seat of his car. It was a single-shot, bolt-action Remington, Model 37 Target Master, in as-new condition. He saw my interest and told Dad it was for sale. Dad recognized my instant love for the rifle, so about a week later he bought it for five dollars and gave it to me. At the time five dollars was one day's wages.

That rifle became my all-time favorite possession because it provided the greatest feelings a boy can experience: the thrill of the hunt, anticipation of the unknown and a sense of being a predator in the wild and natural world. In fact, when I think of freedom, I think of myself as a boy walking out through the sagebrush carrying that rifle. I spent all my free time from then on roaming the hills and canyons with it.

With a single-shot rifle, you have to make the first one count, so before long I became a deadly marksman. I routinely hit targets smaller than the image of my front sight, which I'd filed down to make smaller. This was during World War II when ammo was scarce and I could only shoot on rare occasions, so most of the time I practiced stalking game and observing nature. I soon learned the habits of various game animals and picked up a lot of hunter's tricks. I became so good at tracking that I could run and track a deer at the same time.

When I did shoot, it was usually to kill an animal for meat. In autumn, I hunted for cottontail rabbits and wild ducks. I tried to shoot them in the head so as not to damage any meat, which was relatively easy for cottontails, but harder for ducks. To shoot ducks in the head, I had to crawl up over the edge of pond banks and stalk them to get in range. After I shot them, usually they floated out of reach and I had to throw rocks or clods behind them to create waves that washed them ashore. In spring and summer, when I could get enough ammo, I laid in the fence lines and shot prairie dogs standing by their burrows two or three hundred yards away. In those days, there were thousands of prairie dogs and the "prairie dog towns" were a real problem for farmers.

I remember one autumn evening coming back from hunting with two cottontail rabbits and a male mallard duck. My mother saw me, dropped her arms to her sides and said, "Son, what are we going to do with all this meat?" We had already butchered our animals and now had beef, pork, lamb, chicken, deer, rabbit and duck to choose from.

Bob Sleigh

When we lived on the farm, which was four and a half miles from Monticello, there were no school busses, so students had to make their own way to school, or, in the case of some families who lived way out in the country, simply not go. Sometimes Dad drove us in the green panel truck, which the girls didn't like riding in and called the Green Monster. Other times we managed to hitch a ride, but most of the time, especially in good weather, we had to walk. One year Devon got a certificate for perfect attendance under those conditions and I got the mumps. On rare occasions, I rode Crimpy to school and tied him up in a vacant lot across the road from the school grounds while attending class.

Although I once found a five dollar bill lying alongside the road and used it to buy two weeks' of school lunch tickets, walking along the side of a gravel highway was boring. So one spring day when I was in the fifth grade and didn't have to be at school until noon, I decided to go out through the sagebrush and oaks parallel to the highway. Walking through the sagebrush on a nice spring day, even without a rifle, is the second best thing there is to do. As I walked along looking for Indian paint brush, I saw a young coyote that looked like a female trotting through the sagebrush toward me. There was a stiff breeze blowing. She was upwind and hadn't seen me, so I hid behind a small, bushy piñon tree and waited to see how close she would come. When she got about eight feet away, I jumped out and yelled, "Boo!" She whirled and really took off. I had no idea they could run that fast and jump that high.

In winter, when the snow was deep and Dad couldn't get the Green Monster out to the highway, he took us kids to school in a bob sleigh pulled by Old Smokey and The Black. Devon, Mona, and I wrapped ourselves in blankets and sat on loose hay in the back of the sleigh. We snuggled up to keep warm, smelled the aroma of the alfalfa and listened to Dad sing to himself as he sat on the front seat and drove the horses. They were sweet and sad songs of the type the old cowboys sang at night to calm the herd. My favorite was one with a refrain that went ". . . *that's a picture from life's other side.*"

The elevation along the highway between the farm and Monticello is almost exactly seven thousand feet and the early winter mornings were usually clear and bitterly cold. We left before dawn, when many bright stars were still out and the milky way was a big white swath across the sky. Some mornings there was still a pale moon and we could see billions of dancing lights on the surface of the snow. On most mornings we could hear the coyotes howl off in the distance, and one time we saw shimmering bands of bluish-green lights from the *aurora borealis* in the northern sky just to the west of the La Sal Mountain.

Piss Ants

The farm was located halfway between the Blue Mountain and Montezuma Canyon, both of which were wild and natural areas. The landscape included mountain, high-desert-plateau and canyon country, all rich in flora and fauna. I spent a lot of time outdoors during all four seasons and lived intimately with nature every day. I was also an avid naturalist and spent a lot of my time observing and thinking about the role nature played in everything I saw.

When I was ten years old, I already knew that many species of birds and animals acquired and defended territory. I didn't publish that fact because I thought everyone knew it and didn't learn until I was an adult that a bird watcher in England had discovered it for science and did publish his findings in about 1937, so I was a good five years late anyway and, in any case, hadn't learned the scientific method.

At some point, I began checking in with nature when I was trying to solve a problem. It wasn't a conscious decision; I just started doing it. The process varied with the situation. I looked for repeating patterns, common characteristics, the natural forces in play and aspects of human nature involved. Basically, I was asking, How does nature view it?

I reasoned that if a new problem was similar to an old problem, and the same natural forces were involved, then the new problem might have a similar solution. The trick was to be disciplined and to look at things objectively. I found this most helpful in correctly identifying "the" problem.

My hours alone thinking eventually led to some big philosophical questions, but I usually got hung up on religion or philosophy, which are closely intertwined. Since I was only a boy and not discussing things with Socrates, I wasn't making much progress on any front. In fact, I ran into a brick wall when I tackled infinity.

I was having enough trouble dealing with the finite world. It was hard to believe that light from a star had left it light years before and that the star might not even be there now. Trying to envision how far light could travel in a whole year or how something could have no beginning and no end was impossible for me, despite my active imagination.

My struggle with infinity came into perspective one day as I was walking through the freshly turned earth of a field Dad was plowing. I saw a black ant frantically climbing around in the newly plowed ground and stopped to watch. It was the kind we called piss ants, which according to my boyhood folklore, would bite you and then turn around and pee on the wound to make it sting. I've been stung by them before, but never watched to see how they did it, so that may not be true. They also leave a scent trail to find their way back home.

This little ant was in real trouble. His scent trail was gone, his home was plowed under and he was lost for sure. While watching him, I was struck with the futility of my own pursuit and realized that my trying to envision infinity was about like that little ant trying to envision Hawaii. This insight led me to draw a conclusion that has since been reinforced many times: the truth is usually right in front of us. Although we may not believe it or be looking at it the right way, the truth invariably lies along the most obvious path.

Green Alfalfa

When we moved to the farm, I had to start working and doing chores. I chopped firewood, fed and milked the cows, fed the pigs, hoed weeds in the pinto beans and drove the tractor. The job I spent the most, and worst, time at was herding cows. I don't care how romantic it sounds, herding cows is boring.

I usually rode Crimpy and took Old Bob along. If I wanted the cows to move out of an area, all I had to do was yell, "Here Bob!" and they started running. But one day I was keeping the cows out of the hayfield without my horse or dog along. Cattle can't eat green alfalfa because it causes gas to form in their stomachs, which can blow up and kill them. This day, the cows could see the green alfalfa and wanted it bad. I had to run back and forth all day to keep them out. By now, Old Bob was about twelve and not the terror he used to be, so even if I yelled his name, it wasn't very effective anymore.

Late in the afternoon, a yearling steer managed to get past me and started grazing in the alfalfa. By then, I was so tired and angry that I decided to just let him eat for a while. I suppose it would also be safe to say that I was a little curious about what would happen.

That evening, Dad noticed the steer staggering around the corral and yelled for me to run to the house and get the butcher knife, which I did. He took it and stabbed the steer in the hollow area of the stomach below the bone that sticks up near the rear of a cow's back. A slurry of liquid green manure and gas shot about six feet in the air. Then he took a sharp stick and kept the hole open and venting until the steer was degassed and walking around. The steer survived just fine and we butchered him that autumn.

Crop Circles

One nice summer day, Dad and I were mowing the alfalfa in the lower hayfield and had Old Smokey and The Black hooked up to the mowing machine. The Black was still young and we were just breaking him in as a workhorse. I was driving the team and sitting on the seat located on the mower, which was a simple machine with a standard tongue and doubletree team hookup connected to a pair of steel wheels and axle. It had a gear box connected between the axle and a mowing bar off the right side. The wheels had cleats that powered the gear box as they turned, causing the mower's cutting bar to move back and forth. The gear box ratios were such that the cutting bar moved at the proper speed when the mower was being pulled by a team of horses at a normal walking pace.

I was about to finish the first cut around the edge of the field when a B-17 bomber flew directly overhead going north at an altitude of about two thousand feet. The noise from the plane's four big engines drowned out the mower noise and spooked the horses. The Black bolted, dragging Old Smokey, the mower and me along. The faster we went, the faster the mower's cutting bar moved. We went out through the hayfield and cut some wild patterns in the alfalfa.

The danger of getting mowed down by the cutting bar kept Dad at bay, so he couldn't help me. I had my hands full just trying to stay on the mower and away from the cutting bar myself. Finally, I lost the rein leading to The Black, which turned out to be a good thing. When I pulled on the remaining rein, it caused Old Smokey to turn in a circle, toward his side, which dragged The Black with him and Dad was able to enter the circle and grab their bridles.

Old Slats

Dad's great passion in life was raising and working with horses. We were always "horse poor" and over the years owned many horses, but the only ones I still remember well are Crimpy, Old Smokey, The Black, Patches, a strawberry roan mare whose name I can't remember, and one other.

One day Dad bought a white stallion that was part Arabian. He said, "We can get some pretty colts out of him." He had light blue eyes, which gave him an albino look. His hair was all white, but the skin underneath was actually black and white pinto and the white part was slightly pink. He was a tall horse and very tough; you could ride him hard all day and he never seemed to get tired. He was also an ugly horse. No matter how much we fed him, he stayed so skinny you could see his ribs, so Mother named him Old Slats.

Old Slats had a one-track mind. All he wanted was to get to the mares. When we put him in a pasture by himself, he paced around the fence all day trying to find a way out. When you rode him and got off for some reason, you had to tie him up firmly. If you were just standing there, you had to keep hold of the bridle reins at all times or he would hold his head out to the side to avoid stepping on them and start running. You could not catch him.

One day Dad got off Old Slats to shut the gate and he got loose in the hayfield with Dad's saddle and bridle on. We didn't have another horse around, so the whole family went down to the hayfield and spread out in a big line in an attempt to corner him. Several times we thought we had him, but he kept getting away. Dad was about ready to get the gun and shoot him when we finally caught him.

Dad bred him to a blue mare we had and next spring the mare died giving birth. The colt lived and was a stallion with good lines. He was a unique pinto with a flaxen mane and tail. His spots included almost every horse color there is, not just the usual two, which made him look like a patchwork quilt. Dad was elated and named him Patches.

Dad brought Patches up to the house and put him in the cellar to keep warm. That evening we fed him some cow's milk with a bottle and nipple we had used for the lambs. We all petted him and said good night. Apparently he couldn't tolerate the cow's milk because his stomach blew up during the night and we found him dead the next morning.

Old Slats was still around and since he was a stud, we had to keep him separated from all the horses, not just the mares. When he got in with the other horses, he chased the geldings, bit them on the back of their necks and kicked them. Geldings won't fight a stallion; all they will do is run and try to get away, even if they are bigger and stronger.

One rainy night, Old Slats managed to get in with the other horses and was chasing Old Smokey unmercifully around and around. As they ran by the house I could hear Old Smokey whinny frantically. I knew he wanted us to help him, but to do that I'd have had to get up, go outside in the dark and rain, round up the horses on foot, catch one, and then separate Old Slats from the other horses somehow. Course, I couldn't catch Old Slats and put him in the corral by myself and if I'd even suggested it, Mother would have ordered me back to bed; I was only ten years old. So I laid awake a long time listening to them run and hating that horse.

Big Snake

One summer day, Devon and I were babysitting the little kids. Mother was pregnant with my youngest sister Betty and she and Dad had left early in the morning to see the doctor, so Devon cooked breakfast. We had just finished eating when the first kid out the door came running back in and said, "There's a big snake outside!"

We all ran out and, sure enough, there was a huge rattlesnake lying alongside the house by the back porch. It was about six feet long, three inches in diameter and must have had nine rattles.

Now, this was no problem for the Hansen Clan. Devon and I immediately took charge and marshaled our forces. She told the little kids to stay back and everyone else to start gathering rocks. Since I was an equal branch of government and didn't follow Devon's orders, I ran down to the woodpile and got the axe. I was out of .22 cartridges.

The snake—who would have been better off encountering a pack of wolves—soon realized that he had tangled with the wrong bunch and started crawling across the yard toward the outhouse, which was located in the scrub oaks at the edge of the hill on the west side of the house. He hadn't gone far before we started throwing rocks and hit him several times. With each hit, he whipped his head around, buzzed his rattles, opened his mouth and struck out. You could see big drops of white venom on his fangs.

When the snake reached the scrub oaks, he started crawling up through the branches to get away and keep our rocks from pinning him against the ground. For a while, it looked like he was getting away, but by now we had gathered a pile of rocks and everyone let go with a fusillade, which knocked him down from the oaks and dazed him. I reached in, grabbed his tail, dragged him out and cut off his head with the axe. His venom had a thick, penetrating odor that I could still smell when I went down to the hayfield later, which was about a quarter mile away.

Woodpile

When Mother gave birth to my sister Betty, Dad took her to the hospital in Moab and then didn't come home that night. At the time, Devon had just turned twelve and I was still ten. We knew where Mother and Dad had gone and assumed that we were in charge, which was all right by us. We were perfectly capable of taking care of ourselves and the little kids.

Dad must have asked the Mormon church to send someone out, because two young men about eighteen dressed in suits like Mormon missionaries showed up around four that afternoon saying they were there to take care of us. Their arrival or what they told us apparently upset my big sister, because she gave them her famous silent treatment; the whole thing puzzled me. We were now being taken care of, but having no idea what that meant, we just stood around, waiting.

The two guys tried to make small talk without much success. I was curious why the Church sent missionaries to San Juan County where they already had so many Mormons instead of to other places where they didn't, but I didn't know how to bring up the subject, so I was quiet myself.

After looking over the situation, one of them finally asked Devon how we cooked dinner. Devon broke her silence and told them they had to build a fire first. They looked over at the kitchen stove and the wood box was empty. I anticipated their next question and volunteered to show them the woodpile. One of them went with me, but when we got there all we found was a bed of wood chips a few inches deep covering an area about twenty-five feet in diameter, a beaten-up splitting log resting in the middle and the axe. He picked up the axe, held it for a moment, then dropped his hands and the axe down at his sides and stared off into the distance. I could imagine what he was thinking—How do these people live like this?

He said nothing but had clearly revealed how he felt and I was suddenly ashamed of our situation. The contempt and despair in that drop of his hands to his sides left a lifelong impression on me and whenever I saw that gesture, I always took note of it.

After Mother gave birth, she and the baby stayed in the hospital for several days, which was the custom then. Dad borrowed a car and drove to Moab to pick them up and took RA, Berta, and Dean along. The car was a four-door Ford sedan with rear doors that opened out from the front.

On the way to Moab, RA was riding in the backseat and managed to open the right rear door and, at about fifty miles an hour, fell out. He hit the edge of the highway, rolled off the shoulder and laid there. Dad stopped, ran back and found him unconscious, with an ugly gash on his head that was bleeding pretty badly. When he came to, Dad carried him back to the car, wrapped his head with something and rushed on to the hospital in Moab.

Meanwhile, Mother's room happened to face the hospital entrance and the parking lot. She was sitting up watching for Dad and the kids and was horrified to see her husband come running in carrying her bleeding boy. For a while everyone forgot about the new baby sister, but we made up for it when she got home.

Little Wigglers

Soon after we moved to the farm, Dad bought three pregnant sows, then got at least one more group of pigs later that included some razorbacks. The sows each gave birth to six or seven piglets and by spring we had a whole bunch of pigs.

We called the piglets "little wigglers" and they were just delightful. They were about this long and that big around and had little curly tails. They were very firm, strong for their size, with short, silky hair. When we picked them up, they squealed and struggled to get away and the sows grunted at us. It was a daily ritual we cherished.

When the little wigglers were about a month old, Patches was born and the blue mare died. Dad took the tractor and dragged the blue mare's carcass up to a little draw on the east side of the corrals for the pigs to eat. Pigs will eat anything. Our little wigglers crawled into the carcass and I don't know which stank most, the little wigglers or the carcass. After that we didn't pick them up and pet them anymore.

When the weather got cold that autumn, around my eleventh birthday, Dad and I started killing and butchering six to eight pigs every weekend until we'd done a total of forty-seven. To process them, Dad built a six- by eight-foot wooden platform under a big piñon tree. He rigged a block and tackle to a big limb about twelve feet above the platform and set a fifty-gallon steel barrel half-full of water over a fire beside the platform. Finally, he put some wood ashes in the hot water.

The day we started butchering, Dad hired a young man about twenty to help and let him use my .22 rifle to kill the pigs. When he shot the third pig, the bullet hit the pig too far down on its nose and it started squealing and ran back into the group. I had already noticed that he seemed to be afraid of them and wasn't hitting them exactly between the eyes, so I told him to give me the rifle. He handed it over. I put a round in the chamber, quickly found the wounded pig and shot it directly between the eyes. Dad never said a word, so I did all the shooting from then on. The guy only worked that day.

When the water in the barrel got hot, I'd shoot a pig and Dad would stick it in the throat. Once it was dead, we slit the skin on the back legs to expose the big tendons above the knees and hooked the legs to a singletree[5] connected to the block and tackle.

We used the block and tackle to hoist the pig then lower it into the hot water and wood ashes. After all parts of the pig had soaked for a minute or so, we hoisted it out of the barrel and lowered it onto the platform. The hot water and ashes made the pig's hair loose and we used garden hoes without handles to scrape it off then washed the skin with warm water. Finally, we hoisted the pig again, cut the head off, removed the entrails and put the heart and liver in a clean bucket to be saved.

One Saturday when there was about a foot of new snow on the ground, I shot a black sow, Dad stuck her and we were letting her bleed while we finished scraping another pig. After a few minutes, I looked up and saw her walking slowly out through the barnyard, pushing her way through the new-fallen snow and leaving a big red swath behind. I grabbed my rifle and shot her again, but after a few minutes she was up walking again, so Dad told me to just leave her alone and eventually she keeled over.

As we went along, we suspended the dressed pigs in a round metal granary where the temperature dropped to the twenties or below at night but never got above about thirty-five during the daytime. We kept a couple for ourselves and sold the rest. When we sold them, we loaded three carcasses, cut in two, in the back of the Green Monster and took them to Monticello. We parked near the main gate at the vanadium mill and sold the meat to the workers as they came out at quitting time.

This was during the war when meat was rationed and the buyers were supposed to give us rationing stamps for the meat, but we already had more stamps than we could use, so Dad told them to keep their stamps. "The government didn't raise these pigs," he said. "I did."

---

[5]The wooden and steel bar to which a work horse's harness pull straps are attached.

Book Learning

When I was in the fifth grade, World War II was still going on and teachers were scarce. My class went to school in the afternoon and the sixth grade went in the morning, in the same classroom with the same teacher. Consequently, my grade school education was abbreviated and I was never taught some subjects, like sentence diagraming.

In the cold part of winter, Dad took us to school in a bob sleigh. They let children like me, who arrived early and had no place to go until noon, wait in the library. We were unsupervised and had to be good or they would throw us out in the cold, which was frequently below zero.

After being thrown out a couple of times, I chose to be good and one day I was wandering around the back recesses of the library, where the big books with blank library cards are kept, when I found a gold mine. I discovered three or four long shelves of *National Geographic* magazines stored in chronological order and dating back to before I was born, possibly to the beginning of the magazine.

I still remember opening a volume to a beautiful color drawing of people gathering papyrus in the Nile River delta during the time of the Pharaohs. I paged slowly through each volume looking at the photographs, drawings and maps. Since we didn't take a newspaper or magazines or have a radio, and this was before television, it was hard for me to imagine other places, so what I liked most about *National Geographic* magazine was seeing where a country was on the map, then looking at photographs of the countryside, the plants and animals, and people in their native clothing, which made different parts of the world more real to me.

I usually read all the captions but not the articles because they were too long and had words I didn't understand. I started with the volume for November 1932 to see what was going on when I was born and then went to December 1941 to see what was happening when Pearl Harbor was bombed. I discovered that it was best to look at volumes on each side of an event to put it in context. The articles were usually timeless, so I found the advertisements more revealing; they always showed the latest products, clothing styles and things like that.

I spent the rest of the winter looking through the magazines and probably learned more than I would have in a full day of fifth-grade classes. They opened a new world to me and I started reading books of all kinds, especially nonfiction. I was hungry for knowledge and now I knew where to get it, even in Monticello, Utah.

Leather Thongs

My discovery of books led to a lot of experimenting, which was usually related to what I had been reading. One book about the Plains Indians contained authentic paintings showing how they outfitted their horses, which I found intriguing. I noticed that they rode their horses bareback or with just a blanket for a saddle. Instead of bridles, they controlled their horses with leather thongs around the lower jaw. I decided it would be neat to try out their methods.

One day I had to ride Crimpy to a field down the highway from our farm and bring back about six head of horses. It was an opportunity to try out the Indian tack, so I cut two leather thongs from an old bridle rein, tied one around Crimpy's lower jaw for a bridle and used the other to secure a small Navajo blanket on his back for a saddle.

I rode Crimpy over, herded the horses down the highway and into our upper hayfield, then got off to shut the gate. The horses stopped just inside the gate and started eating alfalfa. Everything was going along just fine.

While I was off shutting the gate, though, one of those little summer thunderstorms came up. Suddenly, big drops of rain started to patter on the ground and a low rumble of thunder came from Montezuma Canyon. Those summer showers always seemed to have the same effect on horses; they invariably wanted to run, fart and kick up their heels, so down through the hayfield they went, all having a great time. Meanwhile, Crimpy was stomping around, very impatient to go with them.

When I swung up on him, my seat had barely hit the Navajo blanket when Crimpy was off on a dead run after the other horses. I pulled on the leather thong and nothing happened. I soon learned that it wouldn't even slow him down. . . . *so much for Indian bridles . . .*

My next plan was to let Crimpy run until he caught up with the other horses, who by now had stopped at the corral. But when we got within a couple of hundred yards, I remembered that the fence corner near the corral was a ninety-degree angle. I knew Crimpy would make a sharp turn without leaving enough room between his side and the fence post for my leg and I could be knocked off. I had to do something.

A painting of an Indian brave clinging to the side of his horse while shooting a bow and arrow under the horse's neck on a dead run flashed through my mind, but I decided not to try it. Instead, I opted to bail out into the soft dirt of the plowed field before we reached the corner.

I got up, dusted myself off, walked over to Crimpy and took off the Navajo blanket and leather thong bridle. Then I looked around to make sure Dad wasn't watching.

Resting Places

During the two summers I herded cows, I learned a lot about them. They have individual personalities, can communicate in various ways, and ours could come up with some ingenious ways for getting into the beans and alfalfa. My observations indicated that they were intelligent and could think, but I had no idea the level that thinking reached until the day one of our cows died.

She had laid down and rolled backwards into an irrigation ditch with her legs up in the air, so she couldn't get up. When that happens to cattle, they die in a short time and cowboys spend a lot of their time pulling them out of holes. Our cow died before we noticed she was down and a few days later her carcass began to stink, so Dad decided to move it farther away from the house. I don't remember why we didn't just let the pigs eat it, but they were bigger by then and we probably had them penned up to keep them out of the garden.

We got the tractor and hooked it to a "slip," which was an eight- by ten-foot wooden structure with several rows of two by fours acting like sleigh runners along the bottom and boards nailed across the top. One lengthwise end was hooked to a tractor or team of horses with a chain bridle. It "slipped" across the ground and could haul a good load. We used ours to haul dry pinto bean plants from the field to the threshing machine.

Dad started the tractor and pulled the slip over to the cow's carcass. The rest of the cattle were grazing peacefully in the field around it. We maneuvered close to the carcass, got off, then each grabbed a hoof and dragged it onto the slip.

When we got on the tractor and drove off, the cattle went crazy. As if on signal, they all ran over and gathered around the slip. They started running alongside, milling around and sticking their noses up close to smell the carcass, while bawling frantically. I have seen this behavior twice. The second time, some cow entrails were on a wagon being hauled through a cow pasture.

Cattle show no outward sign of emotion if one of their own dies, but it obviously bothers them greatly if they are moved from their final resting place, or perhaps, if they are just moved after death. We can't communicate with them, so there is no way to determine the reason for their behavior. All we can do is speculate.

I have considered many explanations, from the possibility that they are like Catholics who place crosses and flowers alongside the road where a loved one has died, to the chance that cows are afraid of ghosts. After all, a ghost is a dead something moving. But, if that were the case, the cows would probably run the other way.

I have yet to come up with a satisfactory explanation for this bovine behavior. One thing is certain, though; cows get upset when they see dead cows, or parts of dead cows, moving. Why, is a really interesting question.

Navajo Blanket

One day Devon and Mona took Crimpy for a ride. Mother let them use my saddle and saddle blanket which was a small Navajo blanket that I used as an Indian saddle in a previous story.

While riding along the highway between Monticello and Blanding, the girls allowed the saddle cinch to get loose. The blanket worked its way out from under the saddle and both girls, then dropped to the ground without them noticing it. When they got home, they had no idea where they had lost it. In fact, they didn't even know it was gone. I was furious and, despite extensive searching, never found it, so I told the girls they could never use my saddle again. From now on when they rode Crimpy, they would have to ride him bareback. They just flipped their hair and said, "Fine."

About a month later, I saw them out riding Crimpy again, bareback this time, with Devon in front and Mona behind. They were headed home along a trail about a quarter mile east of the house and I noticed that Devon was holding the bridle reins loosely near the ends. Old Crimpy had his head down and was slowly picking his way along. Both girls were laughing, talking and having a great time, as oblivious to the world around them as they had been when they lost my Navajo blanket.

I ran down through the trees and sagebrush, hid behind a clump of scrub oak next to the trail and waited. As they came by, I jumped out and yelled, "Boo!"

Crimpy took one quick step sideways and stopped. That was enough. Mona reached forward, grabbed Devon, and they both went off in the sagebrush. . . . *now, we're even!* . . .

CHAPTER FIVE
Monticello

Crop Rotation

We lived on the farm two years, almost exactly, although it seems like I spent most of my childhood there. It was a happy time for me. Dad raised pinto beans the first year and I spent many long days walking up and down the rows hoeing weeds, which were mostly red roots, sun flowers, and Russian thistles which become tumbleweeds when they mature. The rows ran east and west and were a mile long, minus about twenty feet at each end.

We harvested the pinto beans in late summer. Dad had the machinery to pull up the bean plants and form them into rows to dry. He didn't have a threshing machine to separate the beans from the hulls, so he hired a man for that job and paid him with hundred-pound sacks of beans. The man's combine-style threshing machine could cut down the plant to be threshed, like a mowing machine, and also separate different sizes of grains and seeds from the straw or bean hulls. We used it as a threshing machine only.

We parked the combine at the edge of the field and hauled the dry bean plants to it on two slips, one pulled by a team of horses and the other by the tractor. The machine blew the bean hulls into one spot, where we stacked them in a big pile for use later as cattle feed.

When we started threshing, the combine was not adjusted properly or something else was wrong because the beans started coming out with leaves and stems mixed in. Each sack was about three-quarters beans and one-quarter hulls. Dad stopped the operator and they talked a while but never solved the problem, so Dad finally decided to continue threshing and have the beans cleaned at the elevator when he sold them. As we went along, it looked like a bumper crop.

We took the dirty beans to the elevator for cleaning and sale. After paying the elevator and the combine owner, giving the farm owner his share for rent, and keeping two sacks for our own consumption, we didn't have much left, so that year's bean crop was pretty much a bust.

The next year Dad planted winter wheat. To save money, he bought untreated wheat seed, which he planted early that autumn. It came up nicely, grew several inches and looked like rows of lush grass. The deer loved it. When cold weather came, the wheat plants died, which was normal.

That winter there was a lot of snow. I remember looking out one morning and the new snow reached to the top of the fence posts. When the wind came up, drifting snow completely filled small draws that were thirty to fifty feet deep. All that moisture meant we would get a good wheat crop next year.

In spring, the wheat came up from the roots, all nice and pretty, with lots of long, full heads. But when it was almost ripe and ready for harvest, it caught some kind of fungus and the heads turned sooty black. The crop was a total loss.

Shortly after that, the farm owner either sold the farm or kicked us off, because we moved into a house in Monticello. The new place, a three-bedroom house located just north of the Catholic Church in the southern part of town, is still there to this day. Sometime later, Dad bought a small place about two miles east of Monticello on the north side of the highway and we stayed there for the remaining time I lived in Utah.

Buck Fever

One early February weekend during our first winter in Monticello and soon after I turned twelve, Dad and I went down in Montezuma Canyon to cut fence posts. We selected juniper trees with straight trunks at least eight feet tall that tapered from about six inches at the bottom to about four inches at the top. We felled them with an axe then lopped off the limbs and cut out the tops. A good man could cut about a hundred in a day.

By early afternoon, I had cut a couple of dozen posts so Dad told me to take a break. I went back to the Green Monster, got his old 38-40 caliber, lever-action carbine and went deer hunting. Both the octagon barrel and the stock had been cut down to an overall length of thirty-six inches. The cartridges were short, like pistol cartridges, with large slugs of 180 grains each. The maximum effective range of the rifle was probably not much more than a hundred yards and, no doubt, it had a trajectory like a rock. Despite the war, Dad had managed to get six or eight rounds of ammo.

The deer yard up in the canyons during winter, so with about four inches of snow on the ground, there were tracks all over. I hunted along the canyon bench, picking my way through the piñon and juniper trees and skirting the edges of small sagebrush parks. After half a mile, just as I reached the crest of a small knoll and stepped out from behind a large sandstone rock, I spotted a two-point buck. He was in a small clearing to my left at the foot of the knoll, about forty yards away. He was facing me, pawing and eating grass under the snow.

He either saw movement or smelled me about the time I saw him because he stopped eating and looked up. I pulled back behind the rock and waited, my heart pounding. Then I got down on my stomach and inched the rifle out around the bottom edge of the rock. The buck was still looking in my direction, so I cocked the hammer, aimed at his forehead, fired and missed. The buck stood frozen.

I couldn't tell where the round hit, so I pulled back again, quietly jacked another round into the chamber, eased the rifle out, took careful aim, fired and missed again. This time, I saw the round hit a juniper limb, behind and a little to the right of the buck, and realized that I was tilting the rifle slightly toward me, which offset the barrel to the right. The buck still hadn't moved.

I pulled back behind the rock, silently levered in a third round, pushed the rifle farther out, got it straight up and down, aimed, fired and hit the buck right between the eyes. He dropped and never moved. I had killed my first deer.

Shooting three times at your first buck is a common boyhood experience and there is even a name for it, but usually the buck is running away, the boy is hopelessly overstimulated or both. I have no idea why mine went so smoothly and refuse to speculate.

Canned Raspberries

One weekend in the winter of my eighth-grade year, I went out to Aunt Offie's for a visit and my cousin Ray and I decided to go camping down in the canyons. We took our .22 rifles, bedrolls, some food, a frying pan and a few utensils. As I remember, we had about six pieces of bacon, four potatoes and eggs, some raisins and a half dozen baking powder biscuits, which we figured was enough for two meals.

We reached the bottom of Coal Bed Canyon in late afternoon, set up camp in a cave, gathered a large pile of firewood and built a campfire. We were sitting around the fire relaxing when Ray got an idea. He reminded me that we were only about a mile or so from Aunt Ruby's. They lived in town during the winter and no one was home. He thought we might go up to their place, break into the cellar and get some more food, maybe something for dessert, so we decided to give it a try.

Ray managed to break into the cellar and found several jars of canned raspberries. I don't remember if they were quarts or half gallons, but we took one jar back to camp. By the time we got there, it was just getting dark and had started to snow. We cooked and ate our supper, then settled down beside the campfire and started eating the raspberries. We passed them back and forth while watching the fire and thinking our own thoughts.

I loved spending time in the canyons. Most are wild and rugged with a lot of wildlife, breathtaking beauty and sometimes the sound of total silence. There was always something to do: exploring cliff dwellings along the canyon walls; searching for arrowheads and ancient Indian pottery scattered across the benches; or, my favorite, watching the wildlife, especially the big colorful lizards, which were hard to find.

Being in the canyons during the daytime was one thing, but being there at night could be something else. When the sun goes down, the deep canyons get dark faster than the land above, which leaves an unexpected empty feeling and sense of foreboding that is impossible to describe. I'd camped in the wilderness before, so this feeling surprised me the first time I stayed overnight in a deep canyon. Since then, I've learned to expect it, but it never goes away. The bottom of a deep canyon at night is a dark and lonely place, especially in winter.

We were camped not far from the headwaters of Coal Bed, which becomes a big canyon but is relatively small at that point. We had our camp set up in a nice-sized sandstone cave in the bottom ledge with plenty of room in front for the campfire. On one side, oak leaves had drifted in and made a nice foundation for our bedrolls. There was a pile of jumbled rocks in the back of the cave, and a small grove of scrub oaks a few feet wide were growing across the mouth.

By now there were a good four inches of snow on the ground and the empty branches of the oaks were white and fluffy. With the light from the campfire, we could see into the oaks, but not much on the other side. Through gaps between the trunks we got glimpses of large snowflakes falling for a little way into the darkness beyond, then nothing.

We were well into the raspberries when both of us thought we saw something on the other side of the oaks. I thought I'd seen something tan moving along the far edge and Ray thought he'd seen some eyes shining in the dark. We grabbed our rifles, put them across our knees and strained to see any movement in the darkness beyond the oaks. While we were looking, Ray turned to me, nodded toward the back of the cave and said, "I wonder if there's a den back in those rocks?"

We began telling ourselves how safe we were with our guns, the fire and our supply of firewood, but just to make sure, we fired a couple of rounds into the canyon darkness. Then, to be on the safe side, we decided we should stay up and keep the fire going. So, that's what we did, stayed up all night, watched for movement beyond the oaks, tended the fire and ate raspberries.

It was a long, cold night with the only consequences being that I lost a lot of sleep and my liking for raspberries. I couldn't eat them again for many years.

Criminal Record

When we moved into Monticello, I had just come off two years on the farm, where the time consumed herding cows, hunting, and walking to and from school precluded doing much with kids outside my family. Even in Blanding, the only kid I had played with was Larry Hoagland, so the move provided an opportunity to socialize with other kids my age.

One spring day when I was thirteen, two boys asked me to skip school and go hunting. They had a whole box of .22 cartridges and wanted me to get my rifle, which was probably why they asked me along.

We got my rifle and headed out of town going east along the ridge on the north side of South Creek. We took turns shooting for an hour or so, then while we were going through thick timber and they had the rifle, we got separated. I backtracked, picked up their trail and when I found them, they had entered a ranch house that happened to belong to my ex-aunt, who had been married to Dad's eldest brother before he died.

I went in and told them the place belonged to some of my relatives and that they had to leave. They left and headed down toward South Creek carrying the gun, as it was still their turn to shoot. I lagged behind because I was a little unhappy about the situation, but when they got to the creek, they started shooting so I ran to catch up. When I got there, I saw that they had wounded a couple of tame ducks, which were flopping around. I got angry, grabbed my rifle and killed the wounded ducks. I told the boys they couldn't shoot anymore and we headed back toward town, through some fields on the south side of the creek.

Later, as we went through a wheatfield, they showed me some pocket knives and offered to give me one if I'd let them shoot again. When I realized they'd stolen things from my Aunt's place I got even angrier and I pointed the gun in their direction and told them to take off. As they ran, I fired shots near their feet and then they ran really fast. I walked on home alone.

That evening my ex-aunt and her husband came by and told my parents their house had been robbed. They had seen us boys in the field, recognized me, and asked me if I knew anything about it. I didn't know what to do. I didn't want to squeal and just wanted the whole mess to go away, so I made up a story about seeing a redheaded guy near their house. I was never a very good liar so nobody believed my story.

A couple of months later, we went to juvenile court where we admitted the truth. The judge established a value for the stolen property and ducks then divided the fine amongst the three of us. My share was $23, which my parents had to pay, and that was a lot of money in those days.

I wanted to become an FBI agent when I grew up and my sisters knew it. When this happened, they taunted me: "Now you can't be an FBI man because you have a criminal record."

Yearling Does

Perhaps the second time I skipped school, a friend named Dale and I took off at noon one autumn day and went hunting out southwest of Monticello. With a full box of cartridges each, we spent the afternoon shooting prairie dogs and jackrabbits.

When the sun went down behind the Blue Mountain and dusk was coming on, we found ourselves about two miles from town at the head of a long, wide draw that runs north and empties into South Creek. The draw was covered with sagebrush and dotted with groves of scrub oaks. It was ideal deer country. We paused at the head of the draw and Dale said, "Let's run it and see if we can get a buckskin."

I nodded, then Dale discovered that he was out of ammo, so I dug into my pocket and pulled out four .22 long rifle cartridges. My gun was loaded, which meant we had five rounds between us, so I gave him two rounds.

We started running the draw. Dale walked down the east side near the bottom and I walked abreast of him, on a parallel course about a hundred yards away, up along the west side. That way if we flushed a deer, there was a better chance one of us would get a good shot.

When I got down near the end of the draw, I came to a knoll covered with piñon and juniper trees and instead of walking up and over it, I walked around the base on the west side, which put the knoll between Dale and me. When I reached the north side of the knoll, Dale was nowhere to be seen. I waited a few minutes then went back up the bottom of the draw on the east side of the knoll for about a hundred yards, stopped and whistled. Dale whistled back. He was way up near the top on the far east side of the draw. He yelled, "Keep coming, around to the big piñon!"

I walked another seventy-five yards and came to a big, dead piñon tree, where I found Dale's tracks and two expended .22 shell cases on the ground. He yelled again. "Come on up." I found him standing between two dead yearling does about twenty feet apart and the first thing he said was "How far is it, from here to the piñon?"

It was about four hundred yards. He had killed two yearling does, with his only two rounds from a single-shot .22 rifle, at that range.

The Deacon

I don't believe a person can live in Utah without some sort of encounter with religion. Most of what I knew about religion at that point came from Mother, who graduated from the eighth grade in Oklahoma and taught me the gospel with simple country sayings like "The Lord knows about every leaf that falls," which I've heard a million times. I once asked Dad about religion and he said, "I think it's all a bunch of bullshit." I never asked him again, so I'm not sure if that was his final word on the subject.

My family didn't go to church or say prayers. I prayed to myself privately once in a while and had the feeling that I was talking to God and that he was listening. Mother only talked about God, so Jesus Christ was just somebody I read about in books, with no special connection, so he didn't make it into my thoughts.

When you live in Utah, you either go to the Mormon Church or you're an outcast and have no social life, so after we moved into Monticello, I started going to an event called Mutual that was held at the Mormon Church every Wednesday evening. The meetings were opened and closed with prayer, but it was primarily a social event designed to keep the kids off the street. They always served cookies and punch and the regular guys and pretty girls were there, so it was a lot of fun. I learned to dance at Mutual and liked it so much that I started going to the Mormon Church itself, which is officially called the Church of Jesus Christ of Latter Day Saints.

For some reason that I can't identify now, I felt that I should join a church. I had been told that you couldn't go to heaven unless you were baptized and that may have been a factor. I wanted to join the right church, but I didn't know how to go about choosing a religion. I had long since stopped discussing serious matters with my parents, so this was something I had to struggle with on my own. The story about the boy, Joseph Smith, appealed to me because I felt like we were in the same boat, so, since he had chosen the Mormon Church, I decided to take a hard look at it.

Their thirteen articles of faith were a fair and reasonable set of rules and the people who went to the Mormon Church seemed normal. I was impressed with the way they handled their welfare system, and the Mormon Church seemed more democratic and logical than what I had read and heard about other religions, all of which had at least one aspect that was a nonstarter for me. I didn't understand some of the Mormon dogma, like getting baptized for the dead and being married for all eternity, so I decided to deal with that later. I figured that joining wouldn't do any harm as long as my relationship with God was preserved.

I was twelve when I joined the church. Mormon boys of that age are eligible to become deacons, which required completion of several tasks, one of which was memorizing the thirteen articles of faith and reciting them to a priest. I studied the articles and when I thought I had them down, I found a priest one day after school. He was a young man in his early twenties working in the office upstairs at Redd's Grocery Store.

During the recitation, I couldn't remember one article, the third one as I recall, no matter how hard I tried. Assuming that he would flunk me, I admitted that I just couldn't remember it. He said that was all right, that I'd gotten most of them, and signed off my card. I was stunned by his casual attitude. . . . *they don't even follow their own rules . . .*

Premonition

In the summer of 1947, Dad hired a big truck equipped with a wooden cattle-rack trailer and we hauled all our horses, including Crimpy, to Spanish Fork, Utah, where we sold them in the sale ring. I went along and rode in the cab between Dad and the truck driver.

After the sale, we put our saddles, bridles and other gear on some big tarpaulins in the curved front end of the trailer. Then the driver picked up fifty sacks of cement to take back for another party, which they stacked in the trailer over the rear double set of dual wheels. We headed home late in the afternoon.

As we were going over Soldier's Summit between Spanish Fork and Price, Utah, we stopped and I went back to the front of the trailer to get some rest. I got under a saddle blanket and promptly went to sleep. Later, the driver pulled over and stopped in the desert between Price and Green River and I woke up, frightened by a dream I'd been having in which I was somewhere far away from where I should be, with an urgent sense that I should get back to Dad.

I laid there a few moments trying to figure out where I was then went up to the cab, where both Dad and the driver were fast asleep. I didn't want to stay in the trailer, but was too ashamed to wake them, so I just stood there in the empty desert for a while and listened to the far-off whine of truck tires on the highway.

Finally, I returned to the trailer and laid there wide awake. A while later, the truck started up and we went on into Green River, where they stopped for coffee. After coffee, I told Dad I wasn't sleepy anymore and wanted to ride up front with them. We resumed our journey and just at daybreak were coming into Moab.

At that time, the highway came down the canyon from the north, went east about a half mile along the river bottom, made a couple of turns, and then went over the old bridge and on into Moab. When we came around one of the last curves and headed south toward a left turn at the water's edge, we saw the river for the first time. In the first light of dawn, it was an awesome sight. The river was in flood and the water was wide, deep and muddy, with uprooted trees and driftwood floating in rafts down the middle; the mighty Colorado was rocking and rolling.

Dad saw it first and said, "Look, Son! There's enough water to irrigate all of San Juan County!"

Both the driver and I looked at the river and apparently his hands followed his eyes. The right front wheel went off the shoulder and we started sliding around the edge. Dad reached over me to help the driver turn the steering wheel and about the same time tree branches started hitting the right side of the cab. The left front wheel hit a rock or something and we jackknifed into the river where the present-day bridge is, going about thirty miles an hour.

When we hit the water, the cab window busted; glass came back in our faces and a piece cut my upper lip. I first felt water around my feet then it was suddenly all over me. I floated up, hit the cab roof and got a bad feeling. Then we started down and pressure built up in my ears. When the cab came to rest on the river bed, there were twelve feet of water from the top of the cab to the surface and the force of the current caused the cab to tilt to the right.

As we sank, I remembered that Dad's window was open, so when we hit bottom, I dove over his lap and out the window. Dad grabbed my pant leg and I kicked back. He knew I was conscious and could swim, so he let me go.

I surfaced about fifty feet downstream and about thirty feet from the bank. The first thing I saw was my new Stetson hat floating ahead of me in the current and some big, ugly rapids coming up fast. I quickly swam to the bank, grabbed some willows hanging over and hung there to catch my breath. It was hard swimming in cowboy boots and Levi's.

I looked upstream and saw Dad straddling the trailer cattle rack, which angled down into the water. Unable to swim, Dad had left the cab and managed to grab the air hoses then reach across to the cattle rack and climb up the rack to the surface, holding his breath all the way. Just as I had done in that pond in Blanding several years before.

The driver could swim and got out on the upstream side. When I climbed up on the bank, I could see that the right rear dual wheels on the trailer were still resting on the river bank; the left rear duals were off the ground and rolling and the clearance lights were still on. The fifty sacks of cement had slid forward and now buried our saddles, and the place where I had been sleeping.

PART TWO
The Sailor

CHAPTER SIX
First Cruise

Emmett High

In the summer of 1948, I had to leave the high-desert country I love when we moved to Emmett, Idaho. The deep canyons, tall sagebrush and red dirt of my childhood were replaced with rolling sandy hills covered with cheek grass and short sagebrush. As compensation, we lived in a lush green valley with milder winters because of the lower elevation.

My personal situation improved greatly when I got my first job, which gave me more control over my life. I worked with about twenty-five men, mostly college students and men recently discharged from the service, for the Forest Service at High Valley Ranger Station in the Boise National Forest about fifty miles northeast of Emmett. We lived in boarded-up tents, slept on army bunks and ate in a cookhouse. For the first time in my life, I had all I could eat, with meat at every meal and even dessert, so I grew a few inches and gained several pounds that summer.

Our job, called piling brush, was to clean up the forest after loggers. We also learned how to fight forest fires and I went on three big fires that summer. It was hard work, the worst part of which was swinging a big, double-bitted axe all day. I woke up around four every morning with my arms aching so badly I wanted to cry. I had lied and said I was eighteen to get the job, so at fifteen I was a little young for that kind of work. On the plus side, I managed to earn enough to buy some nice school clothes and pay for my books and student activities card.

When I started my sophomore year at Emmett High, it was a regular, all-American high school with about a thousand students, which was a universe away from the schools I'd attended in Utah. My first cousin, Phyllis, who is the daughter of Dad's youngest sister, was in my grade and popular in school. As Phyllis's cousin, I was welcomed into a nice group and began to experience normal society for the first time. Phyllis decided that I didn't "look like a Gerald," so she unilaterally named me Jerry and for the rest of my life that's been the name used by everyone except my parents, siblings and strangers.

I now had an opportunity to turn my life around and knew I'd better take advantage of it. I wanted to graduate from high school, then go to college and take civil engineering, so I signed up for a full load of hard subjects, such as physics and algebra. In the process, I almost bit off more than I could chew. I was far behind in my education and had to struggle just to get Cs. At the time, I think the Idaho school system was rated first or second in the nation, so I was dealing with some tough teachers. My algebra teacher, for example, marked a right answer wrong if you omitted even one step while transposing a formula. But my main problem, which had come with me from Utah, was my family. In the atmosphere at home, I still found it almost impossible to do homework and flunked bookkeeping twice because bookkeeping is all homework.

Shortly after my sixteenth birthday, Dad called me aside one evening and said he couldn't afford me anymore and that I would have to leave home. I believed that he was responsible for me until I was eighteen and he seemed uncomfortable, so I thought that he wasn't serious or maybe didn't like what he was doing. Perhaps he was even trying to tell me he needed help. The same thing may have happened to him, because he did leave home at an even younger age. In any case, I said I wanted to stay until I graduated from high school. He agreed, but on the condition that I pay my own way, so I worked in a small sawmill for the next two summers and earned enough to buy all my school clothes, books and even my class ring.

I enjoyed my last three years of high school, especially my sophomore and junior years. I loved to dance and one year was in the floor show at the annual Mormon Church dance called the Gold and Green Ball. I was in a couple of school plays and joined the Thespian Club. I even took Latin and maxed out my library card by reading sixty-seven nonfiction books in one semester. In the end, I managed to knock off some of the rough edges and got an excellent high school education.

Union Dues

I graduated from high school on May 11, 1951, with the selective service breathing down my neck and the Korean War still going hot and heavy. I was sixth on the list to be drafted and my draft board was taking an average of three men each month. I had eight years of obligated military service staring me in the face. . . . *hello, world* . . .

My friends suggested that I get a job in the big sawmill in Emmett. I'd have a well paying job, belong to the union and, if I got drafted, my seniority would stack up while I was gone and both would be waiting when I got out. It sounded like a good plan. At least I'd save some money for college and maybe things would work out. I got the job and was assigned to the third shift.

The night I reported for work, they first introduced me to the union steward, who said I would be on probation for thirty days and would then have to join the union and pay dues. Then the company man took me to my work station and briefly explained my job, which was to straighten lumber before it entered the trim saws. I stood by a big table with a series of chains running across it from left to right. The lumber came in on a belt from the next building over, and when it dropped on the left end of the table, it was always crisscrossed to some degree and needed to be straightened before the chains carried it across the table, then under a curtain, and on into the trim saws.

When I first started, I couldn't get all the boards straight before they went under the curtain, so I studied the situation and determined that I needed to work on both sides of the table. There was a four-foot walkway along the other side of the table and behind it were several roller ways leading up to the head rig band saws. I assumed lumber came down the roller ways then flew out and dropped on the table, so it was a dangerous area because my back would be to the roller ways if I worked there. But no lumber had come down that way, so I started jumping up on the table and walking over and back to work on both sides. It was a successful strategy that allowed me to keep up even after the volume of lumber increased a short time later, so everything settled into a routine.

I always ate my sack lunch alone. The men seemed to avoid me, which I assumed was part of the probation. One night I noticed another man eating by himself and decided that nobody wanted to visit at that the time of night. I worked there for almost a month and no one talked to me at all, except maybe a "Howdy" when we passed. I never met my boss.

One night, while working on the other side of the table, I had just stepped to my right, when out of the corner of my eye I saw something moving behind me. My left arm was still back and resting on a piece of lumber when something nicked the end of my glove. If I hadn't stepped aside, a sixteen-foot beam that flew off a roller way and crashed down on the table would have slammed into the middle of my back and probably cut me in half.

I whirled and looked up toward the head rigs. More beams were coming and two guys were running toward me, yelling, but I couldn't hear them over the background noise.

Furious, I threw my gloves down, jumped over the table and stomped out to the office at the main gate. I said to the man there, "I just almost got killed; I'm quitting!"

"What happened? You can't leave until you talk to the union steward."

"The union can go to hell; I'm leaving right now and I'll be back tomorrow for my pay!"

Bush Pilot

After quitting the job at the big sawmill, I learned from a buddy that the Bureau of Reclamation had a special program and jobs near Moses Lake, Washington, for guys who wanted to take engineering in college. We both went to Moses Lake, got surveying jobs and were even given a small trailer to live in. I have a vague memory that food was provided, too, but at the least we did our own cooking. There were several teams surveying the area for later construction of some big irrigation canals. My job, which may have been the easiest I ever had, was to hold the pole that the surveyor looked at through his transit and to help measure distances.

On my first day, the team piled into a big station wagon and drove about twenty miles out into the desert. I was sitting by the door, so when we stopped, I opened it and got out. The surveyor told me to get back in and relax. We sat there for a couple of hours, shooting the breeze and drinking coffee, before we finally got out and worked for forty-five minutes. Then we drove fifteen miles to another survey location and did the same thing. On average, we worked a couple of hours a day and the job drove me crazy. . . . *civil engineering ain't for me . . .*

Weekends were almost worse because there was absolutely nothing that two young men considered worth doing. At the time, that area was a bleak desert with endless wind and constant dust storms, a real drag. We played card games, but my buddy beat me every time, another drag, and one Friday night we even went to a local grade school play. Worse yet, we learned that our draft board was taking more men and we probably wouldn't even get to college. By then we both had a bad case of cabin fever, so after an argument over something unmemorable, I decided to quit and join the service.

I was so pleasantly surprised by the amount they paid me on departure that I decided to prolong the joy by saving it and hitchhiking home. My first ride got me to the edge of town at Pasco, Washington, on the Columbia River. I had to walk a couple of miles through Pasco and Kennewick, but I didn't mind; it was a nice day and hitchhiking gives you a great sense of freedom, especially when you have a pocket full of money.

At the south edge of town, I got a ride in a new Buick with a woman and her three-year-old son. She was an attractive brunette about twenty-four who had driven down from Alaska to visit her folks in San Francisco. Her husband had stayed behind to tend to the travel lodge and outfitting business they owned. I told her I was going home to Idaho and would probably join the service soon to keep from being drafted.

We talked and laughed while she drove and really hit it off. After a while, she asked if I would like to go on to San Francisco with her; she had a lot of things to do and I could help. I could even go back to Alaska and work for her husband, who was a bush pilot and could teach me to fly a plane.

At one point, she looked back at her son, who was nodding in the back seat, and suggested that maybe we should pull over for a while and let him get some sleep. I could read clearly both her lips and between the lines, but she was married with a small son and that was always a red flag for me, so I reluctantly passed. When we got to Pendleton, Oregon, she went west to Portland and I went east to Idaho.

Welcome Aboard

Later that summer, another buddy and I planned to meet in Boise to join the paratroopers, probably because I didn't parachute off that cliff into the Dolores River or perhaps because all boys, at some point, want to be paratroopers. In any case, in a pivotal twist of fate, he didn't show up, so I went instead to the Navy Recruiting Office and told them I wanted to join.

Once the chief recruiter had my entrance exams and high school records in hand, he suggested that I go to college and join the NROTC instead. "Why go in the Navy as a peon?" he asked. I thought a peon was a Mexican slave, but feared it might mean more and was too shy to admit it. I was ignorant of college entrance mechanics and had never heard of NROTC. I didn't even know what questions to ask and secretly doubted that I had the brains or could get the money to make it in college anyway, so I said, "I just want to go in the Navy now and get it over with."

They put me on a train to Salt Lake City where I was given a physical and on August 9, 1951, I enlisted in the Navy for four years. I went to eleven weeks of boot camp at the naval training center in San Diego and near the end, when we submitted our choices for duty assignment, I volunteered for and requested submarine duty. My second choice was radioman because I assumed I would get to say, "Roger, over and out," like in the movies.

When everyone got their orders, mine simply said to report back to the naval training center, with no details about what I was going to do. When I reported back after boot leave, they divided a bunch of us into two groups: my group was going to Radioman A School for sixteen weeks and the other was going to Communications Technician School. I was dismayed to discover that I had to learn the Morse code.

When a radioman sent or received messages, he sat at a desk, called a radio operating position, which had a typewriter well in the center with a small desktop shelf on each side of the well. A telegraph key, connected to the radio transmitter, was mounted on the right side. We listened to the code through earphones plugged into a jack that was connected to a radio receiver on a shelf above and behind the typewriter well. We translated the code into characters (letters or numbers) then typed them on a message blank using a typewriter with all upper-case keys.

To graduate, we had to copy the code at 16 words per minute (wpm). We could only count up to about 6 wpm in dots and dashes per character, then had to learn the rhythm of the dots and dashes in a character, which was similar to playing a chord on a musical instrument. I graduated from Radioman A School in March 1952 and received orders to the USS Hanna DE-449, a destroyer escort stationed in San Diego. The Hanna was due to operate out of San Diego for the summer then go overseas in October. The Korean War was still on.

The day I reported aboard, the radio gang consisted of a chief radioman, a first class radioman, one seaman and two seaman apprentices, counting me. The next day, the chief retired and the first class got shore duty in Washington, D.C., so Monday we went to sea with one seaman and two seaman apprentices, counting me.

A ship the size of a destroyer escort normally required two radiomen on watch at all times. One man had to copy the fleet broadcast, called fox, twenty-four hours a day. Usually at sea a transmitter and receiver were tuned to a ship-to-shore circuit in case messages had to be sent out, but the circuit didn't require the operator's presence at all times. In port a transmitter and receiver were always tuned to the "harbor common" voice circuit, which an operator monitored at all times in case the ship was called. Radio frequencies that work at night don't work in the daytime because the ionosphere goes up and down, so transmitters had to be set up on new frequencies at least twice a day, which was a fairly complicated task that took several minutes. There were other duties, such as routing the message board, plus we had to eat during mealtimes, shower during water hours, go to the head and so on. Two men had to be available at all times, even though the second man was only busy about a quarter of the time, so until we got more radiomen, it was a hectic time. One good thing did come of it, I was never assigned to mess-cooking duties.

The radio gang was an independent group and didn't get involved with most shipboard activities. We handled all long-range, ship-to-shore communications. All tactical voice circuits were handled by officers on the bridge or in the CIC (combat information center). At the time, men in the Navy stood three-section duty with watches of four hours on and eight hours off and a dogged watch in late afternoon. A dogged watch is two two-hour watches in a row designed to shift the watch rotation. Radiomen usually stood watches of eight hours on and sixteen hours off and periodically dogged the watch in the daytime or on weekends. Our workload was always heavier in port than at sea because we had at least one extra voice circuit to man.

Since we only had three radiomen and needed six, we did what we had to do and slept when we could, often on a steel deck in the transmitter room. I was aboard ship about a month before I was able to go on liberty the first time. In those days liberty was a privilege and the leading petty officer, from whom you got your liberty card, controlled your life. Mine would have released me, but couldn't because we were shorthanded. We went to sea every week and had to do everything, whether we knew how or not. Under those conditions, you learn fast and I had been promoted to seaman by the time I went on liberty the fifth time. A few weeks later, we got a third class radioman and another seaman apprentice. About a month later, we got a second class radioman and that was the radio gang we had when we went overseas.

One day after I'd been promoted to seaman and had been aboard three months, the operations officer called me in and said the captain wanted to recommend someone from the ship for the Naval Academy. They had looked through all the service records onboard and I was the only one who met all the requirements, so he wanted me to apply.

Well, at that time the Navy was not too high on my list. My navy experiences now included boot camp, learning the Morse code, standing lots of watches and getting seasick. What I wanted to do was raise turkey red wheat, pinto beans and alfalfa, hunt for mule deer and fly fish for rainbow trout. I was a lover, not a fighter.

I also knew exactly what peon meant now, so I told the operations officer that I was going to do my four years and get out. There was no way I would ever make the Navy a career.

Fire Control

In October 1952, the Hanna went overseas. On the way to Japan, we stopped in Pearl Harbor and Midway Island for refueling and some liberty. One day at sea between Hawaii and Midway, I wandered back to the fantail where I could hear small arms fire. The men who stood quarterdeck watches were doing their qualifying shooting.

A first class gunner's mate named O'Leary, whom I knew and liked, was in charge. He had broken out some M1 rifles and .45 caliber pistols for the exercise and they were throwing empty tin cans over the fantail as targets. O'Leary saw me coming and said, "Watch out! Here comes a pussy from O division." I just grinned.

"Want to take a shot?"

"Naw, I don't want to make the guys look bad."

They were just winding up the session and O'Leary had a short clip of five rounds left, so he handed it to me with an M1 and said, "Take a shot anyway."

Putting an ammo clip in an M1 is a little tricky and a good way to bust your thumb if you don't do it right. I couldn't resist the challenge, so I deftly inserted the clip and asked, "What do you want me to hit?"

He motioned toward the last can they had thrown over, which by now was about three waves back and a good two hundred yards away. I took aim . . . *no way can you hit that little can . . . bobbing in the wake . . .*

I torched one off and the can went flying about six feet in the air. I don't know who was more surprised, O'Leary or me. I handed the M1 back to him, shook my head slowly and said, "I tried to tell you," and walked off.

For weeks, O'Leary tried to get them to make my battle station the fire control director for the five-inch guns. I would have loved getting my hands on that trigger and we might have become a more effective weapon, but I was in the operations department and fire control was in the deck department and the Navy just doesn't do things like that.

Near Miss

We stopped in Yokosuka, Japan, for refueling, replenishment and some liberty then headed for Korea, arriving on station off the North Korean coast just above Wonsan Harbor four days before Thanksgiving 1952. We exchanged flashing-light messages with the ship we were relieving and they headed out to sea, leaving us to confront the bleak Korean coast and the enemy alone. The captain called, "Battle stations for the duty gun crew," and told the officer of the deck, "We might as well let them know we're here."

I was off watch and standing on the bridge taking it all in. There was a railroad running along the coast a short way inland. The captain pointed to the nearest tunnel opening, about 5000 yards away, and told the gunnery officer to see if he could hit it. We fired the forward gun and the first five-inch round kicked up dust and smoke right at the tunnel opening. The captain shouted, "Again!"

We fired the after gun with the same result, then repeated the routine for about eight rounds. Each time, the captain made an enthusiastic little jump and yelled, "Again!" We tore up the tunnel entrance before we secured to start up the coast for a scheduled rendezvous with one of our destroyers.

Apparently we hit something that really upset the North Koreans. For the next two nights, as we steamed north along the coast, they fired either high explosive rounds or star shells at us every hour or so. The high explosive rounds usually landed several hundred yards ahead or astern. The star shells burst and floated down farther out to sea as they tried to see us in silhouette. Every so often we fired back at lights on the beach. I understand the destroyer escort we relieved had been there for six months without having even a star shell thrown at them.

The next morning, we met the USS Rooks DD-804 near a couple of small islands called the Yang Do Islands. The captain took the motor whaleboat over to the Rooks to attend a conference then we headed back south. Just before noon the next day, we reached what I believe was the same area where we had fired on the railroad. I'd had the midwatch the night before and was still in my bunk about to get up. We were steaming south along the coast and planned to go to battle stations and work on the railroad again at 1300.

While we were gone, the North Koreans had planted six shore batteries on a small point near the beach. At least one of the shore batteries was a big gun about the size of an eight inch. They were waiting for us and when we came abreast of them they started firing. The first round landed about a hundred yards off our starboard bow. The second round landed close aboard on the port side and splashed water up on the ship. The third round, from the big gun, hit the water a few feet from the ship and blew a five-foot hole in our side, two feet below the waterline where the gangway goes over on the starboard side.

When the first round landed, the officer of the deck sounded battle stations and ordered "right full rudder," which turned the ship toward the coast and caused it to swing to the left. This maneuver happened to prevent round three from being a direct hit and curtains for all of us. Rounds four, five and six landed simultaneously in a row off the port side, where the ship would have been had the OD ordered left rudder and headed out to sea, as the North Koreans obviously expected.

The near miss sprayed shrapnel into the forward fire room and into a third class machinist mate from Pennsylvania named Robert Potts, who was temporarily in that corner of the fireroom logging hourly readings on the evaporators. He was hit badly and as he went down water started pouring in. The other men started evacuating the fireroom and the last man up the ladder, Kit Carson, happened to look back and see Potts lying on the deck plates. He went back down and hauled him out, but he died a short time later.

The third round also ruptured the electrical cables going to the forward guns, leaving just the after five-inch gun and some 20MM and 40MM antiaircraft guns on the after part of the 01 level still operational. It also rocked the ship and knocked me out of my bunk. I grabbed my dungarees and ran to the foot of the double ladder leading up to the main deck, where I stopped and put on both shoes with neat bow knots then climbed up and ran forward a short way to my battle station, a 40MM powder room that we used for emergency radio.

A third class radioman named Davy was already there, sitting on the deck, praying. He had spots on the back of his faded dungaree shirt from water kicked up by the second round as he ran down the main deck from the radio shack. I asked him if we should set up the emergency transmitter. He looked up and said, "The batteries are dead," then bowed his head for more praying.

I sat down on the deck and started listening. The after five-inch gun was now firing every fifteen to twenty seconds and in between I could hear muffled explosions from incoming rounds. Their shock waves hammered the hull like a big steel drum and I couldn't tell if they were hits or misses.

Following several rounds, the 1MC blared, "Fire on the fantail! Fire on the fantail!" We had started laying a smoke screen, which had ignited the painted canvas cover over the smoke maker,[6] and the paint on the adjacent depth charge racks, which contained about six live depth charges each, was also burning. To avoid being knocked down by the muzzle blast, the damage control party trying to fight the fire had to wait until after the gun fired, run like hell past it before it fired again, then fight the fire while still in the blast zone.

Shortly after they passed the word of the fire on the fantail, the quad 40MM on the 01 level just above me started thumping away. I knew the effective range of a 40MM was 4000 yards, which meant we were about two miles from the shore batteries, which was almost point-blank range for them. I got the same bad feeling I'd had when Dad and I rode the truck off into the Colorado River and asked, "How close to the beach are we, anyway?"

Davy stopped praying long enough to raise his head and say, "If we were any closer, we'd be scraping bottom."

The North Koreans were firing both high explosive and antiaircraft shells. The AA rounds were bursting above the ship and showering the topside with shrapnel. The gun crews were hunkered down in the gun tubs, so the quad 40MM was being manned by two chief boatswain's mates, instead of the normal crew of about seven.

We were under heavy fire for twenty-nine minutes, which is actually a long time for things like that. It seemed like all

---

[6]The smoke maker was a fan-shaped device between the depth charge racks on the fantail.

afternoon to me. They fired more than two hundred rounds at us but hit us only once, with a near miss. We fired back a hundred and ten rounds from our after five-inch gun, leaving the paint on the barrel blistered and the loader, a big guy, exhausted. I heard we got credit for one shore battery and a possible. I don't know if it was the big gun.

Near the end or shortly after the action, the Rooks arrived at our location. I don't know if they engaged in the action or not, but they did send their doctor over to examine Potts. He told our chief hospital corpsman not to feel bad and said Potts couldn't have survived if he'd been hit like that a half block from a hospital in the States.

We steamed into Sasebo, Japan, about noon on Thanksgiving day 1952 with a big hole in our side and a dead shipmate in the reefer. All the ships in the harbor had their flags at half-mast.

Patrol Duty

In February 1953, two Canadian destroyers, an Australian destroyer and the Hanna escorted HMS Glory, a small British aircraft carrier, up into the Yellow Sea along the west coast of Korea. The Glory carried propeller-driven aircraft that were giving close air support to our marines inland. One day, while I was in the mess hall taking the exam for third class radioman, we rescued one of their pilots, who had been forced to ditch in the sea after his plane was hit.

A little way above the thirty-eighth parallel, we ran into small icebergs in the ocean, which eventually got so thick that we had to turn back. It has to be cold to freeze salt water and that area has got to be one of the coldest on earth despite being about the same latitude as San Francisco. I was glad not to be in a foxhole on the beach and my decision to join the Navy rather than being drafted was paying off.

One night on our way back south, we were stationed between the Glory and the Korean coast and steaming about ten miles offshore when we came upon about thirty lights scattered over the water off our port bow. It was a group of small fishing boats, each one with a single dim light mounted on a small mast amidship, probably working lights for fishing. The Glory contacted us on tactical radio to say the area was restricted and that the boats had to leave. I had gone to the bridge to route the message board, which the captain was holding at the time, so I got to stick around.

I didn't have any kind of personal relationship with Captain Meredith, who was a lieutenant commander, but he may have gotten word of my can-shooting episode and it was obvious that I liked spending time on the bridge. Anyway, I believe he held the message board on purpose so I could stay. The most exciting place I've ever seen is the bridge of a destroyer in nice weather. I emphasize the part about nice weather.

A South Korean ensign named Kim was onboard to act as our interpreter, so I assumed we'd go alongside the fishing boats and use the bullhorn to clear the area. But that could take a while, and meanwhile the rest of the task force would be steaming over the horizon. The captain had a better idea. He told the officer of the deck to have O'Leary bring a .45 caliber submachine gun and a can of ammo to the bridge. Pretty soon, here came O'Leary outfitted as ordered.

The captain ordered the man on the helm to steer the ship down through the fishing boats, "like you'd steer your own car." He told O'Leary to stand out on the port wing of the bridge and as we steamed by each fishing boat, he said, "Give 'em a burst; don't hit 'em, just scare 'em." There we were at darken ship with no moon and down through the fishing fleet we went with O'Leary firing a burst from the submachine gun as we passed each boat. After a few bursts, the lights started rocking rapidly toward the Korean coast. We kicked up speed and regained our station.

A few days later, after being released by the Glory, we were steaming independently down near the tip of the Korean peninsula and came upon a forty-foot fishing boat riding on a sea anchor twenty miles from land. There was no sign of life onboard. Ensign Kim hailed it several times with the bullhorn and got no response, so the captain said, "Sink it."

The duty gun crews had now moved from the five-inch guns to the twin 40MM mounts located port and starboard just below and forward of the bridge. If we needed to shoot in a hurry, the gun crew could man either 40MM, depending on which side saw the action.

The fishing boat was about three hundred yards off our port side and the captain wanted to use the twin 20MM gun mounted on the after port side of the bridge, so two gunner's mates ran up and manned it. The gunner opened fire with a short burst that went right through the fishing boat, throwing wood splinters and kicking up geysers of water twenty feet high on the other side. Within seconds, three half-naked men exploded from the boat waving their arms and shouting. Asleep and upwind of us, they hadn't heard our calls.

A few days later, shortly after we'd received a message warning us to expect a submarine offensive from the North Koreans, we were steaming along and got a solid contact on sonar. Now we're talking! A destroyer escort was designed for antisubmarine warfare and we could lay a pattern of ten depth charges at one time.

I was on the bridge routing the message board again when the action started. The captain called, "Battle stations depth charge," and we began our attack. When we steamed over the contact, they rolled one depth charge off the fantail. That surprised me as I'd thought we'd lay a whole pattern, but the old man probably wasn't sure he really had a submarine.

When the depth charge exploded, a vicious shock wave ripped the water white in a circle about a hundred feet in diameter, followed by a big geyser with a dark center and the familiar steel-drum-and-sledge-hammer sound when the shock wave hit the hull.

We were turning to port for another pass when, all of a sudden, a two-hundred-foot-diameter circle of white appeared where the depth charge had exploded. The new circle contained thousands of dead fish floating on the surface—and not a fishing boat in sight to collect the bounty.

Ocean Waves

In March we headed for Manila, where the Hanna was to be one of four U.S. Navy ships representing the United States at the 1953 World's Fair in the Philippines. The U.S. pavilion was a big replica of the liberty bell.

We headed south from Korean waters and after a couple of days were in the tropics. One beautiful afternoon I was off watch and lounging around with some other guys on the fantail with our shirts off, catching some rays. Lying on my back, I happened to look down at my chest and noticed a single hair growing near the center. I am Danish and German and have very little body hair, so without thinking and to myself, I said, "I'll be goddamned! I've got a hair on my chest."

The whole bunch jumped up and ran over.

"Where?!"

"Let me see!"

Almost at that instant, a huge wave—it must have been fifteen feet above the ocean surface and traveling at twenty knots—rose up over the fantail from astern and drenched the entire after end of the ship. We were hundreds of miles from land and I always thought it was a tsunami wave, but apparently they are not visible at sea, so I have no idea what it really was. If the men had not been up and alert, such a massive wave would probably have washed some of them overboard. Now we just had a bunch of drowned rats on the fantail and everyone, including me, had forgotten the hair on my chest.

I was excited and eager as we entered Manila Bay, as I had wanted to see the Philippines since my tour of *National Geographic* in the fifth grade. I knew we would pass right by the island of Corregidor and that Bataan was right over there. As we came into the harbor, we passed a forest of masts sticking out of the water from Japanese ships sunk by our air forces when we took back the Philippines during World War II. At the time, there was a sunken Japanese destroyer sitting on the bottom, right off the Manila Hotel, that looked like it was at anchor.

We tied up to a pier in Manila and I had the duty the first night in. I was a seaman with monthly pay of only $90, which was further reduced by my monthly purchase of one and one third $25 savings bonds, but I'd been lending some out at interest, so I now had about $200 and was planning some good liberty. I bought khakis and a nice polo shirt, so I could go on the beach[7] without a uniform, which attracted incessant hassling by everyone from pimps to little beggars.

After four months of nothing but the barren hills of Korea and salt water, I was looking forward to a change. Our liberties in Japan had mainly been spent hanging out in bars and houses of ill repute. Now, I just wanted to relax, see the sights, and, if I got lucky, meet a nice girl who could put a whole sentence together in English on any subject other than the price of sex.

I spent the next morning seeing the sights alone. Just after noon I wound up in a nice cocktail lounge on Escolta street in downtown Manila that was empty except for three American sailors in uniform from one of the other ships. I walked past them to the back of the bar and sat down. The three sailors were drinking American beer and talking to the bartender, a strikingly beautiful girl about nineteen who spoke perfect English. They were trying desperately, but unsuccessfully, to

---

[7]Navy slang for going on liberty.

get her to go out with them and bring some of her girlfriends along. When she waited on me, I ordered a beer and asked to see the menu. She preempted that by confidently recommending a San Miguel beer and some fried rice and lumpia, which I graciously accepted. The fried rice came wrapped in a banana leaf closed with a sliver of bamboo. Lumpia are small egg rolls, mostly meat, served with a sweet and sour sauce. Local San Miguel beer is some of the world's best and the combination was as good as it gets.

A few minutes later another girl, who turned out to be the regular bartender, came in and relieved the first girl, who sat down behind the bar at a small desk near me and started doing paperwork. The guys down the bar switched their attention to the new girl, who seemed to be more interested in their plan. I was still watching the first girl.

After a bit, she looked over and asked if I wanted another beer and we started talking. We had that end of the bar to ourselves and talked for quite a while. Her name was Pilar and her family owned that place and another restaurant. She was a college student and her paperwork was actually homework. I remember being curious about whether students in the Philippines studied English or Spanish in school. It turns out the language is Tagalog, but they also study English.

In turn, I told her that I was a radioman on one of the destroyers visiting for the World's Fair and, after a pleasant hour-long conversation, I got up to leave.

"Where are you going now?" she asked. "Do you have plans?"

"No, no plans, but what I'd really like is a nice date."

"I'll go out with you." . . . *all right!* . . .

I picked her up in a taxi at her home later and we went to a movie, which was the thing to do in Manila at the time as theaters always ran newly released stateside movies. Afterward, we had great Chinese food and a couple of drinks at a nice restaurant, danced a few times, then went to her apartment for an after-dinner drink. We sat around talking for a couple more hours, then she gave me her mailing address and a couple of sweet good night kisses.

It was a great evening. First, because I'd done exactly what I'd set out to do but, even better, because there was a witness; an officer from the ship had seen us in the Chinese restaurant and the word soon got out that Hansen had made out with a beautiful nice girl.

We left the Philippines for Japan, stopping overnight in Okinawa on the way. I had the duty and never got ashore, but Okinawa looked like a pretty island from our anchorage in Buckner Bay. The next morning we got underway and ran headlong into a typhoon named Ruth.

Ruth brought the worst weather I experienced during my entire navy career. She was truly ugly. A destroyer escort was about the worst kind of ship to be on in rough weather. When I went on the bridge to route the message board, I had to look up to see the tops of the waves, which were like mountains. We were routinely taking fifty-four degree rolls. The ship staggered up out of a trough, reached the top of the wave, dropped off the other side, hit bottom, drove you to your knees and your head against anything in the way, which produced many bandaged heads. Then it lurched and shuddered up the other side and did it all over again. Your stomach was slammed up and down the same way and almost everyone was seasick, especially me.

I will never forget that trip. One midwatch, I was sitting at a radio operating position, tied down in my chair with line and a shit-can[8] tied with more line to the side of my chair. I copied the fleet broadcast we called Guam fox for a while, puked in the shit-can, then went back to copying fox again. It was a long time from midnight 'til dawn. I promised myself and Brown, the other radioman on watch, "If I ever see land again, I'm going to put in for shore duty, even if it's in hell."

---

[8]Navy slang for wastepaper basket

We were in typhoon Ruth for five days and I was in bad shape when we finally reached Sasebo, Japan, and calm water. As soon as we tied up, I went down to the ship's office and submitted a request for overseas shore duty in the Philippines.

The P.I.

In May 1953, the Hanna completed her tour overseas and we headed back to the States. When we arrived in Pearl Harbor, I learned that I'd received orders for two years' shore duty at the Naval Communications Facility, Philippines, located at the Naval Station on Sangley Point, just across the bay from Manila. I was going to be transferred when we got back to San Diego, so I wrote to Pilar that I would return to the Philippines by the middle of July.

We tied up at the navy pier in San Diego at exactly 1147 on June 9, 1953, with flags waving and bands playing. I know the exact time because Brown and I won the $500 anchor pool. With the added news that the ship had gotten a letter promoting me to third class radioman on July 1, 1953, my life hit a high point: I would soon be a third class petty officer, had thirty days' leave starting the next day, had just won half of a $500 anchor pool and had orders for shore duty in the Philippines, where there was a beautiful girl waiting for me.

After my leave, I reported to the naval station at Treasure Island for further transfer to the Philippines. That's when the pink bubble burst. Treasure Island had no record of my third class letter and wouldn't try to trace it. As far as they were concerned, I was still a seaman, which meant I had to wait for a troop ship going to the Philippines. Had I been a petty officer (which I really was), I would have gone by plane. I waited a month for a troop ship then spent another nineteen days sailing to the Philippines via Guam, so my "shall return" date became September, not July.

When I arrived at Sangley Point, they also had no word of my promotion to third class radioman, plus my pay record was now missing as well. The disbursing office set up a temporary one, but only gave me a portion of my pay, barely enough for toilet articles, let alone liberty. Finally, a month later, my records were straightened out and I got my back pay and put on my Crow.[9] Then I called Pilar. When she said she had assumed I wasn't coming back and was now dating a guy from the American Embassy in Manila, the natural animosity any sailor has toward yeomen and disbursing clerks, who so freely fuck up their lives, became hatred.

I arrived at Sangley Point in a group of nonrated men that was automatically assigned to the receiving unit for indoctrination, which included classes on the do's and don'ts of a sailor's life in the Philippines, VD lectures and so on.

The naval station occupied the tip of a peninsula called Sangley Point, which extended out into Manila Bay about seven miles west of Manila. The naval station was about a mile and a quarter long and a half mile wide and tapered near the tip. The main gate led directly into a town named Cavite City, which we just called Cavite.

An airstrip ran east-west lengthwise along the north side next to the beach and the rest was occupied by everything needed for Island Americana, including a commissary and navy exchange, barracks and mess hall, hospital and dental clinic, dependent housing, officers', chiefs' and enlisted men's clubs, movie theater, bowling alley, ammo dump and a nine-hole golf course. On the south side of the base, some big seaplane aprons led into Cañacao Bay, the body of water to the south of the base.

The communications facility was in Building 8, a two-story structure with concrete walls two feet thick located a block from the main gate in the southwest corner of the base. It was

---

[9]Navy slang for a petty officer's rating badge.

the only thing left standing after the Japanese bombed the station on December 10, 1941, three days after Pearl Harbor.

The Naval Station was a relatively small base with a few thousand men, all Americans. It had only a few tenants: Commander Naval Forces, Philippines, a Rear Admiral, had his flag[10] there, plus the Naval Communication Facility, some navy VP Squadrons (P5M & P4M), a Mobile Construction Battalion (Seabees) and a Marine Detachment.

The admiral had a sixty-foot motor yacht, the Margaret, which was manned by a Filipino Insular Force crew of six to eight men. He used it to cruise around the islands on weekends and once used it to keep President Magsaysay, who was a famous and popular Philippine president, from being assassinated during an election. She was also used for recreation parties for the troops. When the admiral went out on the Margaret, he always took a U.S. Navy radioman with him to communicate with the base, and for a three-month period, I was the "admiral's radioman." After I left, I learned that Congress found out about the Margaret and she had to be given up.

In the red light districts of Japan and the city of tarpaper shacks called Pusan in Korea, I had merely glimpsed the ravages of war and desperate human conditions. But duty in the Philippines provided an opportunity for me to experience in depth a world far different from the one I had known in San Juan County, Utah.

World War II and Japanese occupation had been over for only eight years and the Philippines had received its independence from the U.S. just seven years before, on July 4, 1946, so it was a new country with the scars of war and Japanese occupation still visible. "Treasury of the United States" was still printed on peso and centavo notes and we got paid in military payment certificates (MPC) to keep greenbacks out

---

[10]An admiral has a flag for his command that is flown on ships and stations indicating that he and his staff are stationed there.

of the hands of communist guerrillas called the Huks who were at large in the countryside. They kept the Philippine Army busy and managed to make their presence felt in town sometimes. One afternoon in Manila, I went to step into the back of a jitney[11] and found myself looking down the barrel of a .45 automatic; he wanted me to take another bus, so I did. I knew a Filipino police lieutenant personally who was killed by a grenade one night in Cavite, so any place outside the base was also a dangerous place.

Our main defense against the Huks was to stay off the streets late at night and out of dark alleys. But in Cavite, a place with lots of sex and multiple partners, venereal disease was the biggest danger we faced, and it was an omnipresent monster.

Sangley Point is located about twelve degrees north and that's deep in the tropics, so much of the time it was a hundred and ten degrees and raining like a cow peeing on a flat rock. There was no refrigeration, so everyone went to market daily. The freshly picked fruits and vegetables included many I'd never seen before and still can't name. Maids, who did most of the shopping, demanded live chickens, swimming fish and shrimp that were still jumping. The pork was freshly butchered and the most expensive meat was pig liver. The open air markets were a festival of colors and odors and sensual experiences you can't get from *National Geographic* magazines. The most enduring aromatic memory I have is of a popular dish in which small silver fish called dillies, which had been dried whole, were sauteed with fresh garlic and served over rice with a dash of patis, a salty, amber-colored fish sauce that smelled like rotten anchovies. I loved the dish, but had to leave the area when it was cooking.

The Naval Communication Facility, Philippines, was a minor relay station, the contact point for ship-to-shore traffic from ships in the ocean areas halfway between us, Guam and

---

[11]Small, colorful bus built on a Jeep body.

Japan and around to Africa, so we covered a larger area than most major relay stations. Each radio room watch section consisted of about fifteen radiomen with a senior first class radioman as watch supervisor. The Coast Guard had two men on watch in a small radio room off to the side that they used to communicate with loran stations located up and down the Philippine island chain.

I was first assigned a split-phone watch, with the station ship Hong Kong in one ear and the international distress circuit[12] in the other. I exchanged messages on the Hong Kong circuit a few times each watch and listened for SOS traffic and transmitted typhoon warnings on the distress circuit. Most of the time I had nothing to do, so it wasn't long before I became interested in the heavy traffic circuits, where the operators used speed keys.

Morse code was normally sent with a standard telegraph key, which limits speed to about 20 wpm, counting five characters per word as in typing, but the code could be sent much faster using a speed key, called a bug. A speed key was constructed on a heavy metal base about a half inch thick, four inches wide and six inches long. A bar was mounted horizontally on jewel bearings about an inch and a half above the base. On each side of the bar were sets of electrical contacts that made or broke the transmitter keying circuit, causing dots and dashes to be formed. My speed key had an oval green plastic handle mounted at the operator's end of the bar, but most had two plastic handles, one round and one oblong. A short pigtail conductor exited from the far end of the base and was connected to the transmitter circuit at the telegraph key.

When the operator pushed the handle to the right with his right thumb, it caused the bar to vibrate, making and breaking the contacts at the far end, which resulted in a

---

[12](500 KHz) A circuit set up by international agreement after the Titanic sank.

series of dots that sounded like a machine gun. When the operator pulled the handle to the left with the inside of his right forefinger, it closed the contacts at the near end of the bar for as long as he held it over, thus creating the dashes. By rolling your hand back and forth, you could send Morse code at speeds up to about 50 wpm. We had to send and receive at 35 wpm to get a license and use a speed key on a navy circuit.

I bought a speed key for $20 from one of the guys being transferred, and when I wasn't busy on watch, I'd set up an oscillator and practice for hours. One of the chief warrant officers gave speed key exams every month or so, the first of which I flunked. He gave me some pointers and told me to keep practicing. I passed on my second try a couple of months later and became a rare bird indeed: a third class radioman with a speed key license.

Speed key operators were in high demand and short supply, so I was immediately assigned to the circuit with Commander Task Force 77, who was the "eyes and ears of the Seventh Fleet." He had his flag aboard a seaplane tender anchored in the Pescadore Islands and we had a lot of traffic with them. Since they were too far away for a radio-teletype circuit, we used CW[13] and speed keys on both ends.

Sitting that circuit made time pass quickly and earned respect from the other radioman, but I never let my rare-bird status go to my head. One reason was Satoa, the man who relieved me, who had once been a commercial radio operator. He was a Samoan and the best radioman I've ever seen. One time I clocked him sending Morse code at 53 wpm. He was

---

[13]Stands for "continuous wave," the normal method of transmitting Morse code. Only the transmitter's carrier wave was used to form dots and dashes, allowing all the transmitter's energy to be concentrated in one radio frequency thus allowing transmissions over long distances.

essentially translating the dots and dashes in a five-character word every second, and that's moving.

Satoa was a seaman, not a first class, because he loved to fight. He was about five feet tall, three feet wide and solid, blue-twisted steel. He could whip any five men at one time, but couldn't handle his liquor, so when he got drunk, he wanted to fight. I never knew whether he would show up to relieve me or be in the brig after putting a bunch of shore patrol in sick bay.

Angelina

By the time the Navy got my records squared away and I had money for liberty, I had also teamed up with a third class radioman named Ernest Lee Conner, whom everyone called Frenchy. He was Cajun French from Lake Arthur, Louisiana, and had worked on Mississippi River tugboats before joining the Navy. Recognizing at the outset the value of a good man covering your back in a place like Cavite, we sized each other up and joined forces. We were exactly the same size and eventually even started wearing each other's clothes because we lived in different Quonset huts and our laundry came back on different days.

Frenchy was more mature than the average sailor our age and the only close buddy I had in the Navy, but he did have a small problem. When we hit the beach, he would lay his money on the bar and spend like a drunken sailor until it was all gone, then expect me to do the same. I had a better idea. Early on, I started stealing some of his money and stuffing it in my pocket, then when he "ran out," I'd spend some of mine. The day after it happened the first time, I asked if he was ready to hit the beach and he said dejectedly, "I'm broke." I told him what I'd done and gave his money back. I don't know if he forgot my game in the heat of things, but he never changed, so I continued covering him.

Frenchy and I had talked about the pitfalls of liberty in the Philippines and carefully considered both of our options. We could pull liberty in Manila, which was my original intention, or pull liberty in Cavite. Going to Manila turned out to be a hassle because we had to ride a converted M-boat seven miles across Manila bay from the tip of Sangley Point to the fleet landing in Manila. The boats only ran every two hours and the last one left Manila at midnight, so you ended up getting Cinderella liberty.

We opted to spend our liberties in Cavite and agreed on a plan to protect ourselves. We avoided the major bars and more popular places where VD or a fight were almost inevitable. We stayed relatively sober and did our drinking in the better restaurants and bars not frequented by the masses. We only went out with the nicer girls who worked as food waitresses in restaurants or had similar jobs. Our goal was to take our time, find a clean, safe girl and "go native."

American servicemen have a way of describing any place in the world and we called the Philippines "the P.I.," the money "P's" instead of pesos, and every girl by her first name. If necessary, we added the name of the bar or restaurant where she worked, because they were all five foot two with black hair, brown eyes and one gold tooth.

Cavite was a town that existed only because of the base. It was composed mainly of bars, restaurants and hotels, although there were some nice residential areas at the edge of the jungle around the main part of town with two-bedroom, two-bath, palm-thatched bamboo huts standing on six-foot stilts in neat compounds complete with coconut palms, plantain and mango trees, banty chickens and long-tailed monkeys.

One day I was headed on liberty in Cavite when I ran into a guy at the bus stop named Knecht, whom I'd met on the troop ship coming over. He asked if I wanted to catch a boat to Manila with him.

"I'll pass," I said.

"Well, I can't handle all three of 'em."

I took the hook and asked for details. It seems he was assigned to special services and had recently escorted some Filipino movie stars and entertainers around the base for a USO-type show and one of the girls with the group had invited him home to meet her family. The family, which was wealthy, had three daughters and owned a private technical college in Manila.

That information created a real conflict for me. I knew there were others like Pilar in Manila, but I was now ensconced in the suburbs of Cavite with a girl named Julie and pulling liberty in Manila was such an effort that I'd ruled it out. At the same time, I did miss intelligent female conversation and had always wanted to go with nice girls, so this sounded like an opportunity to branch out. Perhaps I could have the best of both worlds: a good girl in Manila and a bad girl in Cavite.

It turned out to be an old-fashioned, third-world, courtship scenario. We met the mother, who was nice and friendly, and all three daughters, who were pretty and well educated. We sat around in a semiformal atmosphere, ate cookies, drank punch and engaged in small talk for a couple of hours. Knecht had his eye on Baby, the youngest daughter. I kinda liked the middle girl, who was a chemist.

We wanted to take the girls out, but couldn't without a chaperone and no touching was allowed. Presumably we passed the gentleman test because the mother finally agreed to a movie outing with the proviso that we stay together and be back by eleven. It was a good movie and we each got a good night kiss in the taxi, so it turned out pretty well.

The middle girl and I had a few double dates, but didn't hit it off, so that ended. In the meantime, Baby and I had become good friends, and since I was a gentleman, she wanted to keep me in the group. She knew a lot of nice girls in Manila who wanted to date Americans, but the boat ride to Manila was no fun and I was still in my comfort zone with Julie, so I didn't follow up. Still, I had tasted the wine of Manila—the Asian city of love.

During my brief exposure to Manila society, I was a little intimidated by the atmosphere and couldn't understand what so many nice, beautiful, rich girls could see in a bunch of sailors, even if we were gentlemen. One night we had gone to a party at the American Embassy and I'd started talking to a girl who was bouncing around in an excited state because she was going to Madrid, Spain, the next day for her debut. I'd never heard of anything like that and was at a loss for words. . . . *let's see . . . tomorrow I'll be copying Morse code . . .*

I came to understand that I was seeing the law of the jungle applied to people. Baby and the other girls in the group, at their level in Philippine society, were the most beautiful, most educated and fittest to play the survival game. While I had been hoeing beans and herding cows, they had been going hungry, watching their mothers get raped and dodging incoming rounds. They had experienced nature in the raw, knew the rules and were determined to put their assets to the highest use. In the prevailing culture, they had three options: marry a rich Filipino, become a rich Filipino's mistress or find a third way in a jungle of competition. American citizens were at the top of the food chain in the P.I. and we were a popular third option. I could clearly see the danger, but was also young and invincible. I wanted to live high on the hog and spend time with beautiful, educated, young women, so I ignored the forces of nature.

One evening at the enlisted men's (EM) club, I ran into Knecht and Baby, who told me she had a girlfriend who wanted to meet me. I was cool to the idea, but she was insistent, so I finally agreed to meet them at the fleet landing in Manila next Friday night on the 1600 boat. They and another couple would act as chaperones and we would all come back to the EM club for the evening.

On Friday afternoon I slept in after the midwatch and missed the 1600 boat, so I went to the EM club, got a hamburger and a San Miguel and waited for them. When they arrived, my date wasn't with them because the shore patrol had refused to let her on the boat without an escort, a policy I wasn't aware of. Baby jumped all over me and said to hurry and catch the next boat to Manila, because she was still waiting at the fleet landing, so I raced over and caught the 1800 boat.

When I got to Manila, nobody was waiting, so I sat down to wait for the boat to make its return trip to Sangley Point. Then a taxi pulled up and a young woman got out and stepped up on the landing. Wearing a light blue cocktail dress, black high heels and a sequined black lace shawl over long black hair, she was probably the most beautiful girl I'd ever seen. She saw me, walked over and asked in perfect English if I was Jerry. If I hadn't been, I would have been. She told me her name was Angelina and that she was my date. We shook hands and took the boat back to Sangley where we joined the others at the EM club.

Angelina was eleven months younger than I and had completed two years at Santa Isabella College. She now worked in a department store in downtown Manila and lived with her auntie, who couldn't have children and had "adopted" her. Her auntie was married to an attorney who was a senior official at the National Bureau of Investigation (same as FBI) and they were wealthy and had a luxurious home. Angelina was Spanish, Chinese and Filipino, called a "mestiza," and was not only a beautiful woman, but also a lovely person with a charming personality. She had gone to school with Pilar, whom I later learned had actually called in the second bartender that day so she could be free to visit while I ate my rice and lumpia; she had also been watching me and the predator became the prey.

Angelina was also an interesting person, with a history. Her grandfather had been a famous cockfighting champion.

He had traveled around the Orient before World War II and had fathered a son in Japan who eventually became an officer in the Japanese army occupying the Philippines. Angelina's father and grandfather had been thrown in prison by the Japanese, and her uncle, the Japanese officer, had gotten his father and half brother out without the knowledge of either the Japanese or the Filipinos; either group would have killed them all.

As a chip off her grandfather's block, Angelina was a remarkable and headstrong girl and to know her was to love her. When little, she had been coached by her grandfather and one night we went to a cockfight on the base that was part of a festival to raise money for Navy Relief and I learned the hard way that she could pick the winning rooster every time. Incidentally, that was my first and last cockfight; they strap razor-sharp little swords on the rooster's spurs and the result is a gruesome display of blood, feathers and guts. Along with bullfighting, it was a part of Spanish culture that I never understood. I like chickens.

Angelina and I started dating and the rest of my time in the Philippines is a story about us. It was an adventure-filled time and one that I always thought would make a great historical novel. It all started with our meeting at the fleet landing that night, so our song was *Harbor Lights*. She later became my first wife and the mother of all my children.

Telling the story about her and doing it justice would take another complete book, but that is not the reason I wrote this one. We were married for twenty-two years, raised a family together and in many ways had a successful marriage. She served with me and served this country during my remaining time in the Navy, and to me she will always be the "Little Mommy."

We have now been divorced for over twenty-five years; our children are around and love us both, so there are many things I chose not to write about for fear of tampering with their feelings, but I will tell the story about how we got married.

When I had about two months left to serve in the Philippines, a natural force called love found a way and Angelina became pregnant with our child. Neither one of us wanted her to have an abortion and leaving one of my children in the Philippines was simply out of the question, so we were suddenly faced with a dilemma.

In order to get married, I had to obtain navy approval, which included a six-month waiting period. Getting married without navy approval at the time was a general court-martial offense. If the bride was pregnant, there was still a three-month waiting period and we didn't have that long before my departure. There was also a rumor that, in cases like ours, the navy doctors gave the woman an abortion when she tried to prove she was pregnant.

After a lot of agonizing, I came up with an idea. We were, after all, in a third-world country where any problem can be solved with money, so we asked her uncle, who worked for the NBI, if there was a way we could get married and have it fixed so they couldn't prove it until after I got back to the States and out of the Navy.

Her uncle said he could arrange it, but that it would take money. We didn't have the kind of money needed, but her auntie did, so they made the arrangements and we were married in a brief civil ceremony in Quezon City on June 22, 1955.

On July 1, 1955, I left the Philippines for the States on the same troop ship I'd sailed over on. Angelina planned to stay with her family in the Philippines until the baby was born and then join me. When the ship departed the dock in Manila, I was on the deck looking down at my beautiful pregnant wife, who was on the pier looking up at me.

Leaving her behind was the hardest thing I have ever had to do.

CHAPTER SEVEN
Submarines

Four Corners

I was released to inactive duty after my first cruise ended in July 1955. I returned to Emmett, Idaho, and shortly thereafter my family and I moved back to the Montezuma Valley of Colorado. I wanted to return to the Four Corners and get a farm. The family just wanted to go home, especially Mother and Dad. I tried to use the G.I. bill to get a farm, then tried to use it to go to college and finally decided it was essentially useless for guys like me. Dad and I were both unemployed now and had to make a living, so we got a job with the Vanadium Corporation of America prospecting for uranium with a wagon drill on the Navajo Indian Reservation in northeastern Arizona.

The wagon drill was an ex-army half-track with an air compressor mounted on the back and a jackhammer mounted on a twelve-foot channel beam attached to the front bumper. The beam could be raised and lowered for travel or positioned vertically to drill straight down about fifty feet while prospecting. The jackhammer could be raised to add or remove ten-foot drill steels and we estimated the depth of any ore veins by how many drill steels we had on. We typically worked our way around the rim rocks on top of a cliff, drilling holes at random then looking at the color of the tailings to determine if we were hitting a vein. If we found color, we drilled adjacent holes and attempted to map the ore body.

It was a good job that paid well, but the working conditions were miserable. We lived in a tent, did our own cooking and it was now winter in the high-desert mountains. We stayed at the job site all week, then went home to Cortez on weekends. One weekend while we were gone, a pack of wild dogs broke into our tent and ate all our food, even the macaroni and flour, and licked all the shortening out of a half-empty can. We had to travel seventy miles one way to get more.

After a few months, the joy of being back on sacred ground turned into a grim reality. I still had no plan for getting Angelina and the baby from the Philippines to the States and my memories of her were now becoming more like a dream that never happened. The stark contrast between the life we had shared in the Philippines and the life we would face in the Four Corners made me realize that bringing her there would be like planting an orchid on the moon. As Dad always said, "That country is hard on women and pickups." For my part, I loved the sagebrush, the autumn foliage and the canyons, and especially the way you could see forever across the broad expanse of countryside. My dream—foolish as it may have been—was to find a way to live there. But it was a young, single man's dream, the kind you only get one of per lifetime, and now I had to give it up.

At Christmas time my sister, Mona, and her husband came down from Idaho to visit. Jack had been a corpsman with the marines who were cut off at the Chosin Reservoir during the Korean War. Now, unable to find work in Emmett, he was going back in the Navy. I was beginning to comprehend how complex my life had become and that I needed to get away from the family to concentrate on my own affairs, so I decided to join Jack and go back into the service, just for a couple of years.

When we got to Salt Lake City, I signed up for a two-year tour of duty as a station keeper at the Naval Reserve Electronics Facility in Santa Rosa, California. Since I'd been

Ultimately, I reached the top floor and the office obviously occupied by the Big Guy himself. When I walked in, an old gentleman was sitting behind a big desk talking to a secretary seated near him. They probably didn't expect to see a first class radioman burst into their office with a black look on his face. They both looked startled and started to stand up. I jabbed my finger at the old guy and said, "Sit down and don't say a fuckin' word! I want to tell you a story."

They sat back in their seats with their mouths open. I showed them the INS application form and described the problem in firm and exhaustive detail. He listened intently, and when I stopped, he turned to his secretary and dictated a blistering letter to the American Embassy in Manila. The secretary typed it up, had him sign it and then she put it in an envelope and handed it to him. He handed me the letter and said, "You mail it, Son; it will get there faster." I thanked him; we shook hands and I left.

A short time later, Angelina and Anna flew into Travis Air Force Base and I got to see my number one baby girl for the first time. She was thirteen months old, could talk and was afraid of me. She didn't know who or what I was and there was no way to tell her. Angelina and Anna Maria were now strangers in a foreign land, with only an ignorant country boy to take care of them.

Angelina and Anna had come to the States in March 1957 and our second daughter, Teresa Gail, was born in Santa Rosa, California, on December 15, 1957, almost exactly nine months later. I made first class radioman in November 1956, so by the time my Naval Reserve tour was up in 1958, I was first class with six years' active duty, had a wife and two daughters, and a speed key license. There was a nice little recession going on, and I still had no viable life plan.

Consistent with my college plans, I had checked out the local junior college and realized that I could not carry a realistic class load and do my navy job at the same time. I also knew that I was in a critical rating and could get anything I wanted if I went back in the regular navy.

I always faced my responsibilities head-on and decided the best option I had was to ship over and make the Navy a career. I figured that living in urban areas along the coasts would protect my wife and children from any racial prejudices they might encounter in other areas. I also decided that if I was going to spend my life in the Navy, then I wanted to do it as an officer. I gave myself five years to get a commission. My basic plan was to get as many schools as I could and work hard. I already knew that anyone who put in more than one box top per day would be richly rewarded in the Navy.

The Navy was chronically short of electronic technicians and to relieve pressure, they had just started a new thirty-one week Radioman B school at the Naval Training Center in Bainbridge, Maryland, to train radiomen to repair their own gear. I shipped over for six years on the condition that I be sent to Radioman B School.

B School

When I received orders to Radioman B School, we moved to Maryland and into new navy housing near the base, which meant that I could walk to school. When I reported in, I became one of roughly fifty men waiting to start school. To keep us occupied, they had us attend math classes and taught us how to use a slide rule. I ended up working for a month in the shop building radio receivers for students to use in troubleshooting practice, then attending math classes eight hours a day, five days a week, for two months before being assigned to my first regular class.

Each class had twenty students. All were radiomen and most were chief or first class petty officers. We had a few second class in the school and there was even a marine tech sergeant in my class. Despite our high motivation—our careers were on the line—the school still had a twenty-five percent failure rate, the highest in the Navy at the time. Men who couldn't make it were weeded out in a hurry and sent back to the fleet, where radiomen were needed desperately. Most students failed during the first two weeks, when they taught DC circuits, and that was the easy part.

I was absolutely determined to graduate. I studied hard and did my homework religiously. I knew that I had to thoroughly understand all the basic principles or I would never make it. At first, I feared I wouldn't pass because there were so many things I didn't understand. Electronics is a hard subject anyway, but to make matters worse, many principles can be learned 180 degrees out of phase, as they can appear to work exactly opposite to the way they actually do work.

In desperation, I decided that if I was going to fail, I would go down fighting. I started asking questions in class and didn't let up until the instructor had explained the subject matter in a way I understood. It scared me at first that only a few guys were asking questions. We had lots of pop quizzes and a big test every Friday. To my surprise, I got good grades right away. That also got the attention of the other students because they started asking more questions, too. One day, an instructor stopped me in the passageway and thanked me for asking good questions, which, he said, helped him teach better. The whole situation gave me a new outlook on life and took a big bite out of my inferiority complex.

I graduated from B School near the top of my class and was now a first class radioman with a speed key license and also an electronics technician who could repair my own gear. Consequently, I was hot property and knew it. When I put in my preferences for duty assignment, I again requested submarine duty and this time I got it.

Main Induction

I received orders to Submarine School in New London, Connecticut, then took thirty days' leave before reporting in. During my leave, our third daughter, Susan Lee, was born, on May 10, 1959, in the navy hospital at the Naval Training Center in Bainbridge, Maryland.

At Submarine School, we learned the details of submarine construction and the operating principles of the various submarine systems and components. After learning those basics, we were assigned to a submarine and given six months to get "qualified in submarines," which required being intimately familiar with all parts of the ship and involved tracing out and making one-line diagrams of all the submarine's piping and electrical systems. We had to know how to do every job on the ship, from firing a torpedo tube to setting up a radio transmitter. The final exam consisted of an oral examination by the leading petty officer in each compartment, followed by a walk-through and oral exam on the entire ship with the engineer officer.

A submarine dived and surfaced by changing its displacement, which is the amount of water it pushed aside as it rested in the water. A World War II type submarine had two hulls, a thick inner pressure hull with a thin outer hull around it. Modern nuclear submarines have two hulls in only a couple of sections, but the principle remains the same. In the case of conventional submarines, the area between the two hulls contained both diesel fuel tanks and ballast tanks. The ballast tanks were divided into the "forward group" and the "after group." Another ballast tank called "bow buoyancy" was located in the bow. There was a large opening called a "flood" in the bottom of each ballast tank and another opening called a "vent" in the top. The vent was equipped with a valve that was operated remotely from the control room. The main ballast blow system, a high-pressure air system, routed air from air banks through the air manifold in the control room to connections in the top of each ballast tank. Diving and surfacing was controlled by six men in the control room: one man each on the hydraulic, air and trim manifolds, two men on the bow and stern planes and the diving officer.

When a submarine dived, the hydraulic manifold operator (chief of the watch) opened the vent valves, allowing air to rush out the vents and water to flow rapidly into the ballast tanks through the floods, thus replacing air with water, changing the displacement and giving the submarine "negative buoyancy," which caused it to sink quickly (dive).

Once submerged (under water), the first objective was to achieve neutral buoyancy to halt the ship's rapid decent, so the air manifold operator blew "negative tank" to a mark that was calculated to give the ship "neutral buoyancy." If that action alone didn't achieve true neutral buoyancy, other actions had to be taken. The trim manifold operator could flood or pump water between the auxiliary tanks and sea to achieve a more accurate neutral buoyancy or he could pump water between trim tanks located fore and aft to attain a more even keel. All maneuvering actions were controlled and ordered by the diving officer. Once the submarine was submerged with neutral buoyancy, it maneuvered up and down by changing the angle of the bow and stern planes— sort of like flying an airplane—both of which have been described as "hours of boredom, punctuated by moments of sheer panic."

When a submarine surfaced, the air manifold operator "blew main ballast" by opening valves on the air manifold in the control room, which directed high-pressure air into the top of the ballast tanks. The vent valves were now shut, so water was forced out the floods, replacing water with air and changing the displacement to "positive buoyancy," which caused the submarine to float to the surface. To keep the submarine from coming straight up or tail first, they always blew the bow buoyancy tank and the forward group first, which caused the bow to rise and surface first.

They have a saying in the submarine force: The only thing besides enemy action that will sink a submarine is stupidity in series. Submarines have built-in redundancy and are designed to withstand one equipment failure or one mistake, but they can't handle two in a row. When something goes wrong, the next thing done must be correct. Submarine qualifications are designed to insure that every man onboard knows the correct action in an emergency at any location in the ship because corrective action is usually needed in seconds and the man nearest the problem might not be the regular operator.

The crew actually determined when a man was qualified, and they understood that by doing so, they were putting their lives in his hands, so they took it seriously. The tests they devised to see if a man would panic in an emergency were probably not politically correct and some were pure evil, but it was a system that worked well.

During submarine school, we went to sea on a submarine one day each week for hands-on training. On my first trip on a school boat, I had an experience that was designed to make a point with the students, and which I believe captures the essence of the submarine force.

The ship had just dived and leveled off at periscope depth when the cook in the galley passed the word to the control room, "The main induction didn't sound right when it went shut."

The hydraulic operating mechanism for the main induction valve was located in the overhead of the galley, where the cook was stationed, and the valve itself was located in the superstructure above it, in the after part of the sail behind the conning tower. It was a big valve that shuts the main air intake for the ship when the submarine dives. If it failed to shut, a massive amount of seawater would pour into the ship and the main ballast blow system might not be able to overcome it. Failure of the main induction valve was one of the worst things that could happen to a submarine.

The cook was a first class commissaryman who was qualified in submarines, but I had never witnessed a situation quite like this before and was curious about how the officers would handle it.

When the control room got the word, the captain told the diving officer[14] to "Take her up." He made a sweep of the horizon with the periscope and then we surfaced. The captain ordered the chief of the watch to cycle the main induction valve several times while he and the engineer officer looked at the valve and the operating mechanism with flashlights. For about fifteen minutes, they looked over everything and talked to the cook while everyone waited and watched. We didn't dive again until everyone was satisfied that the main induction valve was operating properly.

This little exercise was designed to teach the students that every man counts on a submarine and that even the cook's word is taken seriously. I am sure the same event or something similar, was staged for every submarine school class. I got the message. But what impressed me was that submarine officers don't just give orders; they dive in and get their hands dirty.

The Ronquil

I graduated from Submarine School and got orders to the USS Ronquil SS-396, a diesel-electric submarine stationed in San Diego. She was originally built as a World War II fleet boat and had been given the Guppy IIA conversion, which included the installation of a fairing, called a sail, around the conning tower and a snorkel system. At the time, the Ronquil was a main-line submarine and we were still fighting the cold war. The first nuclear submarine, the Nautilus, had gone to sea in 1954, only six years earlier, and there were a few other operational nuclear submarines, but the main force was still represented by ships like the Ronquil.

---

[14]Officer of the deck is called the diving officer on a submarine.

A new commanding officer with the rank of lieutenant commander came aboard about the same time I did. He had some definite ideas about running a submarine and was soon dubbed "Bubbles Bothwell" by the crew. Before we got underway on what was the first trip for both the captain and me, the executive officer put out the word that the captain wanted a twenty degree bubble on any change of depth of a hundred feet or more, and that we should take care stowing the ship for sea.

On a diesel-electric submarine, the angle at which the ship was slanting up or down was measured by an inclinometer, which was similar to a carpenter's level, mounted behind the diving stand.[15] It consisted of a half circle of glass tubing mounted flat on a plate with the ends pointing down. The plate on each side of the tube was marked off in degrees—down-angle on the left and up-angle on the right. Inside the tube was liquid and an air bubble.

When the ship was on an "even keel," the bubble rested at the top center of the tube which was zero. When the ship slanted down in a dive, the bubble moved inside the tube along the graduations on the left, indicating angle of dive. When the ship slanted up, the bubble moved in the right half of the tube, indicating up-angles. Technically, the bubble stayed still and the glass tube moved with the ship, but the visual effect was that the bubble was moving. The terms "angles" and "bubbles" are used interchangeably in the submarine force.

The phrase "losing your bubble" meant that the air bubble had escaped from the tube and could no longer be seen. That could happen only if the submarine was going straight up, straight down or was upside down, any of which is a bad place to be on a submarine. I doubt if anyone has ever actually lost their bubble and lived to tell about it, so it is really a derogatory term meaning someone has lost control. At an angle of about thirty degrees, you fall either forward or aft unless you hang onto something.

---

[15]Large wheels which operated the bow and stern planes.

The ship was scheduled to go into the shipyard at Hunter's Point in San Francisco soon for overhaul and a new battery. There was always additional work needed that the Navy didn't have money for, so the crew was left to do it themselves or barter under the table with the shipyard to get it done. The currency for this barter was called "cumshaw," a term that originated in the Far East. Hunter's Point was a naval shipyard with federal civil service employees, who were open to a little graft and corruption, so for months the crew had been hoarding canned hams, coffee, mixed nuts and other goodies to be used as cumshaw during the yard period and it was squirreled away all over the ship.

When we reached a fifteen degree down-bubble on our first dive, shit started flying everywhere and it sounded like an earthquake as the cumshaw came crashing out of its hiding places. The captain took us down to two hundred feet, then back up to periscope depth with a twenty degree up-angle and everything went flying back the other way. We surfaced and the captain got on the 1MC and said, "You have thirty minutes to stow the ship for sea, then we're going to do it again with thirty degree angles." When we went down the next time, it was a wild ride, but I didn't hear anything banging, except my own heart.

Those two dives were my real introduction to the submarine force. We went to sea every week and it took some time to adjust to my new environment. One thing I noticed was that routine emergencies happened two or three times a day. For example, we'd be running along submerged when an electrician pulled the wrong lever and all the lights went out. Nothing is darker than the inside of a submerged submarine without lights and the first time it happened, I yelled, "Bears, skunks and wildcats!" When the lights came back on, the guys looked at me like I'd lost my bubble. It was too much to explain, so I said, "Guess you had to be there."

Submarine duty is impossible to describe in a way the average person can understand. You can only experience it and you can't handle that unless you are about thirteen percent crazy. It's hazardous duty: you have to volunteer and you get extra pay. But from an individual sailor's standpoint, it's not really as dangerous as working in the woods or being a cowboy. The trouble with submarine duty is that when something does go wrong, it usually kills all hands, so I guess it depends on what you consider hazardous and how you play the odds.

We spent a lot of time each day performing exercises to train the crew because a lot of us were new to the ship. One operation we practiced was called "ventilation alpha," in which we surfaced, opened the hatches in the forward and after escape trunks, started an engine and took a suction on the boat, which dragged in a big gulp of fresh air through the open hatches. Then we shut down the engine, shut the escape trunk hatches and dived again. The entire evolution was timed from periscope depth to periscope depth. We sometimes did it by operating the vent valves manually instead of hydraulically, which required a certain degree of coordination.

Since we would soon move off the boat into a living barge, the chief of the boat[16] had assigned me a temporary bunk in the overhead of the forward torpedo room in an area called the "hanging gardens," which was typically used by lower-rated men. The only disadvantage of sleeping there was that you heard any word passed on the 7MC, which was the PA system between all control stations. Late one night while we were running on the surface, the 7MC clicked on and a sleepy-voiced diving officer said, "Dive, Dive." The low rumble of the main engines stopped, the forward group vents popped open and air rushed out. The ship slanted down and it started to get quiet.

I was anticipating a leveling off and was almost back to sleep when the 7MC blared "Flooding in the engine room!

---

[16]The senior enlisted man onboard a submarine.

Flooding in the engine room!" The scream of high-pressure air hit bow buoyancy and the forward group, and the ship started back up. My mind told me that we would surface all right, but there was always that two percent chance, so it was still a bad way to wake up.

The problem was that the man on watch in the forward engine room had not gotten the inboard exhaust valve shut in time and the outboard exhaust valve had hung open. Seawater came back through the diesel exhaust system and reached the pistons while the engine was still rolling, which busted some of them.

Another time, we were acting as a target for some destroyers who were making passes over us and dropping concussion grenades called PDCs to simulate depth charges. Because a PDC could sink and explode on or near us, we were rigged for "hit shots," which meant we had installed double hatches and protective metal covers for the exercise. We were at battle stations and my station was with the reload crew in the forward torpedo room.

That day either the sonarmen on the destroyers were good or sonar conditions were ideal, because they were really kicking ass. They were making figure eights over us and hitting us on every pass. We got tired of that shit and went down to test depth, rigged for quiet and waited. Nothing happened for about twenty minutes, then suddenly another PDC exploded close by and almost immediately the bow started moving up and down and around and around in a corkscrew motion. We just stared at each other with our mouths open; there was no way this could be happening.

About that time, someone in the after torpedo room got on the 7MC and stuttered "Aba! Aba!" But before he could get the word out, the control room told us to fire a red flare to warn the destroyers topside that we were making an emergency surface. We fired a flare, surfaced and discovered that the last PDC had blown off the quarter-inch metal cover welded over the after torpedo room loading hatch. The metal cover had floated back and caught in the port propeller, then acted like a big propeller blade, making the stern wiggle and the bow wobble.

But it wasn't all stress. One Sunday afternoon, we were tied up alongside the Sperry in San Diego Bay and I was in the forward torpedo room working on my qualifications. Several other men were present, including a third class torpedoman who was performing maintenance on a torpedo, which was routine for a submarine, but not your normal Sunday afternoon activity.

A couple of suitcases crashed down from the forward escape trunk followed by a full fleet ensign in dress uniform. When he landed, he turned and said, "Hi men. I'm reporting for duty; my name is Peterson." The torpedoman looked him up and down then said, "No it ain't. You're too little to be called Peterson. Your name is Pete." He turned out to be a good officer and even the captain called him Pete.

To me the submarine force was an exciting world full of tough men with strong character. They were an odd lot to be sure, but they could all tap dance and if you don't believe that, just ask one.

CHAPTER EIGHT
Nuclear Navy

Homework

Shortly after the Ronquil returned to San Diego, I qualified in submarines and received my "dolphins," a pin worn above the service ribbons by submariners signifying that they are qualified in submarines. Enlisted men wear silver dolphins and officers who qualify while officers, wear gold dolphins.

A short time later, Commander, Submarine Force Pacific, sent out a message that any man in the force could apply for Nuclear Power School, without excluding radiomen, who were in a critical rating. I had never considered nuclear power as a possible career path, but it was an opportunity for more education, which did fit my plans, so I jumped on it. I applied and passed the qualifying tests, something I could never have done without the math I learned in Radioman B school. A short time later, I got orders to Nuclear Power School at Mare Island Naval Shipyard in Vallejo, California. We moved to Vallejo and into navy housing just outside the base and, again, I could walk to school.

When Admiral Rickover, a captain at the time, first conceived the idea of a nuclear submarine force, he went to academia for proposals on how to teach a bunch of sailors to operate a nuclear reactor. They told him it would take at least four years of schooling. He said he could do it in one.

His program consisted of six months of classroom instruction followed by six months of hands-on experience at a prototype nuclear reactor located in the desert near Arco, Idaho. The classroom portion included mathematics, classical physics, thermodynamics, water chemistry, metallurgy, nuclear physics, health physics, reactor kinetics and systems and components. Systems and components was an umbrella class that covered the operating principles of all kinds of mechanical and electrical devices and involved learning almost every basic engineering principle there is. Students destined to be reactor operators received additional training in specialized electronic circuits used in radiac instruments and various reactor control and instrumentation systems.

Class time was eight hours of tough work, five days a week. More homework was assigned than any human could finish, then grades depended on how much was completed. My normal schedule was to come home, take a couple of hours off to eat dinner and get the kids settled down a little, then do homework until at least 2300 every night, plus all day Saturday. I started my study periods by transcribing my daily class notes into smooth form in a small notebook, which I still have. Homework always involved complex math problems, which we did using slide rules because handheld scientific calculators were not yet available at the corner drugstore.

The thing I remember most about nuclear power school was the collision between science and country boys. Learning about science was hard on us. I can remember standing flat-footed and arguing with my instructor who was trying to explain that I couldn't throw a baseball any farther from the top of a hundred-foot cliff than I could standing on a level playground. Well, vector algebra doesn't lie, and once I understood that, I moved on to the hard stuff, like the revelation that the element krypton is an inert gas, not a green metal that zaps Superman.

They didn't teach English, anthropology, psychology or any of the other liberal arts subjects. It was all meat, which gave the country boys a vaudevillian stage for corny material like "Yesterday I couldn't spell engineer; today I are one;" or when confronted with the formula for the area of a circle, someone in the back saying, "No, pie are round; cornbread are square."

Halfway through basic school, Angelina broke our all-girl jinx and delivered our first son, Brian Peter, on December 31, 1960, in a civilian hospital in Vallejo, California. We got a timely income tax deduction and one of the two sweetest boys on this planet.

I graduated from Nuclear Power School "with distinction" then received orders for the second six months involving hands-on training at the S1W[17] Prototype in Idaho. We moved to Blackfoot and into civilian housing.

Generally, men in three ratings attended Nuclear Power School: electricians, machinist mates and electronic technicians. At that time, there were exceptions to the rule, such as enginemen who qualified as machinist mates and IC electricians who qualified as electricians. The electricians operated the electrical plant, the machinist mates operated the steam plant and the electronic technicians (called reactor operators) operated the reactor itself and maintained the reactor control systems.

Everyone got the same basic instruction, but the reactor operators received more specialized training and took a month longer to qualify at the prototype. I qualified as a reactor operator and made chief radioman on November 16, 1961. That made me one of only two chief radiomen in the Navy who were qualified as reactor operators. A total of six radiomen actually attended Nuclear Power School before the Bureau of Naval Personnel put a stop to it. Two of us qualified as reactor operators, three qualified as electricians and one dropped out on purpose, because he wanted to remain a radioman.

---

[17] Submarine, First design by Westinghouse; the USS Nautilus power plant.

The Cowboy

After I qualified at the prototype in Idaho, I was told that I would remain there as an instructor, but the orders were changed a week later and I was transferred to the Pollack SSN-603, which was under construction in Camden, New Jersey.

I took thirty days' leave and just as winter was coming on, we loaded the kids in our new station wagon and moved to New Jersey. En route we stopped in Cortez, Colorado, to visit my folks. It was still nice autumn weather, so Dad asked if I would like to go to the ranch with him for a week. He was working as the cattle boss at Indian Creek ranch, located about thirty-five miles northwest of Monticello, Utah. Although it was the tail end of the fall roundup, there was still work to do. One of his cowboys had gone on vacation, left his boots and saddle at the ranch and Dad thought they would fit me. I could see that it was important to him, so I agreed to go. I left Angelina and the kids with Mother in Cortez and we drove to the ranch in Dad's Scout, which was a four-wheel drive vehicle. The boots fit, so I took over his string of horses and became a cowboy for a week, which is nothing like being queen for a day.

Indian Creek was a big operating cattle ranch and working there was like stepping back in time a hundred and fifty years. But riding a horse is like riding a bicycle—you never forget—so I jumped right on. I'd done it many times before, but now I was under the watchful eyes of a bunch of hardened cowboys who weren't necessarily impressed by my chief petty officer title.

I knew there wasn't a dime's worth of difference between submarine sailors and cowboys. They're both a bunch of arrogant bastards who think they can do anything, give no slack to anyone and reserve all their sympathy for little animals and pretty girls. I saddled and bridled my own horse, swung up in the saddle and stuck when it bucked a couple of short jumps.

We were riding big, well-trained saddle horses who knew what to do as soon as they got a clue. All I had to do was provide the hint and stay on, which you do with your legs, so by the end of the first day, the insides of my legs were raw. I wasn't getting paid, except by Dad's grinning, so I got with the program. . . . *what the hell . . . I'm on vacation . . .*

After supper the second evening, Dad said a couple of the guys were going to take the Scout out to see if they could spotlight a deer and he thought I might want to go along. I borrowed a 30-30 Winchester carbine and three of us piled into Dad's Scout, with me in the front passenger seat, which is the best shooting position.

We drove around for an hour without seeing anything, so the driver decided to go farther down the valley to take a look in some alfalfa fields. I knew the real problem was a full moon, but didn't say anything because they were doing it for my benefit. We got there and were headed out through a big hayfield at about thirty miles an hour when we hit an area where the irrigation water was still on. The Scout went about fifty feet into the wet area and just settled down.

There is a saying, "You're not stuck, until you're stuck in a four-wheel drive," and we were stuck. We had a winch, but the nearest tree was three hundred yards away, so our only option was to walk out. "How far?" I asked and they reckoned about nine miles. In cowboy boots, carrying a rifle, with the insides of my legs raw, I faced a long and painful trip in the moonlight. While we walked, though, we talked about a lot of things and I picked up a tone of respect for my dad that I had never witnessed, or felt myself, and it gave me pause.

Dad and I had never gotten along when we worked together, which I'd blamed on two things: He was intimidated by my education and I could see his faults. Being a father, he could also see mine and tried to help using bits of cowboy philosophy, which were probably all he had and how he learned it himself. Unfortunately, I didn't understand their real purpose and ignored most of them. He did have one saying I liked though: "I've never seen a horse that couldn't be rode, or a cowboy that couldn't be throwed."

The next day we rode over to some corrals where they had a couple of hundred head of cattle, including about forty calves waiting to be branded, dehorned, castrated, earmarked and inoculated. There were a half dozen irons in the fire and even a small salt shaker on a nearby rock for the rocky mountain oysters.

A couple of guys on horses did the cutting and roping. The rest of us hogtied them and did the rest. The little heifers made out pretty well; they just got earmarked, branded, dehorned and shot. But the little bulls got castrated as well, so they wobbled off bleeding at both ends and bawling for their mommy. Mixed in with the smoke from the fire were the whistles and shouts of the cowboys, the bawling of cattle and the rich aroma of cow shit and burning hair.

I jumped into the melee and after I'd helped process three or four calves I suddenly felt nauseated, walked over and leaned against the corral poles then puked. Dad hurried over and asked what was wrong. I told him I didn't know; I just got sick all of a sudden; it must have been something I ate. Dad looked at me and said, "No, that ain't it. You can't do this kind of work unless you're used to it."

He told me to take it easy and they'd finish the calves. I noticed that he didn't call me Son now and thought back to my conversation with the cowboys on our walk in the moonlight. It dawned on me that I was looking at my dad for the first time as an adult. I'd already seen him take management actions and make leadership decisions with ease and confidence that I recognized as a petty officer in the Navy and, for the first time, I saw that while he might not always have been truthful or a good farmer, he sure as hell was a good cowboy. I guess in the big scheme of things that's not too shabby. Some think it's almost as good as being a Jewish carpenter.

The Pollack

We traveled back East from Cortez in the new station wagon, arriving in Philadelphia in the middle of the night. I got confused in traffic and wound up on Petty Island, but eventually we got across the Delaware River and into a motel in Woodbury, New Jersey, for the night.

The next morning I reported in to the Naval Shipyard in Philadelphia with Angelina and all four kids in tow. The second stop was the disbursing office for more money. I was almost broke after the cross-country trip and we had to rent a civilian house and completely restock the larder from the commissary.

A first class disbursing clerk looked over my orders and pay record then told me they could only pay me one month's back pay. I'd get my travel pay and per diem when the ship went in commission. I just stared at him; the ship wouldn't go in commission for at least another year and a half. I knew the money managers in the government had some creative ways to defer expenses, but this was ridiculous. "There must be a misunderstanding; my back pay isn't enough," I insisted.

There was no misunderstanding; he had checked and those were the rules. Pre-commissioning crews generally went to a ship only a couple of months before commissioning, but in our case, the Navy had sent all officers, yeomen, cooks and nuclear-trained men early, to assist the civilian test engineers and technicians during the reactor plant test program. The rest of the crew wouldn't arrive for months. I asked him for ideas and he suggested that I go to Navy Relief or the Salvation Army.

Many times I'd been screwed over by yeomen or disbursing clerks, who take care of all your personal records, but this was serious bullshit. I had a family to worry about. I asked to see the disbursing officer and was escorted into his spacious office. Realizing that he was a commander increased my stress level somewhat, but didn't stop me.

I explained my situation then said, "I'm a chief petty officer in the Navy and I don't think I should have to ask for charity through no fault of my own. I want some money." He quickly reviewed my pay record and said, "Wait outside, Chief; I'll see what I can do."

I'm not sure how he managed it, but I got over $400 that day. When the other crew members started arriving, some were worse off than I was and it became such a mess that the Navy had to change the rules in the case of our ship.

With our new-found wealth, the whole family shopped in the commissary, and we found a nice house in Deptford Township, New Jersey, about fifteen miles from the shipyard, which was located on the east bank of the Delaware River just upstream from the Walt Whitman Bridge. By the time we arranged for our furniture to be delivered and had moved in, the larder was full from another visit to the commissary.

The Pollack was a Thresher-class nuclear attack submarine under construction at the New York Shipbuilding Corporation yard in Camden. It was still on the building ways and several months away from launching. Although New York Ship had built the SS Savannah, the only nuclear-powered merchant ship ever built, the Pollack was their first navy contract for a nuclear-powered ship, which is why the nuclear crew had been sent in early.

I was the first crew member to report in, then later that day, a first class machinist mate named Conway arrived. Within a day or two the executive officer and yeoman showed up, so we were now in business. The crew moved into a living barge equipped with a galley, mess hall, crew's lounge, wardroom, living quarters and offices. For the first week or so, a whole lot of moving and organizing went on.

As a chief radioman, one part of my rating was to handle classified publications, so when the engineer officer got settled, he made me his administrative assistant and put me in charge of the technical library, with a couple of men to help. The tech library would play a major role in our training. The nuclear-trained men had already qualified on a reactor plant prototype and some had qualified on other classes of submarines, but we now had to qualify on an S5W[18] reactor plant, which was the latest and most advanced design.

We had a large amount of material to study, including the reactor plant manuals, technical manuals, electrical diagrams, electronic schematics, piping diagrams and so on, most of which was classified and much of which had to be updated periodically with the latest changes. I got my own office and a nice place to study.

A chief electronics technician senior to me was designated the leading reactor operator. We became friendly and he confided that he planned to get out of the nuclear navy. His current enlistment would be up shortly, so he was going to take his discharge, stay out for a few days, then go to a Navy Recruiting Office and offer to ship over if they did two things: withdraw his volunteer for submarine duty and give him a non-nuclear electronic technician billet. Before long he left and I became the leading reactor operator by default.

Since I was still a radioman, I needed to change my rating to electronics technician. I had two options. I could present my case in writing to the Bureau of Naval Personnel to make the change or take the next fleet-wide exam for chief electronics technician. With a bunch of hot-running first class electronic technicians working for me, I didn't want any doubt about my qualifications, so I took the next exam, passed it and made chief electronics technician the old-fashioned way. In the process, I became a chief petty officer in two ratings, which is also quite rare in the Navy.

The reactor operator (RO) gang consisted of three first class electronic technicians, six more electronic technicians who were second class and below, plus me. I divided our systems and the junior men among the three first class. I told them to become experts on their systems as they would be responsible for all maintenance and for qualifying the other crew members

---

[18]S5W stood for Submarine, Fifth design by Westinghouse.

on them. Then to get their attention, I offered a challenge: "I'll ask a question a day on your systems that you can't answer." I stumped them about ninety percent of the time, but I'm not sure if they recognized my use of the Phil Donahue principle, which is: You can make anyone look bad, if you're asking the questions.

Although the S5W reactor plant was at the cutting edge of technology at the time, this was before the computer chip, when electronics was a world of refrigerator-sized cabinets with six drawers of lights, meters, toggle switches, potentiometers and chicken guts. We had to troubleshoot electronic problems with multimeters, signal generators, oscilloscopes, tweaking screwdrivers and solder guns. Our primary plant instrumentation had a lot of magnetic amplifiers, which are fancy coils with a core and control windings, that were very reliable and had first been used on German pocket battleships during World War II. Our nuclear instrumentation had vacuum tubes and our reactor protection and alarm system was the only circuit with transistors. The electronic schematic diagrams that accompanied each system were typically three feet wide and thirty feet long.

The RO gang was a great group and my job as leading reactor operator on the Pollack was the most rewarding and satisfying job I had in the Navy. A chief petty officer's job is the best there is anyway, because they actually run the Navy.

At one point, we had to make a field change in the rod position indication system, which involved changing some electromechanical parts in several units. It was a very delicate and complicated operation that had never been done in the field, so my division officer told me to supervise the entire process personally. We set up a clean room between the panels in the forward end of the auxiliary machinery space and two of my RO's started in, with me watching over their shoulders.

They read the instructions out loud, then proceeded slowly and carefully with the first unit. Everything worked fine. From then on it was just a repeat for each unit, so I went up to the mess hall and sat down with a cup of coffee. A short time later my division officer came through the mess hall and gave me a startled look. "Why aren't you doing the field change?"

I looked up. "They run me off."

He gazed at me, turned on his heel and walked off. Being a Naval Academy graduate, he either recalled the rules and knew that officers tell chiefs what to do but not how to do it or he considered my relationship with the captain, in whose eyes I could do no wrong and vice versa.

The Captain was Commander Harvey Lyons, who later became a rear admiral and was Commander, Submarine Force Atlantic, the last I heard of him. Captain Lyons and I liked and respected each other. He was a good man and a good leader. He was head and shoulders above any other commanding officer I encountered in my navy career. Whenever we met in the passageway, I stood at attention with my back against the bulkhead and he would punch me in the stomach and say, "How ya doin', Chief?" When I could breathe again I usually said, "Fine, Captain." I am proud to say that I was a Lyons-trained man.

One day a guy came running into the barge to tell me the captain wanted me at the shipyard test engineer's office, on the double. I ran over and entered a room with about thirty people, including men from the naval reactors office, test engineers and electronic technicians from the shipyard and electrical engineers from Westinghouse.

They had a problem they couldn't solve. A welder's lead had induced a voltage spike in the source range nuclear instrumentation, which was a no-no and couldn't be allowed to happen. The shipyard technicians had identified the circuits involved, checked them out and decided there was no way this could be happening. The question was, Where is there a connection between those two circuits? Captain Lyons had said, "Get Chief Hansen," and everyone waited.

When I arrived, the captain described the problem. By blind luck, I had just been studying the power distribution diagram for the vital bus, which supplied electrical power to both circuits. I paused a moment for effect, walked over, pulled the diagram from a pile on the table and said, "Right here—they're adjacent windings on the same magamp."

The captain said, "Thanks Chief," and I left. The whole exchange, which took less than thirty seconds, made it Navy one, shipyard zero, and my captain 10 on the happy scale.

The executive officer was Commander Porter, who held quarters every morning on the pier and put out the word for an hour or so. He was very thorough. One morning he said some scuttlebutt was going around about the shipyard going on strike but that we should ignore it because the contract specified no strikes during construction of the Pollack. He finished by saying, ". . . and you can chip that in stone."

Well, the next morning the shipyard was on strike with pickets at all the gates and we had to show our navy ID cards to get in. At quarters, Commander Porter was very businesslike. He told us that we would have to start wearing our uniforms in and out of the shipyard, that there was no way of telling how long the strike would last, that they might not even pick up our garbage and that there were more questions than answers. He finished by asking if we had any questions. A small voice in the rear ranks asked, "Sir, how do you erase something that's chipped in stone?" There was a burst of laughter and Commander Porter was gently reminded that he was still in the submarine force.

Speaking of Commander Porter, on one sea trial that happened to coincide with Easter—must have been Easter 1964—Commander Porter came up with the bright idea of having an Easter egg hunt. The mess cooks had colored several dozen eggs and Commander Porter came into the chief's quarters to tell us that he wanted us to hide the eggs and then the white hats[19] would hunt for them. No one was brave enough to tell him what we really thought of that idea, so we went off to hide the eggs.

The inside of a nuclear attack submarine was a maze of nooks and crannies with literally millions of places to hide an object the size of an Easter egg. Well, we got with the program. As I remember, when the white hats were turned loose on the hunt, they found only a few. Of course, it is reasonable to assume that they didn't look very hard and that they probably ate some, but I heard that they were still finding Easter eggs years later.

Test Program

Soon after we arrived, in December 1961, the engineering department was organized to support the test program, which started long before ship construction was completed and continued twenty-four hours a day, seven days a week for a typical period of about fifteen months. Four officers and four chief petty officers were teamed up in four sections to be trained as engineering officers of the watch and engineering petty officers of the watch. The rest of the men were put into three-section duty, which was standard in the Navy at that time. I was teamed up with Lieutenant Frank Kelso, who eventually became a four-star admiral and served as Chief of Naval Operations and Acting Secretary of the Navy. He was the best officer I met in the Navy, and I am proud to say that he was a Hansen-trained man. He was also a Lyons-trained man, which helps explain why he got the top four stars.

Mr. Kelso and I had the duty for twenty-four hours at a time, were off for a day then worked regular hours the next two days. The duty section's job was to assist the shipyard test personnel as they conducted the reactor plant tests. Captain Lyons had a rule that either the engineering duty officer or the

---

[19]Enlisted men below the rank of chief petty officer.

engineering duty chief must be physically on the ship whenever any testing was in progress. When we had the duty, one of us carried a copy of the test procedures around, supervised the men in the duty section and coordinated things with the shipyard test engineers. We relieved each other when we could, but frequently we were both up most of the night, and at best, only slept part of it.

In other shipyards, the navy crew didn't get involved until the final phases of the test program, but in the Pollack's case, the shipyard had never gone through a reactor plant test program before, so the Navy wanted the ship's crew to assist them. We hadn't done it either, but we were nuclear trained and understood the rules, the technology and the dangers, which makes a world of difference. In our case, the shipyard test engineers and technicians supervised the tests and ran the test equipment while the navy crew operated all ship systems, turned all the valves and flipped all the switches. Consequently, we became much better qualified than was normally the case. I read all the test procedures and was involved with the decision making process, which gave me a rare opportunity to go completely through a reactor plant test program at the test engineer level.

Aside from the test program, my time on the Pollack was consumed by two pursuits: qualifying on a nuclear submarine, which was similar to qualifying in submarines themselves, and qualifying as a reactor operator and engineering petty officer of the watch.

Before we could take the reactor critical, which occurred during the last phase of the test program, every nuclear-trained member of the crew had to pass an oral examination administered by personnel from Naval Reactors in Washington, D.C. (Admiral Rickover's office). Reactor operators were the most critical personnel and required to be the most highly trained, so for months my three first class electronic technicians and I spent Friday afternoons in the wardroom in practice oral board sessions. The captain, executive officer and engineer officer asked the questions and we were expected to know everything about everything: the reactor plant, steam plant, electrical plant, health physics, water chemistry, operating procedures, casualty procedures and all the theory and gory details involved. Any question was fair game.

Sometime around early February 1962, I rode the USS Thresher SSN-593 on a two-day indoctrination trip from the navy ammo depot in Earl, New Jersey, to the submarine base in New London, Connecticut. I believe the Thresher then left New London and went to the Portsmouth Naval Shipyard in Kittery, Maine, for her post shakedown availability (PSA) and was on her first trip to sea after PSA[20] when she sank.

On St. Patrick's Day, 1962, the Pollack was launched, which is when some notable lady busts a champaign bottle over her bow and the ship slides off the building ways into the water. I stood on the port sail plane and rode the Pollack down. One evening a few weeks later, I was watching television and the news came out that the Thresher had sunk killing all 129 men onboard. I can still remember staring at the TV in disbelief. My trip on her was still fresh in my mind and our executive officer and some of our forward gang had been scheduled to ride her on that fateful trip, but hadn't because there was not enough room.

The Thresher sinking had a major impact on our test program and a profound effect on the Navy and American industry in general because the term "quality control," which hadn't existed in this country prior to that time, was introduced into our lexicon. In classic Monday morning quarterbacking style, changes were made in virtually every aspect of submarine design, construction and testing, from the way material is identified to the way a weld joint is confirmed to be sound.

---

[20]Three-month overhaul period when all problems found during the shakedown cruise are repaired.

As the leading reactor operator on a Thresher-class submarine under construction at the time, I was not only knowledgeable, but also right in the middle of the evolution. I was amazed at the depth and breadth of the changes and the short time frame in which they were implemented, which makes me think that the proper procedures were already "on the shelf" waiting for some excuse to use them. Well, a hundred and twenty-nine men is a damned good excuse, but a hell of a price to pay for not doing it right in the first place.

The Thresher disaster set our schedule back about a year while the shipyard recertified all welds and silver brazed joints to new standards, modified various seawater systems, redesigned the main ballast blow system and made other changes, some of which are probably still classified. Our test program and our qualifications continued at a slower pace and in May 1964, the ship was commissioned and became a ship of the line and the USS Pollack SSN-603.

On April 15, 1962, Angelina and I got our second sweet boy; our youngest son, Gary Dean, was born at the hospital on the base at the Philadelphia Naval Shipyard. I now had my three beautiful girls and Angelina had her two sweet boys, so we called it quits.

By November 1962, I had been a chief petty officer for one year and was otherwise qualified to apply for a commission, but I was still relatively new onboard and had not yet been visible enough to establish the exceptional shipboard reputation I wanted and needed, so I decided to delay applying for one year and changed my five-year goal to six.

Regarding my reputation, I didn't have to wait long. One day Mr. Kelso asked if I would help train some officers to trace signals through the reactor control schematic diagrams. I agreed, even after he added, "The only time available is late in the evening, for a couple of hours, after about 1900."

For a couple of months, I went up to the wardroom on my own time and taught several officers how to trace signals through reactor control circuits. These sessions frequently degenerated into a refresher course in electronics—like How does a capacitor really work? It was interesting and mutually beneficial; teaching is the best way to learn a subject, too.

A few months later, I submitted my request for selection to ensign under the limited duty officer program. The whole process required getting a recommendation from my commanding officer, passing a series of four tests that took all day to complete, being evaluated by a board of three officers on the ship and then being chosen from fleet-wide competition by a selection board in Washington. There was a saying about the process: "Many are called; few are chosen."

The day I walked into the wardroom to be examined by the board of three officers, all the men sitting there were lieutenants from the top half of their Naval Academy class and every one had been my student.

Gory Stuff

Rather than leaving things entirely up to your imagination while reading some of the following stories, this "sea story" is a brief description of the nuclear reactor plant and its operating principles for the type of plant that was on the Pollack, which has long since been cut up for scrap. Virtually all power reactors in the U.S. are of this type and operate basically the same way.

The complete plant consisted of a "primary" and a "secondary" system. The primary system was the "reactor plant" and the secondary system was the "steam plant." While producing power in a dynamic condition, both systems operated as a single power plant.

The primary system (reactor plant) consisted of two large-diameter piping loops. Each loop contained a steam generator and some main coolant pumps mounted in parallel. The two loops came together and mixed in the reactor vessel, which contained the nuclear core. The two loops were identical, so you can think of the primary system as a single piping loop containing the reactor vessel and core, a steam generator and a main coolant pump with primary water (called main coolant) being pumped around the loop and through the core in a big circle.

The core was housed inside the reactor vessel, a cylindrical thick-walled pressure vessel. The control rod drive motors, used to move the control rods inside the core, were mounted on the reactor vessel head. The core was made up of a series of fuel plates a fraction of an inch thick, with water channels of about the same size between them. The control rods were interspersed among the fuel plates and from the end it looked like a metal filter. The uranium fuel, enriched with the isotope U-235, was canned inside the fuel plates by a thin layer of corrosion-resistant metal.

The control rods were not rods, but more like swords. They were made of hafnium an element (metal) that has several isotopes with high "absorption cross-sections" for neutrons, which means they will readily absorb and neutralize neutrons, similar to a sponge soaking up water.

The steam generator was a large cylindrical tube-and-shell heat exchanger mounted vertically. The main coolant loop piping entered at the lower end, then the primary water flowed through the inside of small tubes arranged in an inverted U-shaped bundle then also exited at the lower end. The shell side of the steam generator was filled two-thirds full with secondary water, which was allowed to reach saturation temperature and pressure and turn to steam. Saturation is a precise technical term for the boiling point. The secondary water surrounded and came into contact with the tube bundle, which was the interface between the two systems and where heat energy was transferred from the primary system to the secondary system.

The main coolant pumps were large pumps that produced a lot of flow. The primary coolant was pure (distilled and demineralized) water.

For efficient heat transfer reasons, the primary water inside the main coolant loops and reactor vessel was maintained at a high pressure to keep it from boiling. This high pressure was generated and maintained by a pressurizing system that consisted of a large cylindrical pressurizer vessel connected at the bottom to the main coolant loop via a surge line. The lower section of the pressurizer contained electric heaters, and a set of spray nozzles was mounted in the top.

The pressurizer was filled with primary water and a steam "bubble" was formed in the upper half, by draining as it heated up. The water inside the pressurizer was maintained at saturation temperature and pressure. The electric heaters raised the water temperature a couple of hundred degrees above the temperature of the primary water in the loops. Heating the water inside the pressurizer also raised the pressure, and when a set pressure was reached, the sprays came on, which cooled the steam bubble and thus maintained a band of pressure. This high pressure was transmitted and applied to the main coolant loops via the surge line and gave the reactor its name: pressurized water reactor.

All primary system components that emitted radiation or contained radioactive material were located inside the reactor compartment, which was normally unmanned. A shielded tunnel passageway ran through the upper part of the reactor compartment from the auxiliary machinery space (aft) to the amidship compartment or missile compartment (forward), allowing personnel to travel fore and aft. Personnel entered the reactor compartment from the tunnel.

The secondary system (steam plant) was a conventional steam cycle. A main steam line exited the top of both steam generators and ran aft through the auxiliary machinery space to the engine room. Two main steam stop valves, located just inside the auxiliary machinery space, were remotely operated from the reactor plant control panel in the maneuvering room.

The maneuvering room was the control room for engineering operations. It was a small room located in the forward starboard corner of the engine room. The steam plant, reactor plant and electrical plant control panels were mounted left to right in the forward side of the room and each was manned by an operator. The engineering officer of the watch was stationed at a small desk behind the panel operators.

When the steam reached the engine room, it was used to run the main propulsion turbines, ship service turbine generators (electricity) and other steam components, such as evaporators for making fresh water, air conditioners and so on.

Steam was admitted to the main propulsion turbines through throttle valves controlled from the steam plant control panel. The steam passed through the main turbines, which propelled the ship via a set of reduction gears, that reduced the high turbine speed, about 5000 rpm, to a more efficient propeller speed, about 300 rpm.

The exhaust steam from the main turbines flowed down into the main condenser which was another large tube-and-shell heat exchanger mounted horizontally. The exhaust steam flowed over the tube bundle on the shell side. Cold seawater was pumped through the inside of the tubes by main seawater pumps, which took a suction from and discharged to sea.

The steam condensed back to water in the main condenser and fell down to a collecting tank in the lower section called the hot well. Main condensate pumps then took a suction on the hot well and pumped the water to a surge tank and the suction side of the main feed pumps. The main feed pumps increased the water pressure and pumped it back into the secondary side of the steam generators, thus completing the steam cycle and another big circle.

Although the primary and secondary systems operated as a single plant while producing power, the primary system (reactor plant) could be operated by itself and did so while it was being started up and while the primary system was being heated up to operating temperature. The primary plant produced steam and the secondary plant used it. The secondary system (steam plant) was totally dependent on the primary system and couldn't operate without steam.

There are three areas regarding nuclear power that are intertwined but are easier to understand if they are separated: how a nuclear reactor is started up; what nuclear radiation is; and how a nuclear reactor plant works. In this story I explain how a nuclear reactor plant works. The next story explains how it was started up and a little about nuclear radiation and radioactive contamination.

A pressurized water reactor plant, with both systems operating as a single plant, actually controls itself, as amazing as that may sound. The density of the primary water is the control mechanism that allows that to happen. The density of the primary water controls reactivity, which controls the fission process, and is the thing that makes it work. A pressurized water reactor cannot and will not work without water.

The primary water flowing around the loops and through the core served two functions. It carried heat energy from the core to the steam generators and acted as the moderator in the core. Water has a negative temperature coefficient for reactivity, which is fancy language that essentially means, when water is heated it expands, becoming less dense, and when cooled it contracts, becoming more dense. Reactivity is the name for anything that increases or decreases the intensity of the fission process. Think of the fission process as the number of fissions per cubic centimeter per second that are occurring in the active part of the core, which I visualized as a small oval cloud.[21]

---

[21]I've seen photos and it actually has an eerie green glow.

When a U-235 fuel atom absorbs a neutron, it rapidly comes apart in a process called fission. When fission occurs, the fuel atom splits, usually into two pieces called fission fragments, releases some energy (heat), and expels about three neutrons. The newly released neutrons can go on to cause more fissions, resulting in a chain reaction.

Before another fuel atom will absorb one of the new neutrons, the neutron must be in thermal equilibrium, that is, at about the same energy level (temperature) as the fuel atom, and is then called a thermal neutron. When the neutrons first emerge after fission, they are traveling very fast and are called fast neutrons. They must be slowed down to thermal energies before they can be absorbed and cause another fission.

That slowing-down process, called moderating, is accomplished by collisions between the fast neutrons and other matter. The best kind of collisions are those between neutrons and matter their same size. A proton is about the same size as a neutron and hydrogen has one proton in its nucleus. Water has two atoms of hydrogen and one atom of oxygen in every molecule, so water contains a lot of single protons and makes a good moderator.

While the primary and secondary systems were operating as a single plant and when the main turbine throttle valves were opened, thus increasing steam demand, the pressure on the shell side of the steam generators decreased. The secondary water was now hotter than the saturation temperature for the new lower pressure, so more water flashed to steam to meet the new demand. The secondary water became cooler, dragging more heat energy from the primary water, causing the primary water to get cooler and more dense, thus making it a better moderator.

The primary water leaving the steam generators and entering the core was now cooler and more dense. This increase in density put the hydrogen atoms in the primary water closer together, which caused more collisions between fast neutrons and the single proton nucleus of hydrogen atoms. More thermal neutrons were created and made available to be absorbed by fuel atoms.

More neutrons were absorbed, more fissions took place, reactor power went up and more energy was released, causing the primary water leaving the core to get hotter and providing the heat energy needed to support the new higher power level. If the throttle was shut, the reverse happened. It was a natural and automatic reaction and required no action on the part of the reactor operator.

The change in density of the primary water entering the core caused the change in reactivity and the change in reactivity caused a change in intensity of the fission process. If the water got cooler and more dense, it added reactivity (more fissions); if it got hotter and less dense, it subtracted reactivity (less fissions).

For better or worse, the response time was essentially instantaneous. You could spin the throttle open and do zero to sixty in nothing flat. A nuclear attack submarine was also a hot rod.

Powers of Ten

Sometime in 1963—my memory says autumn, but it could have been earlier—we got the Pollack's reactor plant together and sufficiently tested to load the reactor core, which was a big event. The core contained uranium fuel, which was naturally radioactive, but the radiation being emitted couldn't penetrate the thin layer of canning metal, so even the fuel plates themselves were harmless as long as they weren't eaten. If you were to put the core in water, pull out the control rods and take it "critical," however, you would probably be dead before you could touch it and walk ten feet.

Critical is a specific term that I will use a lot, so I'll explain it. In a nuclear reactor core, at the atom level, when the control rods are pulled away from sections of the fuel plates and "expose" fuel atoms, the rods stop absorbing neutrons in that immediate area, so the adjacent fuel atoms are no longer "protected." Neutrons start buzzing around, colliding with hydrogen in the water, slowing down, being absorbed, causing fissions, and the neutron population, called neutron flux, starts increasing in a process called subcritical multiplication.

This process continues as the rods are pulled slowly up in the core until the neutron population, the number of fissions taking place, and the amount of exposed fuel increases to a critical mass, which basically means that the whole mess has reached a point where it can sustain itself at a constant level of activity. This condition is called critical, which is equivalent to describing an internal combustion engine as turned on or running.

A critical mass is like a beehive containing enough bees to maintain a constant bee population in the hive with a constant number of bees flying in, flying out, dying and being hatched. Neutrons are like bees. Criticality occurs when the active part of the core has a constant level of activity: the neutron population is not increasing or decreasing; a constant number of fissions are taking place; and, on average, there are as many neutrons staying in the core as are leaking out.

The reactor's condition was determined indirectly by neutron detectors, which were similar to Geiger counters and were the sensors for the nuclear instrumentation system. They were located around the outside of the reactor vessel. They detected and measured the number of neutrons leaking from the core, which were proportional to the number inside the core.

To determine when the reactor reached criticality, the reactor operator monitored two meters in the nuclear instrumentation system. When criticality was achieved, one meter, which indicated rate of change in neutron flux called the start-up rate, wavered from below zero to above zero and hung there. The other meter, which indicated neutron flux level, started a slow and steady rise. When those two conditions were met, the operator declared the reactor critical. Technically, the reactor was slightly super critical at that point. Sometimes the start-up rate dropped back below zero and the rods had to be bumped out a bit more. There were usually a few moments of uncertainty, but no bells or whistles.

At the point of criticality, the number of fissions taking place was in the order of ten to the tenth fissions per cubic centimeter (pea size) per second. The active part of the core was about the size of a watermelon and generated tens of millions of watts (megawatts) of thermal energy.

The reactor was shut down by simply driving the control rods in, to the bottom of the core. If an abnormal condition was detected by the electronic reactor protection system, it would automatically drive the rods in a short distance, called a cutback, or release the rods from the drive motors, in which case they were spring-driven to the bottom of the core, instantly shutting down the reactor, called a scram. The reactor operator could scram the reactor by flipping a switch on the reactor plant control panel.

The fission fragments generated during the fission process are actually new atoms, usually of unequal size. They are frequently highly radioactive and decay to lower energy levels by emitting nuclear radiation in the form of x-ray and gamma ray photons, alpha and beta particles and neutrons. A core that has once been critical contains a lot of decaying fission fragments and is lethal. When an atomic bomb explodes, the fission fragments are scattered over the countryside, get in air currents and are scattered over the world. When they finally land, they're called fallout and the area is said to be contaminated.

Radioactive contamination occurs when fission fragments or radioactive isotopes (atoms) from other sources are spread around. The amount of radioactive material present is expressed in units of curies. I always thought of contamination as cow manure. On the other hand, nuclear radiation is the particles and rays being emitted by the radioactive material and is expressed in units of roentgens, which I always thought of as the odor coming from the cow manure. Being a country boy, it was easier that way.

Since I was the leading reactor operator, I got to go into the clean room and examine the new core up close. I ran my white-gloved fingers over the fuel plates and wondered if they contained any of the uranium Dad had mined or any of the yellow cake we had scooped from that petrified log in Utah when I was a boy. It could have and I always wanted to believe that it did.

Once the core was installed, we had to set a continuous watch in the engineering spaces, start operating the radiation monitoring equipment, wear film badges and dosimeters and begin the regular regime of radiation surveys.

A short time later, after we had loaded the core in the reactor vessel but before we had filled the primary system with water, I had the duty. About 0630 the next morning (a Monday), I was standing alone in the reactor compartment tunnel when the forward watertight door opened and the chief hospital corpsman, who was the leading health physicist, stepped in with a concerned look. "Don't go forward; keep everyone aft; we got a problem."

"What's wrong?"

" I just took a swipe under the midship hatch and it's hot as a firecracker."

"Well, it sure as hell ain't coming from my reactor!"

About that time the executive officer stepped through the door and from his look he already knew about the problem. By chance, the local first team was now assembled so no explanation was needed. If the deck under the midship hatch, which was where the men first landed coming aboard, was contaminated with highly radioactive material, then the source of contamination was logically somewhere outside the ship. We looked at each other and you could hear the wheels turning.

The chief corpsman mustered the first idea. "I wonder if anyone washed their car yesterday?"

The executive officer said he had, about 1500, and that it was parked in his spot on the pier. The chief corpsman put on some booties and went out on the pier, passing a line of men waiting to get onboard. He took a radioactive sample, called a swipe, from the top of the executive officer's car. We counted it and the car's roof was contaminated with radioactive material to a level of about 39,000 micro micro curies per 100 square centimeters, according to my memory. I distinctly remember the number was just under 40,000 and way over our limit.

Our limit, at which we were required to stop work and decontaminate, was 450 micro micro curies per 100 square centimeters. A micro micro unit is now called a pico which in scientific notation equals ten to minus twelve, so we had 3.9 times ten to minus eight curies of typical fission isotopes scattered on the ground in every surface area 100 centimeters square. One curie of radioactive material generates 3.7 times ten to the tenth disintegrations per second, which meant there were roughly 1,443 subatomic particles or photons being emitted every second from every surface area the size of a single sheet of toilet paper.

We knew that the contamination had fallen on the roof of the executive officer's car sometime in the prior fifteen hours. We also knew that the Chinese had recently exploded an atomic bomb in the atmosphere, which is a fission reaction that generates the same cross-section of fission fragments (isotopes) as a nuclear reactor. A logical conclusion was that a plume of radioactive fallout from the Chinese bomb tests had descended on that part of Philadelphia, Pennsylvania, and Camden, New Jersey.

The radioactive contamination (fallout) was a fine dusting on the ground that was invisible to the naked eye. We took radiac meters out on the pier, but couldn't get a radiation reading at waist level and had to hold the probe near the ground before we got a reading above background. We didn't try to deal with the health ramifications associated with ingesting the contamination or drinking milk from cows that had; we couldn't do anything about that anyway. Our main concern was in keeping the contamination out of the ship or being forced to follow our very strict rules for dealing with it.

In this case, the radiation was effectively harmless, but the danger from the radioactive contamination was another story and we can only guess what damage, if any, it caused.

Deep Dive

We completed the Pollack's test program, passed our oral boards, took the reactor critical, completed all reactor plant testing and were set for our first sea trail. When the day came, we steamed down the Delaware River and out into the Atlantic. Admiral Rickover was always onboard for a new submarine's first sea trail and the Pollack was no exception.

The purpose of sea trials was to test all the things that can't be adequately tested alongside a pier. One of the first tests was called the deep dive, during which they dived the ship to its design or test depth and performed a hydrostatic test of the pressure hull. The Thresher was performing this test when she sank with all hands. We were the next Thresher-class submarine to go to sea on the East Coast and now it was our turn.

The deep dive was an all-hands evolution. The engineer officer stationed me in the upper level of the auxiliary machinery space where all the reactor control instrumentation equipment was located. The man stationed in the lower level was Conway, the second crew member to have reported in to New York Ship.

The deep dive was performed in increments of a hundred feet at a time. The ship went down to an even hundred-foot mark, leveled off and stayed there until all compartments checked for leaks and reported in to the control room. Then the ship went down another hundred feet and so on. The initial dive to test depth was a time when anything could go wrong and usually did. The Thresher disaster was still fresh in everyone's mind and the crew members, who were normally tense on a deep dive anyway, tended to avoid eye contact. The situation affects everyone differently, but it does affect everyone.

We had just leveled off at a few hundred feet and had all the watertight doors on the latch, so I was surprised to see the after reactor compartment tunnel door open and a rear admiral in wash khakis step in. He saw me and said, "It's a little crowded up there; mind if I stay back here?"

He went on to say that he'd been the supervisor of shipbuilding at New York Ship during most of the time the Pollack was under construction and was going on our first sea trial to sort of guarantee his work. He asked if there was anything he could do. I found my voice and said, "Yes Sir. You take the starboard side and I'll take port." I was sure he knew what to do.

While talking, our eyes met and each probably knew what the other was thinking. I knew he was there because of his principles, not because of any official requirement. He wasn't a submariner and probably didn't feel comfortable around people right then. I figured he had really come aft to find a place where he might have to face death. Finding such a place is not an easy thing to do, especially on a submarine.

I was there because I had volunteered and it was my job, but I wasn't very comfortable either; it was my first time to go deep. . . . *if this is it . . . I'm in damned good company . . .*

We completed the deep dive with no real problems, after which the admiral went forward and I never saw him again. I never knew his name, but I will always admire him.

Full Reversal

After the deep dive, the next big test was the full reversal. When it came time, I was on watch as the engineering petty officer of the watch with an engineering officer of the watch who shall remain nameless. He had the distinction of being the first officer from the bottom half of a naval academy class to be accepted by Admiral Rickover. He was also the ex-division officer who had come close to telling me, a chief, how to do my job when we were making that delicate field change in the rod position indication system. He was intelligent and a reasonably good officer, but had some gaps in common sense and bad hand-eye coordination.

The full reversal involved diving the ship to test depth then increasing speed until the ship stabilized at full speed, at which time the control room signaled "back emergency" on the engine order telegraph. When this signal, called a bell, was received in the maneuvering room, the operator on the steam plant control panel shut the ahead throttle then opened the astern throttle on the main turbines. This action rapidly reversed direction of the main turbines, reductions gears, shafting and propeller, which in turn caused cavitation near the propeller and violent shuddering of the ship's stern as forward motion was slowed.

The timed test started with the back emergency bell and ended when the ship was dead in the water at test depth. It was a scary and violent maneuver that we didn't look forward to. We knew the kinds of things that could go wrong.

When a submarine submerges, the pressure hull compresses inward, which can cause interference problems between mechanical components. On a recent West Coast sea trial for another submarine in our class, this compression had caused the emergency propulsion motor housing to start rubbing against the main shaft. The contact occurred during their full reversal test when maximum compression occurs, and when the stern of the ship was shaking violently and the main turbines, reduction gears, main shaft and propeller were all rolling at high speed and couldn't be stopped quickly. The rubbing caused rapid heat buildup that generated wispy blue smoke and then started throwing sparks and globs of molten metal around the after part of the engine room.

When our test started, the steam plant control panel operator didn't get the ahead throttle completely shut before he started opening the astern throttle, and we dragged too much steam. Well, once the reactor is critical, steam demand determines reactor power level, so when the operator opened both throttles, reactor power rapidly went up over 100 percent. The siren went off; red lights started flashing on the reactor plant control panel; and the reactor protection system actuated, driving the control rods in and reducing reactor power with a cutback.

When the siren went off, the engineering officer of the watch reached over and tried to shut the ahead throttle himself, instead of telling the operator what to do, which caused confusion and delayed proper corrective action.

I was in the lower level of the auxiliary machinery space, and when I heard the siren, my first thought was that the reactor had scrammed. That would have put all control rods on the bottom, shutting down the reactor and the primary system. The main steam stop valves would also have slammed shut, which would have shut down the secondary system. Without steam, the propeller stops, and so does the air conditioning.[22] Meanwhile, we were playing games at test depth and would have had only the main ballast blow system left to get us to the surface. That was part of what had gone wrong on the Thresher, so I ran to maneuvering to see what the hell was going on.

---

[22] Not just an inconvenience. The engineering spaces were a mixture of steam plant, electronics, and people inside a submarine. The temperature and humidity go up about two degrees and two percent per minute and it's a tossup which fails first, electronics or people.

When I got there, the red alarm lights were out, indicating that the condition had cleared. The reactor operator, my man Fredrick Wolfgang Finger III, ET1(SS), caught my eye and mouthed the word "cutback" so I knew that we were all right. By then we were going full astern; the ship was shaking violently; we were getting a big up-angle and the propeller was pulling us backward below test depth. Either the engineer or executive officer was present in maneuvering, which meant they didn't need my help, so I went around the engine room looking for problems.

After we got stabilized and back above test depth, I went back by maneuvering and the engineering officer of the watch was standing at attention, looking like a jellyfish washed up on the beach, and Admiral Rickover was chewing him up one side and down the other. I knew that the admiral's behavior was inappropriate because officers praise in public and criticize in private; and since we had just gone through a violent maneuver and everyone was on edge, his tirade was not helpful to the men on the control panels. The whole situation put me on full alert with adrenalin pumping. My job was to get us through this and if anything else went wrong, it would be over my dead body—I was now in don't-fuck-with-me mode.

A tense half hour later, they passed the word, "Shift propulsion to the EPM." We were going to shift propulsion from the main turbines to the emergency propulsion motor (EPM). To accomplish this operation, we had to shut off steam to the main turbines, allow the turbines, reduction gears and main shaft to slow down, then open the clutch and use the emergency propulsion motor to propel the ship.

The clutch was a hydraulically operated disconnect device located in the main shaft between the reduction gears and the EPM, which was a large DC motor whose rotor was wound on the main shaft with its field mounted around the main shaft. The whole assembly was enclosed in a metal housing. Opening the clutch disconnected the main shaft from the reduction gears and main turbines, thus allowing the EPM to independently turn only the remaining portion of the main shaft and the propeller.

As engineering petty officer of the watch, I stood a roving watch and was in charge at the scene, so when I heard the word passed, I went back to the clutch control station in the after starboard side of the engine room. A second class electrician was already there putting on a set of sound-powered phones to communicate with maneuvering. I glanced at the shaft rpm indicator and stood by, waiting for the main shaft to slow down.

At the same time, Admiral Rickover and two shipyard machinists were crawling around in the bilges aft of the EPM looking at clearances between the main shaft and the EPM housing with flashlights to see if we had any lack-of-clearance problems like those our sister ship had encountered.

When the electrician started the clutch control oil pump, it made a noise and the admiral stood up. He saw us, waved his flashlight at the electrician and yelled at me, "Relieve that man! He doesn't know what he's doing!"

I knew the man did know what he was doing because I'd qualified him on that station myself, so I didn't hesitate. "No, Sir," I said firmly. "He knows his job."

The admiral repeated the order loudly and the electrician started taking off the phones. I turned to him and said just as firmly, "Do your job. I'll handle this."

The admiral may have been a question mark, but Chief Hansen was a known quantity, so he put the phones back on and disengaged the clutch. The admiral glared at me for a few seconds then dove back into the bilges.

I looked forward and saw the executive officer and some civilians from naval reactors standing in the passageway just forward of the reduction gears. They had overheard the conversation and the executive officer's face was contorted with disbelief. One of his chiefs had just defied an order from Admiral Rickover.

A few minutes later, the electrician told me they were going to stay on the EPM for a while and do the EPM test, so I walked forward with my insides churning, the adrenalin rush now gone, and believing that my world was about to come down around me. The executive officer and civilians were gone and the guys in the engine room looked the other way as I passed. I glanced in maneuvering and all eyes were fixed on the control panels. I walked behind the panels and leaned against the ladder to the after escape trunk. . . . *you've done it this time Hansen . . . you are out of the nuclear program for sure and you can kiss a commission goodby . . .*

Later that evening the engineer officer came aft, found me and said he wanted a word. As we stepped aside, my heart was pounding. . . . *this is it* . . . The engineer, who was very sober and subdued, said quietly, "Chief, you saved our ass tonight."

"What?!" I exclaimed.

He told me that during the evening meal in the wardroom, Admiral Rickover had asked Captain Lyons who that chief was back there and the captain had said, "Chief Hansen, my leading reactor operator," and the admiral had said, "I told him to relieve a man because he didn't know what he was doing and the chief refused. If he'd relieved that man, it would have been the same as admitting incompetence, and your ship would be headed to port right now for requalification."

It seems that I had passed one of Admiral Rickover's infamous tests.

PART THREE
The Mustang

CHAPTER NINE
Groton

Chosen One

Shortly after the Pollack went in commission, the ship left Camden and went to New London, Connecticut, for a couple of weeks. After that we traveled to Norfolk, Virginia, to have the ship depermed. Upon arrival in Norfolk, I got the word that I had been selected for ensign under the limited duty officer (LDO) program and was to be commissioned on March 1, 1965.

The limited duty officer program was designed to obtain officers with skills in specialized areas. Since they received their commissions through the ranks and without benefit of a college degree, they were commonly called "mustangs," a name that reflected their reputation for being tough, mean and untamed officers with a wild horse side to their character. They could only advance to the rank of commander, or pay grade O5, and had to serve ten years as an officer to retire with officer's pay. Their assignments were supposed to be limited to billets involving their speciality, which in my case was either electronics or nuclear power, but they were also line officers and eligible for command at sea.

After finishing in Norfolk, we got underway again and went to Charleston, South Carolina, which was to be our homeport. By the time the ship had left Camden, most of the families had already gone to Charleston, but I had gotten encouraging indications about my LDO selection, so I decided to gamble and leave Angelina and the kids in New Jersey until I was certain of my next assignment.

Our arrival in Charleston was accompanied by a lot of fanfare from the community and a lot of grief for the crew. It seems that when the Pollack families had started moving into the new navy housing, the first kid out the back door came running back in and said, "There's a big snake outside!"

The mommy had gone outside and found a copperhead in the grass and a four-foot alligator under some bushes, so a group of the Pollack wives told the Charleston housing office to go pound sand then picked up their kids and moved back to New England. I can still remember one of the engineering petty officers of the watch, a senior chief electrician named Philbin, standing there with his arms hanging down at his sides when he learned the details, including that his wife had been a ringleader in the episode. I was relieved that my family had remained in New Jersey.

A short time later, I got orders to report to Main Navy in Washington, D.C., for my interview with Admiral Rickover. All officers were interviewed personally by the admiral and his staff before acceptance into the nuclear power program as an officer, even if they had already been in the program as enlisted men. These interviews were famous for tough or weird questions and the stories surrounding them were legion.

I was interviewed separately by four, although it was supposed to be three, individuals in civilian clothes, who might have been either civilian engineers or navy officers. The ushers who escorted us from one office to another, including the admiral's, were all prospective commanding officers of nuclear submarines and they, too, were in civilian clothes. When I finally reached the admiral, he asked me five easy questions without even looking up. The old bastard knew exactly who I was and had already dropped one of his little tests on me.

Later that summer, the Pollack went south to conduct sound tests and torpedo trials off the Florida coast near Fort

Lauderdale, then on to San Juan, Puerto Rico, for some liberty. In San Juan, I received orders to report to Naval Reactors Representative at General Dynamics, Electric Boat Division, Groton, Connecticut, for duty. This meant two things: I had not only been accepted by Admiral Rickover to serve in the nuclear power program as an officer, but I had also been assigned to work directly for the admiral as a naval reactor's representative in Groton. Of the twenty-eight newly selected officers, all nuclear-trained chief petty officers who had interviewed with me in Washington, I was the only one accepted into the program. I was now the chosen one from the chosen few.

I was transferred when the Pollack got back to Charleston and took thirty days' leave. When I got home to New Jersey, I learned that we had to wait a couple of weeks before we could move into navy housing at the submarine base in New London, Connecticut, which is a few miles up the Thames River from the Electric Boat shipyard in Groton, so we had a little vacation.

One day I made a short trip to the local drugstore and while waiting for the pharmacist to fill a prescription for the girls, I got a call from Angelina to come right home. Fearing some catastrophe with the kids, I raced home and found her crying. A telegram had arrived saying that her father had passed away nine days earlier. Since she seldom wrote her family in the Philippines, they had finally traced me through the Navy and the telegram was actually a navy message.

It was a bad situation for her and bad timing for us. Although she never shared her deep feelings with me, I'm sure Angelina wanted to go home, but we couldn't afford to fly her to the Philippines and it never occurred to me to ask if the Navy would do it. In any case, with the funeral long over, I viewed a visit by her as just that, so I probably wasn't much help. To make matters worse, I had just finished a tough tour of duty on the Pollack and was headed for a job that would be even more demanding of my time. Angelina was left to cope alone with a life-shattering blow and she never seemed quite the same to me after that.

When we got to New London and checked with the navy housing office, we were assigned to enlisted housing, despite the fact that I would become an officer in a few months and still be stationed there. On the up side, we moved in next to the Russells, the family of a black nuclear-trained first class machinist mate stationed on one of the nuclear submarines in New London. Russ and his wife were two of the most delightful people I have ever met. We had kids the same age and the wives loved each other, so we were soon one big family. Russ made warrant officer a year or so later and served with me later on.

Naval Reactors

Naval reactors representatives were required to wear civilian suits because they routinely gave orders to officers senior to them. Although I was still a chief petty officer and would not be an ensign until after the first of March the next year, to everyone there I was simply Mr. Hansen.

The Naval Reactors Office at Electric Boat had about ten officers and two secretaries. The guys were all nuclear-trained mustang officers like me, except the boss, Commander Martin, who probably had a degree in marine, or possibly nuclear, engineering. When I reported in, Commander Martin said, "You wouldn't be here if you didn't already know what to do," which meant I shouldn't expect any formal training. He told me to follow the other guys around to learn the ropes, then he would assign me to the joint test group on one of the submarines.

After observing for two weeks, I was assigned to the joint test group for the James K. Polk SSBN-645, a fleet ballistic missile submarine, that was still on the building ways. A joint test group (JTG) was a group of five men who directed and oversaw the construction and testing of the reactor plant on a particular submarine. It consisted of the chief test engineer from Electric Boat, an engineer from Westinghouse (the prime contractor), a navy officer from the supervisor of shipbuilding office, the engineer officer from the ship's crew and the naval reactors representative.

The Westinghouse engineer was our technical advisor; the engineer officer was our interface with the ship's crew and the navy officer from the supervisor of shipbuilding paid the bills and interfaced with the rest of the ship. At its core, the JTG amounted to an adversarial relationship between the Electric Boat chief test engineer, whose job it was to manage the test program, and the naval reactors rep, whose job it was to make sure it got done right. The naval reactors rep was responsible for reactor safety and had the ultimate veto.

Anything done to a navy nuclear reactor plant had to be done in accordance with a preapproved plan, test, operating and casualty procedure or a repair procedure that had been approved by the joint test group. Our routine was to review, make necessary changes and approve all test procedures that were issued by Westinghouse. During the construction and test program, if something went wrong or changes had to be made, the chief test engineer produced a written repair procedure, which the JTG reviewed and approved. The shipyard workers or test group then followed it. In many cases, the Westinghouse engineer, chief test engineer, engineer officer and I (the hard core) would put our heads together, figure out what to do, then write the repair procedure.

When the James K. Polk's JTG was formed, we had a get-acquainted meeting, then the chief test engineer and I waited until everyone was gone to have our little philosophical discussion, something we both knew would happen. When the time came, Norm leaned back in his chair and said, "Well, Jerry, how are we gonna handle this?"

I had put some thought into what I would say and have often thought my little speech would make one hell of a wedding ceremony: "I think we should play it right down the middle.

Let's do the job carefully and right the first time; it is easier that way. I don't expect anything more and won't accept anything less. I don't believe in crystal balls, supersafety or Monday morning quarterbacking. I won't let them push you. Don't lie to me or try to fuck over me and we'll get along just fine."

He smiled, stood up and we shook hands. Norm and I became good friends and were on the same JTG for two submarines. We never wrote an incident report. In fact, we never had a serious problem and on the second boat set a record for the least time from start of testing until initial criticality. It was eleven months and I'll bet a Nutty Buddy that it still stands.

On March 1, 1965, I signed some papers in Commander Martin's office and became an ensign. There was no ceremony or fanfare and afterward I went to a JTG meeting. Shortly thereafter, I went to Officer Candidate School for eight weeks in Newport, Rhode Island, and learned how to be an officer. I reported back to Groton about the time the James K. Polk's reactor plant test program got started.

The job at naval reactors was interesting and challenging and could have been a solid ten, but like an ex-wife, it was only a nine; it had one thing that no one could deal with. Every Tuesday we had to write a letter to Admiral Rickover identifying a problem, providing a solution and providing current status. It was a clever form of cruelty. We needed to find at least one problem every week despite the fact that Mother Nature puts out problems like grapes, in bunches.

My new duties required that I operate on a different plane than the one I was accustomed to, even as a chief petty officer and leading reactor operator. What Commander Martin had said when I arrived was partially right: I was accomplished in nuclear power. It remained to be seen how well qualified I was for other aspects of my new job.

As a senior enlisted man, I had been insulated somewhat by the navy chain of command structure. I was always on familiar ground, complete with rules, traditions and order and was responsible only for knowing the technical answers and training my men. Now I was in new territory, wearing civilian clothes and operating like a civilian manager with an awesome amount of authority as well as responsibility. I wouldn't just give answers anymore; I would have to ask the questions and be able to recognize the right answers. I would have to look at things that I had never seen before, from a new perspective. I would have to solve problems that had never been solved and do things that had never been done and all of it would involve a complicated, expensive and dangerous nuclear reactor plant. I was in for a challenging time.

The exotic business of building and testing nuclear reactor plants turned out to be many things, but not necessarily the great calling that most people might imagine. Yes, it was exciting and challenging and I loved the technical complexity of the job, but I soon learned that it was also a major, big-ticket, cutthroat federal government spending program, or for short, the Big Time. Few aspects of the job could be described as mundane or routine. We faced a staggering array of technical problems and conflicts of every kind and spent a majority of our time in intense discussions or negotiations with sharp, experienced civilian engineers and managers who could best be described as man-eating sharks.

Admiral Rickover once said, "If something goes wrong and you can't point to one person who screwed up, then no one was ever responsible in the first place." That statement is true, and in some respects, a naval reactors rep was the designated target. And although we had enough authority to meet our responsibilities, we also had a handicap reserved for soldiers, policemen and other public defenders: we were expected to have god-like qualities and be politically correct at all times. Any mistake in judgment or behavior flashed the spotlight of responsibility on us, no matter what the other guy did.

On a more personal philosophical level, if I had not worked for naval reactors, I might have gone through life believing that I was your average Joe. But I already had a deep distrust of conventional wisdom—meaning that not everyone looked at things the way I did and in my view they were frequently wrong. I believed that natural forces (Mother Nature) controlled everything and my management and problem solving techniques were closely associated with those precepts.

I actually liked to visualize Mother Nature as a sweet lady who spends most of her time creating and perfecting things like Indian paint brush and mountain bluebirds. Except when she is really upset, she leaves the petty day-to-day stuff to her main man Murphy, whose basic law is familiar to everyone: anything that can go wrong, will.

Murphy, like all natural forces, is vigilant and relishes opportunities provided by failed leadership, bad management, poor planning and inattention to detail to get in and muck around. From experience, I knew my job at naval reactors would involve mortal combat between me and Murphy. This understanding tipped the scale my way a bit, but there is a difference between knowing what to do and having the ability or will to do it. I don't like to fix things after they break and play the blame game; I like to keep them from breaking in the first place. Naval reactors, as envisioned by Admiral Rickover anyway, had the same attitude, so in that sense, I was the perfect man for the job, which is not to say that I was guaranteed success. I was, after all, operating in a world where everyone has an agenda.

I can honestly say that while I was stationed at Electric Boat, I won virtually all of my battles and there are many stories I could tell about that period of my career, most of which I am very proud of, but they usually involved gory technical details and a lot of classified information. But I let Murphy win our last battle, so I'll just tell three stories about how that happened.

They will give you an insight into the kind of job it was and, of course, a little insight into me.

The Iceberg

The other naval reactors reps at Electric Boat were nuclear trained as electricians or machinist mates. I was the only ex-reactor operator and one day my past caused me to hit the tip of an iceberg.

I'd been at Electric Boat over two years and was on my second submarine, so by then everyone knew my background. One evening two shipyard electronic technicians approached me in the test office and asked if I'd help them with a problem.

They said they were having trouble aligning the primary plant instrumentation and since I had been a reactor operator maybe I could give them some pointers. I asked them to describe the problem, which they did, but what they told me didn't make sense and couldn't be right. I normally wanted to use what I called the laying-on-of-hands method with a gnarly problem, so I said, "Show me."

We went down to the ship and they demonstrated the problem. They were right: something was wrong. I thought back to my alignment days on the Pollack and remembered that if the alignment procedure wasn't followed exactly, word for word, the results could be wrong. "Let me see the alignment procedure," I said. One of the technicians reached around to his back pocket and pulled out a sheaf of papers and handed them to me. I took them slowly.

I didn't need to look because I knew the pages he so casually kept in his back pocket would be marked CONFIDENTIAL in big red letters, at the top and bottom, but I looked anyway. They were pages from the highly sensitive reactor plant manual, probably outdated versions of the alignment procedure.

"Come with me," I said. "We got a problem." They were quiet as we walked back up the pier.

By then I was not only an ex-chief electronics technician who knew about alignments, I was also an ex-chief radioman who knew about security matters. I'd run a technical library, taken care of reactor plant manuals and had read them all at least nine times. They knew, or should have known, when they came to me in the first place that they had a white rat[23] by the tail.

Digging into the problem was like peeling an onion. Most instrumentation alignments were done on third shift when things were relatively quiet. The alignment procedure was included in a volume of the reactor plant manual, a series of classified publications. The appropriate volume had to be checked out from the technical library, which closed at 1600. To obtain the alignment procedures properly, they had to check out the manual before the library closed, be responsible for a large volume of classified information all night, then check it back in before going home the next morning.

The electronic technicians had a better idea. They checked out the volume one time, removed the applicable pages and squirreled them away in their lockers, which was a security violation. When they checked the volume back in, the librarians obviously didn't do a page check, so if and when they did discover the pages missing, they had no idea who had taken them. They probably covered up to avoid a security violation of their own. When the alignment procedure was changed and technicians attempted to align the instrumentation using the outdated procedure, the results were wrong. Clearly, the system was broken.

I wrote several letters to the admiral on the subject and it caused Electric Boat a lot of grief and cost them a lot of

---

[23]Derisive name for naval reactors reps. A "white rat" is navy slang for a person who tattles on his friends.

money. Before it was all over, they had to convert the test engineer's lunch room into a technical library and, at great expense, hire technical librarians with proper security clearances and skills to man the library twenty-four hours a day, seven days a week.

Like the five-inch rounds the Hanna lobbed on the North Korean railroad, this incident pissed off both labor and management. The electronic technicians now had to jump through hoops to get the alignment procedures and the test engineers no longer had a place to eat lunch and read the newspaper, so morale plummeted. Electric Boat could handle the routine problems uncovered by the naval reactor reps and had even made allowances for them in the contract, but I was costing them hard money and becoming a real pain in the ass.

I'm sure they didn't have a conference with the union to plan my demise, but let's just say there was a commonality of purpose on their part and a weakness to be exploited on mine. In any case, Murphy saw an opportunity and jumped on their side and his was a foolproof, two-step plan.

I was making a tour through the boat late one night and stopped to chat with some civilian electronic technicians. When the subject of the new security rules came up, my joking retort to something said hit a nerve and one of the technicians raised his hackles over it. In all fairness, it should be noted that I am famous for spontaneous responses that are lethal. I didn't take the incident seriously and don't even remember the conversation—but there were witnesses.

The next morning, Commander Martin called me in and said the union had filed a grievance against me. At first, I couldn't imagine what he was talking about, but after we figured it out, I explained what happened and said I was just joking, surely they knew that. He told me to apologize to the technician, "make the problem go away," and be more careful in the future. I contacted the electronic technician and apologized.

Also in the office at the time, listening to every word, was our soon-to-be new boss, a young civilian fresh from the headquarters of naval reactors. He didn't say anything then or later, but his first impression of me was bad and it never changed.

The Cook

The Will Rogers SSBN-659, a fleet ballistic missile submarine, was the second ship for my joint test group. The skipper, whose name was Kaufman, was a navy captain, commonly called a four striper. By now my JTG was like the Colorado River in flood and the test program was rocking and rolling along, until a short time before initial criticality, when several things happened in rapid succession.

At the time, Electric Boat was awash in nuclear submarines, but the cold war was going hot and heavy and the Navy wanted even more, so there was a big push on. They even towed the Flasher SSN-613 to another shipyard for reactor plant testing because the Groton shipyard was so overloaded.

To complicate matters, our new boss, the young civilian fresh from the marbled halls of naval reactors, was now in charge and Commander Martin was gone. The new boss was not too high on my list, either. He reminded me of the young man from my childhood who couldn't shoot pigs exactly between the eyes. He was afraid of the admiral, the management at Electric Boat and his shadow.

My office mate, Lieutenant Bradley, and I both had one submarine deep in its test program, plus another one on the building ways. We were both members of two joint test groups and on call 24-7, yet we wasted hours each day in the boss's office answering an endless stream of questions. He had the Phil Donahue principle down cold, but he didn't have enough experience to deal with the answers and we didn't have time to hold his hand.

I think the Will Rogers was the first submarine scheduled to take the reactor critical after he took over, so I was in the hot seat. Instead of asking me what remained to be done, all of his questions focused on why we couldn't do it right now. If he had understood that my sole job was to insure that the reactor was not taken critical until the primary systems were ready, he might have been on my side, but he couldn't tell the difference between a big problem and a little problem; to him they were all big. He was buckling under the pressure to take the reactor critical on the Will Rogers and didn't know how to deal with it. I did, but he didn't trust me because I'd made a union member angry, which in his mind, was a problem of equal importance.

After one hectic JTG meeting in the chief test engineer's office ended, I sat there for a few minutes with my eyes closed while Norm shuffled papers at his desk. The shipyard was in a full-court press and Norm was getting a lot of pressure from management to proceed with initial criticality, but we still had too many uncorrected deficiencies and were finding more every day, so the primary systems were not yet ready. With no smoking gun to show my new boss, though, I couldn't stop them. I could see the problem clearly, but was still working on the solution.

Finally Norm turned and said, "You know what your problem is? You need to look the other way once in a while." He wanted some slack and an argument can be made that he was trying to help me, but that was a slippery slope I wasn't about to get on. Although some men would have welcomed the easy way out, for better or worse, that wasn't my way.

I leaned back and my thoughts drifted back to the union incident, which still bothered me. . . . *you got a union working for you? . . . I belong to a union, too, the International Order of Submarine Sailors, and I need a little talk with the union steward. . . .*

I went down to the wardroom of the Will Rogers, where Captain Kaufman and several officers were having lunch. The captain looked up as I entered. Without preliminaries I said, "Captain, we got a problem." Things got very quiet and I went on. "The shipyard is going to take you critical soon. I can't stop them and you're going to live with the problems. We've got to do something."

Without hesitation, the captain said, "Thanks, Jerry; let us handle it."

I left and as I walked over the gangway, I smiled to myself. I had just told a wardroom full of men wearing gold dolphins that the main induction didn't sound right when it went shut. . . . *If I can't solve it as a God . . . I'll solve it as a cook . . . .*

The officers and crew of the Will Rogers worked day and night going over the primary systems with a fine-toothed comb. Then they flooded the shipyard with hundreds of deficiency reports and buried them in paperwork, which accomplished several things. It gave us the time we needed; it pissed off the shipyard; and it gave me three days off, my first in eleven months.

At the same time, a few days of nice weather hit New England and I took my boys for a nature walk at an estuary between Mystic and Groton where there is a big hill surrounded by marshland teeming with wildlife. It was a beautiful day. I felt like a boy again and my sons were having a great time. On the way back, we paused to watch some ducks and my boys turned to me with their faces filled with joy and Gary said, "Why don't we do this more often, Dad? Why don't you act like you used to?"

His question will haunt me the rest of my life. I was so obsessed with my job that I was losing my family and suddenly, belatedly, I became aware of the cost to them of the career choices I had made. I liked the nuclear power program and was good at my job. As long as I stayed, I would get 4.0 fitness reports, make commander, then retire and walk across the street to become an NRC agent, but I loved my wife and children. I could be a naval reactors rep or a father to five children. Gnawing at me now was whether or not I could do both at the same time.

Fallen Star

A few days before we were to take the reactor critical on the Will Rogers, the Flasher started critical operations at another shipyard and ran into a problem when they performed their radiation shield survey. The purpose of the shield survey was to determine if the lead shielding installed inside the reactor compartment bulkheads was doing its job.

To create the radiation shield, lead bricks were laid next to each other and any cracks were filled with lead wool, which was pounded into a solid mass by air hammers to form a tight bond. Steel plate was then welded over the bricks to "can" them inside the bulkhead. The shield survey was performed by taking the reactor critical and to a low predetermined power level, then all areas along the bulkheads were marked off in a grid and surveyed with radiac meters to see if any radiation was coming through.

The Flasher test group found spots in the shielding where gamma radiation was streaming through. They noted the spots, shut down the reactor, investigated and found that the lead inside the bulkheads had not been installed properly. The skilled union workers had stuffed the cracks with lead wool, but pounded only the "face" solid and left loose wool on the inside. The result was insufficient lead thickness to stop the big nitrogen-16 gamma rays that occur during critical operations. To correct the problem, it was necessary to remove equipment, cut into the bulkheads and reassemble the lead bricks and lead wool properly.

There was another part to the problem. The lead shielding had been installed on both the Flasher and the Will Rogers at the same time by the same workers, so it was possible that the Will Rogers had the same problem. We had a couple of JTG meetings to address the potential problem and Norm and I personally went over our safety precautions to keep personnel away from the reactor compartment until our shield survey was done. We hadn't written an incident report yet and we were not about to start.

Whenever one of the submarines performed critical operations, three naval reactor reps went into three-section duty to cover the ship around the clock. The shipyard also set up a test shack on the pier adjacent to the stern of the ship. It had a counter running down each side and chairs to sit in. Above the counter was a shelf with closed-circuit TV monitors showing the control panels in the maneuvering room, various system readouts, telephones, a coffee pot and an intercom system with the ship. The test engineer, technicians and members of the JTG usually observed things from the test shack.

On an initial criticality, it was also our custom for the naval reactors rep assigned to that ship to stand the day watches and stay on the ship from the time they started pulling rods until criticality was achieved. Since the process began with a small neutron population that had to multiply many times, reaching initial criticality took several hours and the Will Rogers was no exception. When we finally got there it was about 2300, so I passed the word to my relief and went home. I hadn't slept for two days.

I slept five or six hours, then returned to the test shack and relieved the other rep. There was a lull in testing for the watch relief, so I poured myself a cup of coffee, walked to the door and gazed out the window at the Will Rogers. It was shift-change time and third-shift workers were coming across the gangway leaving the ship.

I watched casually for a few minutes before realizing that I was watching cleaners, mostly black guys, come up out of the superstructure around the missile tube outer doors just forward of the reactor compartment. They were indifferently stepping over the exclusion-area tape, which was adorned with magenta and yellow radiation hazard signs.

The shipyard normally waited until critical operations to clean out the coffee cups, candy wrappers and other junk that accumulated in the superstructure during construction. Like moving day for me in Blanding, though, nobody had told the cleaners this day was different. The reactor was still critical and the radiation shield survey had not been done, yet cleaners had been working inside the exclusion area the whole shift and might have received a dose of gamma radiation. A serious, full-blown incident was staring me in the face.

At that point, I could have done a lot of things, like go to my new boss and point out that the naval reactors rep on the midwatch had his head up his ass and didn't check on things or that the ship's crew had been asleep at the wheel, or give a long list of failings by Electric Boat. By playing the blame game, I could have made myself an innocent bystander and probably a hero in his eyes.

But as Dad used to say, I'd reached the end of my rope. My subconscious took over and it apparently focused on two things. First, if this had been the Pollack, with Captain Lyons in charge, a watch would have been stationed forward of the reactor compartment and nobody would have gotten anywhere near that bulkhead. Second, since my nature trip with my boys, I'd had a hopeless feeling and at that moment viewed my job as pissing in the ocean to raise the tide line.

I knew that yelling at somebody was the worst crime a naval reactors rep could commit and that getting out of the nuclear power program was easier than getting a divorce in Saudi Arabia—you said the magic words "I want out" just once and you were history. So I executed the *coup de gras* in Murphy's plan and called the test manager's boss, who was a vice president, I think. I yelled a lot of things, probably several times, but only have a distinct memory of saying, ". . . if you don't get this fuckin' ship squared away, I'm gonna shut it down like a bull's ass in fly time!"

Vice presidents don't like to be yelled at, so with my run-in with the union technician as a backdrop, he called my new boss and complained. A couple of hours later, one of the guys relieved me and said the boss wanted to see me. I don't remember thinking about anything on the way to his office, which means I probably wasn't thinking.

I went in and he started in on me. He wasn't concerned that a group of cleaners might have received a dose of radiation, only about my telephone call to the vice president. He'd barely launched what was clearly going to be at least one hell of a raking when I raised my right hand with the palm toward him and said, "I don't want to hear it; I want out."

He sat back in his chair and I could see from his lips that he was terrified, which actually surprised me. I told him that I was fed up, didn't know my family anymore and wanted out. He said to go home and await further word.

I went home and told Angelina, who was shocked but didn't say much. Then within what seemed like only a few minutes, Lieutenant Commander Brown, the senior navy officer in our group, came driving up, rushed in the house and growled, "What the hell's going on?!"

Brown and I were good friends. He was a country boy like me—no, much worse. His shipmates named him Iron Balls and coming from a bunch of submarine sailors that says it all. He had two coonhounds and on the occasional dark winter night after a sixteen-hour day, we stumbled around the woods together in the snow or freezing rain with six-volt flashlights listening to his hounds chase raccoons, which was a new sport for me. I'd seen ringtails in San Juan County but never a raccoon, and, of course, we didn't own a flashlight or a coonhound. The objective, I learned, was to listen for the changing tones of the baying hounds as the chase reached its climax and the coon was "treed." It was a down-home, country-style way to get rid of tensions and I loved it.

I told Brown what happened and he said that he was upset with the boss himself and would call Washington; he didn't think the admiral had been told yet; maybe we could stop it and he didn't want to lose me. I told him not to bother. "It's not just the job; it's the price; I'm losing my family."

Later, the submarine officer detailer at the Bureau of Naval Personnel in Washington called and he was very diplomatic. We were both mustang officers and I knew why he was calling, but our first conversation didn't go very well. I told him I wanted out of the fucking submarine force, volunteered to go to Vietnam and I don't know what else. He said he would check to see what was available and call me back.

At this point, I should mention that a high percentage of naval reactors reps ended up in similar straits: they quit or got fired and they got a divorce. It was a grueling job that took its toll on everyone. Although I had a short-term shitty attitude and wasn't thinking clearly, I did know—if I'd seen it on a multiple-choice questionnaire, anyway—that the Navy still viewed me as hot property and quitting or even being fired wouldn't be a black mark against me, officially.

I stewed for an hour before the detailer called back to say that he'd found a job as the electronics officer on an aircraft carrier that was on an around-the-world cruise at the time. She was currently in a liberty port in South Africa, Durban, he thought. . . . *that took an hour? . . .*

"Can't you do any better than that?"

He sensed from my tone that I was calming down and said, "Jerry, I know how you feel; I've seen fallen stars before; it will get better. But the submarine force needs you."

"OK, where do you want me to go?"

He'd set the hook and didn't pause a nanosecond. "The Simon Lake in Holy Loch."

"What the hell," I said. "I always wanted to see Scotland."

I told Angelina and after a family conference, we decided the logical course was for her and the kids to stay in New London until school was out in June, then join me in Scotland. She wanted enough time to finish getting her U.S. citizenship before they left, too.

A few days later, I got orders to the USS Simon Lake AS-33, a submarine tender stationed in Holy Loch, Scotland, and plane tickets to Prestwick.

I left JFK in the late evening and the plane flew out over Long Island, with its thousands of lights below, and headed into the darkness over the Atlantic. I leaned back in my seat and the significance of what had happened began to sink in. I now understood what Dad had meant when he said, "I've never seen a horse that couldn't be rode or a cowboy that couldn't be throwed." I had been bucked off and was now alone in a deep canyon after sundown.

CHAPTER TEN
Holy Loch

Site One

The flight to Scotland took all night, which gave me a long time to think. I tried to put recent events in perspective, but not very successfully, then spent half the night feeling sorry for myself before I finally got a grip on things and was able to focus on tomorrow.

I was plunging back in by going to the Polaris base in Holy Loch, Scotland, which was regarded as the main cold war station for the submarine force. I would be working with the first team at site one. I wasn't concerned about being able to do my job; my worry was that everyone would know who I was and assume that I had been fired.

The submarine force was a small outfit and, at the least, I would be on probation, so I had to get my shit together in a hurry. I would be back in the navy command structure as an officer, in uniform, and with all the duties and traditions that go with it. I had been a civilian wearing a suit and tie for over two years, and by now what I'd learned in Officer Candidate School had begun to fade. I probably had the orders to the engine and rudder down all right, but doubted if I could still recognize all the signal flags and would definitely need to brush up on the Uniform Code of Military Justice. I was deep in thoughts like that when we dropped through broken clouds and I saw the green fields of Scotland spread out below.

When I arrived in Holy Loch, I was jerked back into the real world by the activity, precision and ceremony of a major ship. A submarine tender is a large "mother ship" that "tends" submarines, and is a floating repair activity with all the same repair shops and almost the same capabilities as a shipyard, but this was no dirty shipyard. The Simon Lake had five fleet ballistic missile submarines (FBMs) tied up alongside, an officer of the deck and a marine guard at the gangway—everything but a red carpet.

I told the OD that I was reporting for duty; he took my orders and had the messenger escort me up to the stateroom of the executive officer, who was a commander. We talked a little, then he said they had dispensed with the traditional formal meeting with the captain and that I was being assigned to the repair department. He welcomed me aboard.

After stowing my gear in my stateroom, which I shared with the communications officer, I changed into wash khakis and reported to my new department. I met the repair officer, another commander, and my real boss, Lieutenant Commander Jack Sousa, the assistant repair officer and a mustang. At the time, I was a lieutenant, junior grade.

Jack said that it was standard policy to assign all new repair officers to the duties of ship superintendent for the first six months to learn the ropes, which made me the ship super for the next submarine going into refit.

There were ten FBM submarines in Submarine Squadron Fourteen, whose flag was aboard the Simon Lake. Each one had two crews, the blue crew and the gold crew. One crew took the ship out on a sixty-day patrol then came back to Holy Loch and was relieved by the other crew. The off crew then flew back to the States for sixty days. The ship then stayed alongside the tender for a twenty-eight day refit during which any needed repairs were made and the ship was restocked and rearmed with the desired weapons load. The new crew then went out on patrol and repeated the procedure.

My job as a ship super was to follow the refit on a particular submarine, coordinate the work between the various repair shops and the submarine and keep the assistant repair officer informed. The repair shops had the same numbers as those at a shipyard and the work was very familiar, so I was already overqualified for the job. For me, it was like going from college back to the first grade. The only problem was that before I could go on to second grade, I had to pass first grade, again.

I also had military obligations. I was the duty repair officer for twenty-four hours every four days when I was in charge of the repair department duty section. I also stood watches as the officer of the deck at the quarterdeck. A few days after I reported aboard, the executive officer called me in and said that since I was still a junior officer and this was my first ship, I would also have to complete the junior officer journal (JOJ), which was another creative form of cruelty. . . . *first ship, my ass* . . .

The JOJ was essentially an extended version of Officer Candidate School and consisted of twelve lessons. There were lessons for each department aboard ship, for navy regulations, for the Uniform Code of Military Justice and so on. Each lesson had about a hundred and fifty completion-type questions for which you provided an answer, a chart or diagram, a description or whatever. The lesson on navigation, for example, required "a day's work in navigation." At least one lesson had to be submitted each month or it meant trouble with the executive officer.

Since my family wouldn't arrive for four months, I plunged right in and never went on liberty; I wanted to get as far ahead as possible. The Navy likes new junior officers to have plenty to do, so I was also elected wardroom mess treasurer, despite my sharing of the fact that I had flunked bookkeeping twice in high school. If the books didn't balance, I just paid the difference out of my own pocket. Most people don't know it, but navy officers have to pay for their own food and keep books on how much it costs–even in combat.

When I started as ship super, I was running up and down ladders all day checking on repair jobs, which was not the way to break in my new pair of brown shoes. About the second evening, when I finally limped into my stateroom and took off my shoe and sock, I found an ugly blister on the back of my left heel, which was now a nickle-sized pool of pus with a red band of infection around it. I had to do something soon or I wouldn't be able to walk. I toyed with the idea of going to sick bay, but that's all it would take after such a short time onboard to prove that I was a candy-ass, so I rejected it.

I filled my washbasin with hot water, lathered up soap, then sat down and stuck my foot in. I fell asleep then woke up with a cramp in my leg and a cold foot, but the blister was now a nice pink color with white, crinkly skin replacing the infection band. I bandaged it, went to bed and in a couple of days it was well. When I completed my first refit, the submarine captain told the executive officer that I was the best ship super his ship had ever had and he gave me a letter of commendation. . . . *on my way . . .*

About two months after I arrived in Scotland, I received a personal letter from Captain Kaufman of the Will Rogers. It was a nice letter asking for my side of the story about how and why I had left naval reactors. He said some nice things about me, the only one I remember being "Many times you were a lone voice in the wilderness." It was a nice gesture, but that didn't seem to be its purpose. Enough time had passed for the truth to come out. Captain Kaufman was a senior captain in the nuclear submarine force and probably had a direct line to Admiral Rickover. I figured it might be an opportunity to go back to work for naval reactors, which I thought long and hard about, but in the end I tore up the letter without answering it.

Wildcats

Before my six months were up as ship super, one of the lieutenants in the repair department got transferred back to the States and Jack told me to relieve him. He was the repair services (RS) division officer, who was responsible for the non-destructive test lab, quality control shop, print shop, photo lab and technical library. I learned later that he was also handling the submarine shipalt program, but, frankly, I don't know what else he did. Jack said that I would also be the planning officer and nuclear systems repair officer. I don't recall the officer I relieved being called by either of those titles.

The RS division was a specialized support division that operated pretty much in auto. Nuclear systems repair, which included a lot of quality-control and non-destructive testing matters, was my speciality. The print shop, photo lab and technical library had been put in the RS division because they needed a home, but I was qualified in technical libraries and a logical choice all around.

Jack said the main area he wanted organized was the planning office itself, but that first he wanted me to look into the submarine shipalt program, which was not working very well and generating a lot of flack from the squadron. His final remark was, "You got a free hand; just fix it." That's how I gave orders and how I loved to get them.

A shipalt, which is shorthand for ship alteration, is basically the same as a field change or a recall on your car. Shipalts were issued by the Naval Ship Systems Command in Washington and consisted of a several-page document that specified the shipalt number, hull numbers of applicable ships, a brief title, work description and a list of plans and materials needed for the work. When a shipalt was issued, all applicable ships were required to get the work done as soon as possible, which frequently required access to a shipyard or repair activity such as the Simon Lake.

My new office, which would eventually become the planning office, was a small office with about six men assigned who had been handling the submarine shipalt program. It was in a spacious spare torpedo magazine down in the bowels of the ship in the weapons repair department trunk. I had to go through a marine guard to go back and forth, even to the head. Of the five or six men, three were seamen, and, I believe, one second class and two third class petty officers. The petty officers were all rejects from other repair department shops.

I had rarely seen the lieutenant I relieved and now I knew why. He had spent most of his time holed up in his office, out of sight and out of mind. I had noticed that he usually showed up in the repair office at liberty call with his daily one-box-top report. While I was relieving him, I asked about the submarine shipalt program. He told me it was going along slowly but smoothly and basically how it worked. It sounded to me like a system full of pitfalls, so I figured the sooner he was gone, the better.

When I took over as planning officer, I mustered the men in the office and asked them a series of questions about how the submarine shipalt program worked. The deeper I went into their system, the wormier it got. They had created the most elaborate filing system possible, with a separate cabinet for each submarine, for a total of ten three-drawer file cabinets, plus an additional four file cabinets for general correspondence. In many cases they had ten copies of the same shipalt document filed in ten separate files with all related correspondence. The men had been spending all their time filing. Clearly, I'd have to do some housecleaning, as well as basic research, just to identify the problems. I'd need at least one good petty officer to help.

After a two-hour session in which I gave specifics about what we would be doing and how, two of the men started for the door. I called them back and asked where they were going.

Each had a different destination, one to pick up his laundry and the other to get a haircut. I stood up. "When I give an order, you do it now, not tomorrow, right now. Is that clear?" Looking confused, they sat down and went to work.

I had told the men to go through the files, sort all the documents and records and combine everything into two sets of files. One set would contain a copy of all shipalt documents in numerical order. When completed, that set of files took up less than two drawers. Then they were to file all the miscellaneous correspondence and records in another file by shipalt number regardless of which submarine it pertained to. The idea was to have all the information we had on each shipalt in one place. The final two sets of files took up less than two three-drawer file cabinets, so we ended up with the world's market cornered in folders and cabinets, which we gave back to the Navy.

After I got the men lined out, I went up to the repair office where Jack was waiting. I told him I had a real mess and a bunch of rejects to work with. He just sat there listening, so I went on, "You've got to give me at least one good man." At that, he smiled broadly and pointed to a first class electrician sitting off to the side in the repair office. "This is your man." His name was Miller, a nuclear-trained, surface-craft sailor and one of the best petty officers I ever met.

I took Miller down and introduced him to the men, saying that they would be taking orders from him now. Then we huddled at my desk and I briefed him on the situation, the possible solutions I saw and my basic plan for proceeding. I told him to exercise his own judgment with the men and the job and if he came up with any ideas to yell.

If there were contests for such things, I'd nominate the squadron fourteen submarine shipalt program as the biggest mess ever created. To sum it up, no one was in charge and no one wanted to be because it wasn't romantic, exciting nor challenging and involved a lot of detail and status keeping. In short, it was the kind of area that left Murphy to his own devices, which was too bad because getting shipalts done was important.

When I took over, the shipalt program operated basically as follows. Each submarine ordered the material needed for any shipalt that applied to them. When the material came in, the supply department stored it in a storeroom (cage) on the Simon Lake that had been assigned to each submarine. When a submarine came in from patrol, it gave the material and a work request to the repair department. The assigned lead shop did any research needed in the technical library and did the work.

It sounds like it might work, but in the real world it didn't. We had waded only ankle deep into the program when we discovered that the records tracking the various shipalts had every kind of status problem imaginable, although they did fall into three categories: applicability, availability and completion, each of which would take a whole story to describe. The program had degenerated badly and it was clear that it would take years to dig our way out, unless we found a way to gather and update a lot of information quickly, efficiently and accurately.

The Simon Lake had an automated data processing center (ADP) that produced daily computer printouts for the various departments, so I collared the ADP Officer, an ensign in the supply department, and asked if there was a way to get a small weekly printout with just one line of information per item. He said there might be, using an "80-80 listing," which was made up from IBM cards with a maximum of eighty spaces of data for each line item. If we could give ADP our information efficiently, the duty section could cut the IBM cards during the weekends and produce a printout on Sunday night.

The executive officer personally controlled all use of the ship's computer, so I went to him for approval and he promptly threw me out. Nobody! was getting any more shit out of his ADP!

But we couldn't live without it, so I went to my office and designed a printout line that contained all the information that was absolutely necessary on each shipalt. This included the ship's hull number, shipalt number, a brief title and some columns where single letters could indicate status (a blank meant nothing done, O meant on order, X meant done.) I included a short remarks column for exceptions, because Mother Nature does things that way. I managed to get everything to fit on one line, then designed input forms that the print shop printed and glued into pads.

To make changes, we completed blocks on the input forms, held them until the weekend, then ADP cut an IBM card from each form and produced a printout on Sunday night. During the next week, we entered changes on the printout with red felt-tipped pens then completed an input form so the change would show up on the next printout. We added and deleted items the same way. We could operate more than a week without a new printout and two men could handle the job easily.

When everything was ready, I took samples to the executive officer and after a lot of pleading and promises, he approved our use of ADP time. Our first printout worked, so I took it and my plans for the submarine shipalt program to the repair officer.

I told him the present system was a hopeless mess, wouldn't work in a million years and that I could explain why in great detail. But I think Jack had already softened him up because he approved it without the whole song and dance. I also told him I wanted out of the weapons magazine and asked for an office somewhere in the repair department spaces where the planning office could be part of the team. It was a deal he couldn't refuse, so he didn't. At the time, the squadron engineer was ready to try anything to make the shipalt program work, so he approved it also and we got a nice new office on the main deck just aft of the inside machine shop.

Under my plan, which was to take over the submarine shipalt program completely, the squadron told the planning office which shipalt they wanted done on each submarine. Then we did all research, obtained plans, ordered and then stored the material in one small storeroom, which allowed us to return storeroom space to the supply department. The squadron interfaced with the submarines, moved money around and signed all material requisitions, which allowed the planning phase to proceed while the submarines were on patrol.

When we had everything ready for a shipalt, the submarine gave us a work request when they came in for refit and we transferred the material and planning package to the lead shop, which did the work. When the work was completed, the shipalt showed up as done on the next printout and then was deleted on the following printout. Everyone got a fresh printout each week showing the status of all shipalts in process. Any printouts a submarine had missed while on patrol were included in their arrival package, so they could update their records as well.

During the first several weeks, we spent most of our time gathering information, correcting status items and resolving glitches in our computer program, but for the first time we were able to quickly and accurately track a lot of information. In the process we discovered that virtually all existing records were inaccurate, incomplete or misleading, and, to make matters worse, that records kept by the individual submarines were also a hopeless mess. In this initial research and update period, we also uncovered problems that no one had imagined. For example, in some cases the engineer officer on a submarine hadn't wanted to bother with a shipalt, so he'd signed it off as completed although the work had never been done.

As the true condition of the shipalt program emerged, the squadron engineer became so alarmed that he began to follow our progress personally. It got so bad that the squadron gave us lists of past shipalts for each submarine and we had to do ship checks to determine if they had actually been done. Fortunately, the planning office was revealing the problems, not causing them.

To complicate things, we had problems with our computer printout. Almost weekly we relearned the rule "garbage in, garbage out" and a new one, "everything you put in, comes out." We had one problem that defied solution. Like a computer virus, it kept showing up in different places and in different forms and we spent hours romancing it.

One time my men tried a fix that I had specifically told them not to try, because my check with nature convinced me it wouldn't work. Well, it didn't and resulted in a real mess, so I raised hell with the whole bunch and when I was finished, they were all sitting at their desks looking straight ahead and things were very quiet. I thought about how hard I'd been on them and realized they were just trying their best, so I turned in my chair and said, "You know, if I had to take orders from me, sometimes I think I would tell me to go to hell."

One of the seamen whirled around and said, "Sir, you would have to fuckin' stand in line." We all cracked up laughing and things went back to normal. It was another reminder that in the submarine force you earn it or you don't get it.

Meanwhile we were still saddled with the repair department rejects and had our share of personnel problems. Miller and I made the best of it. A couple of the seamen turned out to be good men and we moved a second class to the technical library where he worked out better, but that still left one problem child. I don't remember his name and desperately wish I could.

I believe he was a third class hull technician. He was a good kid, a willing worker and quite intelligent; but he had absolutely zero common sense. If you told him to do even the simplest task, he would go all ahead flank right into the nearest bulkhead and screw up, usually by coming up with a better idea for what to do or how to do it. He came up with a new idea about every fifteen minutes and what he lacked in common sense, he made up for in enthusiasm. He wrote a lot of notes, which were truly works of art; his spelling and English were atrocious. I took some of the better samples up to the wardroom and passed them around for laughs. He was a challenge Miller and I could not pass up.

Whenever he came up with a new idea, one of us sat him down and patiently explained why it was the dumbest fucking thing we had ever heard, what was wrong with his thinking, what he had failed to consider and how he should have looked at the problem. We actually proved that common sense can be taught—it just takes a long time. Gradually his ideas got more organized and less wild. One day I came into the office and Miller told me our man had an idea he wanted to tell me about. . . . *not again . . . Miller wouldn't do that to me . . . we're friends . . .*

I sat down at my desk and gave him the go-ahead. He carefully outlined a plan to fix our computer glitch that covered all ten bases and solved all the problems. The plan was foolproof, so I said, "Do it." Miller flashed a big, satisfied grin and said, "We already have."

That was the first time we hadn't criticized one of his plans and it made a big difference in the kid's life. He made second class the next time around and turned out to be one of the best men I had. I am probably prouder of that accomplishment than anything I did in the Navy. Miller, who did most of the work, made warrant officer after I left the Simon Lake and he, too, I am proud to say, was a Hansen-trained man.

Finally, our new shipalt program began rocking and rolling. On one of the first refits, after we had the status lined out and our system operating, we completed nine shipalts, which was equivalent to six months' work under the old system, and eventually got to the point where we had so many ready to go on any given refit that the squadron had to pick and choose and that made the assistant repair officer and squadron engineer downright giddy.

As any manager should know, you can manage a large number of jobs effectively just by knowing five things about each one, but it's absolutely mandatory that those five things be accurate, which is probably why Mother Nature gave us four fingers and a thumb. In the end, our computer program gave us only a few pieces of information about each shipalt, but they were all accurate and up to date, which allowed us to concentrate on the exceptions and manage the program effectively. But our system did create one small problem.

It didn't take long before the rest of the repair department saw what we had. As they say, monkey see, monkey do. The repair shops were stuck with the official printout, which was so extensive and required so much complicated and time-consuming input that it was unreliable as a management tool. A lot of the input was gun-decked[24] or done haphazardly and the result was a printout with lots of bells and whistles, but none that could ring or toot.

So, the inevitable happened. Some repair shops took elements of my system and bribed ADP to create weekly printouts covering just their repair jobs. These short, handy printouts allowed the shops to work more effectively and everything went along fine until the repair officer discovered them and put out a written order forbidding any more unofficial printouts. There's a lesson in there somewhere.

A few months after that, a group of officers from Naval Ship System Command came aboard to conduct our annual readiness inspection. When they arrived, a navy captain walked directly from the quarterdeck to our office and asked if this was the planning office. I told him it was and he said, "You guys are doing more shipalts per refit than all the other submarine tenders in the Navy combined and I want to know how the hell you do it."

I had the duty and had to leave, so I introduced Miller and said he could answer all his questions. Miller was holding a chair open when I left.

---

[24] Navy slang. To record made up numbers or readings in a log or record.

Command Duty

Every so often the Simon Lake went to sea for several days. We steamed down the Firth of Clyde and out into the North Atlantic and when we got beyond the thousand-fathom curve, we dumped our radioactive effluent in the ocean.

Whenever a nuclear submarine came in for refit, it normally shut down the reactor and went on shore power supplied by the Simon Lake. During the twenty-eight day refit, the primary system cooled down, causing the primary water to contract, and in order to maintain proper level in the pressurizer, they had to pump water into the primary system. If they had to cool down and depressurize the primary systems, even more water was pumped in.

When the refit was over, the submarine took the reactor critical and heated up the primary system again. Now, they had to discharge primary water due to thermal expansion of the water. Rather than dump the discharged primary water (effluent) directly into Holy Loch, which would have upset the Scots no end, they discharged it into holding tanks on the Simon Lake. That was the radioactive water we were dumping at sea. Water that had been inside the primary system of a nuclear reactor plant was radioactive by definition, but I have seen the numbers on it and am sure there are springs in Southern Utah that are more radioactive, but over time it all adds up.

I had continued working on my junior officer journal and each time we went to sea I also worked on my qualifications for officer of the deck underway. After a number of trips, I had qualified and had completed my JOJ.

One evening around the end of February 1968, when I'd been in Scotland for a little over a year, I was sitting in the wardroom reading a copy of *Navy Times* and saw a list of officers by lineal number who were in the zone for selection to lieutenant. I was surprised to see my number on the list, as I didn't think I'd be in the zone for another year. The next morning I asked the admin officer about it. After a confusing few seconds, he said, "You already made it; you put the bars on in three days!"

Normally it takes four years to make lieutenant, but I'd made it in three and so did a lot of other guys; apparently Viet Nam had taken its toll and they needed more lieutenants. A few days later, I put on the railroad tracks and got a big pay raise.

Then I sat down, counted on my fingers and went to see the executive officer. I told him that I had completed my junior officer journal, was qualified as officer of the deck underway and was a lieutenant, so I was now eligible to stand duties as a command duty officer (CDO). He dropped his arms down at his sides and just looked at me, obviously thinking. Finally, he said, "Jerry, you are a pain in the ass; don't you realize the problems I have?"

"No, Sir," I said.

His sad tale was that there were five lieutenants on the ship senior to me who had not yet qualified as OD underway and some had not completed their JOJ. If he made me a command duty officer, I would be junior to men working for me and the Navy doesn't like that. But he said he'd talk to the captain about it. The next day the captain came through and made me a CDO and I went into seven-section liberty. . . . *back in the saddle again . . .*

The command duty officer acted as the captain while he stood duty, which was for twenty-four hours at a time. He was senior to everyone onboard except the executive officer and captain for whom he acted as a filter by handling everything except big problems. He ran the normal routine of the ship, received all routine reports and, in an emergency, had to get the ship underway with all the authority and responsibility that a captain normally had. He received a letter saying he was qualified for command at sea.

Contrary to what one might expect, being a command duty officer was a pretty routine job most of the time with few tough decisions or crises to deal with. The duty officers in the various departments handled most problems, so the job boiled down to answering questions, giving permission, taking reports and being ready in case the shit hit the fan, which can happen quite suddenly.

One Sunday night, for example, I was the CDO when the wind came up. The west coast of Scotland is famous for sudden, violent windstorms. Normally they lasted only a few hours and had other common features: usually they didn't go over twenty knots; if they went over twenty knots, they could go to forty knots; if they went over forty knots, the sky was the limit. They clocked wind at Prestwick over a hundred and thirty knots while I was there and that is serious wind.

I told the officer of the deck to let me know if it got to twenty knots and every five-knot interval it hit thereafter. I was watching a movie in the wardroom and got a string of reports, so at the end of the reel I went to the quarterdeck; the wind was now about thirty knots. I watched the situation for a while and it seemed to be leveling off, so I went back up to the wardroom. The next report was a steady forty knots with higher gusts, so I ran outside and down the starboard side toward the quarterdeck. By the time I got there, the wind was over seventy knots.

There had been a yacht race in Holy Loch that weekend, so many visiting yachts were anchored in the harbor and red flares were going off all over.

I told the officer of the deck to call away the duty damage control party and have all duty officers meet me on the quarterdeck. When they arrived, I told everyone to be prepared to get underway if we had to. Then I told the duty repair officer to take one of the Box-L's[25] and a couple of men from the damage control party, get underway, and do what he could to save lives in the harbor. Finally, I told the OD that I was stationing myself in the pilot house and would take all reports there.

---

[25] A very seaworthy boat that had been used on the Rhine River Patrol.

I had just started up the starboard side toward the pilot house when a thirty-foot sailboat that was adrift came out of the darkness off our starboard quarter, rode up over the turtle-back[26] of a submarine, which I think was the USS George Washington SSBN-598, and lodged between the submarine and the tender, where it beat itself to death and sank in a couple of minutes.

When I got to the pilot house, I found two quartermasters busily taking bearings to see if we were dragging our anchors; they were still holding. A short time later, the telephone rang and it was the captain. I briefed him on the situation. He told me he couldn't get out to the ship and said, "You're on your own, Jerry." I told him I had a lot of help and wasn't worried.

The windstorm lasted only about four hours, then started dying down. When the duty repair officer reported back, he had some wild tales to tell. They had found red flares going off all over the harbor and people screaming everywhere. The visiting yachts and our small boats were breaking their moorings and being blown into the tender itself and the submarines tied up alongside then drifting south through Holy Loch toward the Firth of Clyde. As the Box-L had come alongside one yacht with two couples onboard, one of the women had thrown a bundle to him. When he caught it and looked down, he was holding a little baby and he realized that the woman, whom he couldn't hear, had been screaming, "Save my baby!"

Summary Court

About 1900 one evening, I was the command duty officer and had walked back to the quarterdeck to check in with the officer of the deck and noticed a seaman messenger, who was making a report. I recognized him as one of a group of men who had come aboard recently. As I remember, they were called

---

[26] Tapered area between the main deck aft and the vertical rudder.

"group eight" personnel. They were mentally challenged and couldn't pass the regular exam to join the Navy, but some had been accepted on a trial basis in the belief that they could perform some jobs. As a group, they were dedicated, patriotic, refreshingly cheerful and would do anything they were asked. They actually could do some jobs well.

I talked to the man for several minutes, asking him where he was from and how he liked the Navy. His chest swelled with obvious pride to be talking to the command duty officer. I am absolutely sure that he wrote to his mother about it and it was a neat, uplifting experience for me.

Afterward, I went back to my office, did some paperwork, then returned to the quarterdeck after the watch had been relieved and the 2000 to 2400 watch was on duty. As I approached the quarterdeck, I saw the same group-eight man and asked why he was still on watch. The OD told me he'd been trying to get him relieved, but the duty supply officer had said there was no one available. I knew that was a bunch of bullshit; the supply department had lots of men.

I should have done a lot of things; telling the OD to exercise his authority and call the duty supply officer to the quarterdeck and give him a direct order to relieve the man comes to mind. Instead, I said, "Let me handle this."

I went to the supply department office and found three third class storekeepers sitting around a table playing cards. My first questions were calm and designed to gather information. They told me there was a policy in the supply department that only nonrated men had to stand duties as messenger or fire watch and that they couldn't relieve the man because there were no more nonrated men in the duty section; besides, the man had said he didn't mind standing two watches in a row. I knew we had second class petty officers standing fire watches in the repair department, so I said, "If one of you doesn't relieve that man in two seconds, I'm going break all three of you into little bitty fucking pieces with my bare hands!"

The man got relieved in short order and I wound up on the executive officer's carpet. The supply officer, who was a commander, had complained to the executive officer, but managed to leave out one critical detail, that the man involved was a group-eight person. When the executive officer discovered that—the group-eight project was his own personal baby—his big guns swung from me to the supply officer and the rules in supply changed real fast. But like most submarine sailors, the executive officer had a memory like an elephant when it comes to unfinished business.

A couple of weeks later the Marine Corps had its annual Birthday Ball which happens to coincide with my birthday, November 10. One of the marines did something at the party that upset the captain in charge of the marine detachment. He took the man to office hours, which is the same as captain's mast, and threw the book at him with a summary court-martial.

Since I was the new lieutenant on board and in such good standing with the executive officer and all, I was designated summary court officer, the judge in the proceedings who could render real punishment. In fact, he could give more punishment than the commanding officer and it was a judicial sentence, so a boot lieutenant could be more lethal than the old man and that enhanced the effectiveness of a summary court-martial.

I brushed up on the Uniform Code of Military Justice and held court. Everyone was in dress uniform, the witnesses and accused were all scared, and I was nervous—this was the real thing. I read the charges and specifications, interviewed the witnesses, and finally called in the marine himself. I listened to his story, asked him several questions and thought about what the witnesses had said. No matter how hard I squinted my eyes and gritted my teeth, I just couldn't see where this rose above a relatively minor offense. The real problem was obvious; the marine captain had it in for him.

I found the marine guilty and sentenced him to two days' restriction with no extra duty. When the marine captain found out, he went ballistic, but there wasn't a thing he could do. The boot lieutenant was also a jury.

The Navigator

While writing these stories, I could remember the events well, but the order they came in is a little fuzzy. I believe this event happened shortly after I made lieutenant and started standing command duty officer duties, but before I got too far into the planning office job. Anyway, we were seeing daylight with the submarine shipalt program.

Early one afternoon I walked into the repair office and found Jack looking glum. He told me the executive officer wanted to see me. As I walked up to his stateroom, I was trying frantically to figure out what kind of trouble I was in, so I wasn't prepared when he said, "You're going to relieve the navigator."

I dropped into a chair, my mind spinning. As navigator, I would be a department head and on a submarine tender that would also make me the operations officer. I had started out as a radioman in the operations department, which included the navigator, but had left that world when I went into nuclear power, which is in the engineering department, and now I was in the repair department. . . . *Jesus . . . my career is about to make a complete circle . . .*

The job was actually appealing. I had always wanted to learn navigation, but knew I wasn't qualified and that was the thought that hit me first. I told the executive officer that although I thought I had piloting down pretty well, I didn't know that much about celestial navigation. Then I had another thought: "What about my job in repair? No one else is qualified to do it." The main battery of a repair ship is the repair department and to my way of thinking should have taken precedence, but the navigation wheel was squeaking loudly, apparently.

He went right by that and started explaining that the detailer couldn't find a relief for our navigator, who had orders back to the States, and that the captain was assigning me to the job.

"You're the best we've got, Jerry. I can help and you can take the correspondence course; you understand the operations department; I know you can do it."

By now I had my own stateroom, so I went there and sat down to think, mostly that it would be nice to be in the Royal Navy and have a shot of good whiskey. As an LDO, my duties were supposed to be limited to electronics and nuclear power. . . . *how can they do this?* . . . Then I remembered someone once saying that even though I was an LDO, I was also a line officer and that one day some captain would look down at the star on my sleeve and assign me any job he wanted.

Eventually I walked back down to repair and Jack already knew. We had a cup of coffee and I said that I would help him any way I could. He said, "Don't worry; you'll have your hands full."

I went to the ship's office and ordered the correspondence course on navigation, got a copy of Dutton's *Navigation and Piloting* and started reading. The next morning I started relieving the navigator who, by the way, was a mustang lieutenant also born on November 10, 1932. He had become what I'd always wanted to be, so I wish we had spent more time comparing notes. I once met a bartender in Honolulu who also shared my birthday. I never asked what she thought about navigation, but I'm betting she sailed her own boat around the islands.

I was almost finished with the relieving process, had signed for all the classified publications and even sent in my first lesson on navigation, when the executive officer called me in again; now it was his turn to be glum. It seems they couldn't make me navigator after all. There had recently been several groundings and other problems associated with bad navigation and the ship had just received a message from Commander, Submarine

Force Atlantic, that from now on, the only officers in the force who could be assigned navigator duties were the captain or executive officer of the ship and officers assigned by the detailer in Washington.

This left the executive officer to assume navigator duties and me to go back to the repair department. Jack had a big grin on his face when I walked in this time. "Get to work; you're a week behind."

The men in the planning office were actually glad to see me.

Bears

When I took over as planning officer, it was only a title, and even that was not on the list of officer billets for the Simon Lake. Jack and I had both been in shipyards with planning departments and knew the kind of work they did, so it was an opportunity—and a challenge—to set it up any way we wanted. When I started organizing the planning office itself, the submarine shipalt program, which was one planning function, was already done, so the next area I dived into was nuclear systems repair.

The Simon Lake already had the basic building blocks to do nuclear repair work. There was a radiological control division with personnel trained to install glove boxes and handle radioactive contamination. We had hull technicians who were qualified as nuclear welders and trained personnel in the non-destructive testing lab and quality control shop. What we didn't have was the glue that held the blocks together. The repair officer and the assistant, while both qualified and experienced as repair officers, were not nuclear trained, which had left exactly no one to set up an organized system for nuclear work.

The Simon Lake had done nuclear repair work only when they absolutely had to and then had just bungled through. Several factors were at play. The nuclear submarine force was still growing and the pipeline of mustang nuclear-trained repair

consisted of a short length of small pipe with a stop valve and an end that was capped and seal-welded shut. In order to tap into the system to connect test equipment, you simply cut the seal welds, opened the valve and you were in. But the test connections were rarely used and the short lengths of pipe were becoming "crud" traps. Crud was the name given to the fine metal wear particles that became entrained in the primary coolant then flowed through the reactor core, where they got zapped by a neutron flux and became radioactive themselves. The term crud was an acronym for Chalk River unidentified deposits, because the phenomenon was first experienced at a nuclear reactor named Chalk River in Canada. The crud was settling out, building up in the test connections and becoming a radiation hazard. The new shipalts directed that they be eliminated.

The grizzly part came in when you considered their locations. Many of them couldn't be isolated from the main coolant system by simply shutting a valve. This meant we had to create a stop valve by installing a freeze seal to isolate the piping that contained the test connection. If something should happen to the freeze seal while the system was open, there could be what is called a "loss of coolant" casualty which had the potential to damage the reactor core and spread radioactive contamination into the environment.

The freeze seals were made by installing a foam coffer dam around the pipe to be isolated. The foam was secured with duct tape then liquid nitrogen was poured into the coffer dam to freeze the water inside the pipe and thus create a stop valve. We kept it frozen by dripping liquid nitrogen on the pipe every so often, the way ether used to be administered. The seal had to be maintained until the system was welded back together, which could be several days later. The method may sound crude, but no highly technical project has been accomplished in this country in the last fifty years without the aid of duct tape, and that includes saving Apollo Thirteen, so we were operating on the leading edge of technology.

Finally, our nuclear work organization was ready. We scheduled one of the nuclear shipalts for the next submarine refit. I wrote the procedure, welders qualified, nuclear work coordinators were assigned, and we were set to go. When the submarine came in from patrol, I went down to the wardroom to brief the officers on what we planned to do.

To get this briefing in perspective, it may be helpful to understand some things about the officers I was briefing. They were well-qualified reactor plant operators, but they were not necessarily nuclear system repairmen. Most of them had been through a typical test program but were not generally familiar with repair work involving abnormal reactor plant conditions. They tended to be conservative-minded and had about the same attitude toward their reactor plant as a pair of Dobermans have toward a little blonde-headed ward.

When I told them we wanted them to shut down, cool down and depressurize their primary systems and where we wanted to install a freeze seal and what we wanted to cut out, the engineer officer leaped to his feet and said, "You want to put a freeze seal where? And do what?"

It didn't get any better when they learned that I was serious and that the squadron was going to make them do it. I gave them a pep talk about our new nuclear work organization, which helped a little, but they had a point. Normally, when this kind of work was done, the patient was "dead," meaning there was no core in the reactor. At site one, though, the situation was quite different; we were going to castrate a live grizzly using only a local anesthetic.

The job turned out well. Better than anyone expected, in fact, including me. I was all over it day and night and took a lot of notes for changes we needed to make. When the job was completed, the squadron breathed a sigh of relief; the repair officer and assistant were happy campers; and the whole repair department got a lift. We now had a good system for doing serious nuclear repair work and we were the first team!

It didn't take long to groom our nuclear repair organization and after we had completed several jobs, we were confident the system was up and running. During one submarine refit, we completed a total of four nuclear repair jobs, which either equaled or exceeded the number of nuclear jobs done the year before on all our submarines combined.

Meanwhile my leader, Jack Sousa, had been waiting like a big tomcat watching a sparrow, and about the time I got my head above water, he pounced. When I heard his plan, I knew it was a natural, but have to admit that I hadn't looked that far ahead. I suppose if you're a nuke, you think that is the all that ends all, so it came as a surprise that he was going to start routing all major, non-nuclear repair jobs to the planning office for the same treatment we gave a nuclear job.

He wanted us to plan them, write a work procedure if needed, do all the research in the tech library, identify the material, obtain the plans, then present everything in a neat package—tied with a pink ribbon—to the lead shop. The lead shop would then order the material and do the work. What had once been a mess of files in the bowels of the ship was now going to be a real planning office on the main deck. He also gave me two more good petty officers.

By now, the submarine shipalt program was running smoothly, so Miller and I tackled our new responsibilities and entered another field with no sleigh tracks in the snow.

We had to develop a comprehensive way to organize all the information needed to accomplish any major, complicated repair job on a nuclear submarine. This "planning" function was currently being done by the individual repair shops, with degree of success varying with the capabilities of the shop, and consumed a lot of senior petty officer time. The possible jobs, which did not fall into easy categories, needed a list as long as your arm. We kicked it around and came up with a bunch of questions. We asked several leading petty officers what kind of jobs they needed planned and what kind of information they'd like to have in the planning packages. We had our own ideas, but I knew from experience that we had to check with the troops. They might not know what to do, but they sure as hell knew what not to do.

We were flooded with enthusiastic feedback. They readily gave us lists of specific jobs that needed planning. Mostly, they needed things like plans, stock numbers and material lists. They normally didn't need a written work procedure, and in cases where they did, a ten-step set of general instructions of the kind you got from a good petty officer would suffice. The big advantage they could all see clearly was having knowledgeable and experienced petty officers do the research and organizing, which resulted in better overall results and took a load off the petty officers in the shops.

I designed the format and contents for a typical repair procedure and left plenty of room for exceptions. When we planned a job, we did the research in the tech library, assembled copies of the plans, made up material lists, and if a work procedure was required, we got verbal instructions from a senior petty officer in the shop and then put them in writing. Finally, we put everything in a folder with the work request and gave it to the lead shop's division officer. He acted as a final filter and was kept in the loop. When the package got to the lead shop, they ordered the material and did the work. After they completed a big job, we debriefed the shop and made changes as needed then kept the work procedure as a sample for future jobs, so we had to plan many of them only once.

We got the system up and running in a relatively short time and the officers and men in the repair department decided that having a planning office was a neat thing after all. They dropped by, visited and even asked questions. We now had three irons in the fire—the submarine shipalt program, nuclear system repair, and major job planning—which was about right for our outfit.

Steam Stop

Shortly after we got the planning office completely organized and running smoothly, we were hit with a big challenge. One of our submarines came back from patrol with steam leaking by the seat of its port main steam stop valve, which was potentially an ugly problem.

There were two of these valves, one in each steam line leading from the steam generators in the reactor compartment to the engine room. They were eight-inch gate valves located high in the overhead of the auxiliary machinery space near the after reactor compartment bulkhead. Since steam demand determined reactor power level, the valves were remotely operated by switches located on the reactor plant control panel in the maneuvering room.

The valve was leaking "by the seat," so it was not leaking unless it was shut. It was always open while on patrol, so the squadron decided to gamble and send the ship back on patrol and repair it during the next refit.

The potential problem with that gamble was that if the crew had to shut the valve for some reason, the odds were they'd want to shut both main steam stops, but steam would still be coming down the line going to wherever, demanding reactor power, dragging steam (water) from one steam generator, possibly making it go "hot and dry" if the steam cycle was interrupted in some way, so there was some risk. With a steam plant inside a submerged submarine, some complicated engineering casualties are possible and they can cascade into a real mess, but there was no way we could plan the job, get the material and do the repairs during this refit. So they left on patrol with the leak.

The valve could not be repaired in place, so it had to be replaced and that presented an array of problems. In order to gain access to the weld joints to replace the valve body, we had to remove a lot of equipment and piping. Replacing the valve was a nuclear repair job. In addition, we had to remove and reinstall about a half dozen other nuclear system valves and connected piping, which were also nuclear jobs. Replacing a main steam stop valve was a job that had never been done before, even by a shipyard.

The repair officer told me to start planning the job. When I got all my ducks in a row, he wanted to sit down with me and make up a bar chart for the whole project. There was still some question about whether or not the work could be done in a twenty-eight-day refit. They might have to send the ship back to a shipyard in the States, which would mean taking a fleet ballistic missile submarine off the line and that involved political considerations.

I took a flashlight, tape measure and notebook down to the submarine and did a thorough ship check. I determined the minimum amount of equipment and piping that had to be removed, measured everything and took lots of notes. Meanwhile, Miller got copies of the plans involved and we started planning the project. If one counted a typical job, such as replacing a valve that involved two weld joints, as a single job, then this project actually involved about a dozen typical nuclear repair jobs.

Any nuclear job is complicated. When we cut into a piping system that might contain radioactive material, we had to install a glove box around the work area to contain it. In order to do most welds, we had to have an inert gas purge flowing through the pipe to keep oxygen away from the heat-affected zone to prevent oxidation. In order to set up the purge paths, the ship's crew had to establish and maintain abnormal plant conditions with odd valve lineups, The welders had to qualify on each weld in a scaled mockup, and in order to do some welds, the welder had to literally stand on his head and look at a mirror to see the joint. All welds had to pass stringent non-destructive testing, such as liquid penetrate inspections and radiographs. These tests were time-consuming. Gamma ray sources were used to radiograph the welds and the area had to be cleared of personnel when a shot was made. In some cases, we had to establish and maintain freeze seals to isolate the work area. It was a complicated and difficult project by any standard.

We worked on the planning for several days and when I had a good understanding of the project, I told the repair officer I was ready to talk. He set aside a full day for our conference and early the next morning we started. He had a three-foot by ten-foot piece of graph paper taped to the bulkhead in the repair office with actual dates along the top and plenty of room down the left side to list the individual jobs. He also had a big ruler and several colors of felt-tipped pens. He had a degree in marine engineering and had done this kind of graph before.

I gave him a list of the individual jobs. We discussed them and decided on the order in which they would probably be done. He listed them down the left side by the name of the system valve being replaced or by other brief titles. Next, we decided which jobs could be done in parallel, which ones had to be done in series and the sequence in which the series jobs had to be done. Then I estimated how long each job would take. Finally, he constructed a bar next to each job starting at the proposed start date and ending at the estimated completion date. Bars for jobs that could be done in parallel occupied the same time periods and bars for series jobs were placed end to end.

Construction of the bar chart took all day. We broke for lunch and dinner and finally in the early evening we had it done and stepped back to take a look. According to the bar chart, the project would take thirty-three days. We only had twenty-eight.

I knew that we were looking at a series of estimates that probably equaled one wild-ass guess. The computer between my ears had already calculated a different scenario, but it wasn't something you could integrate into a bar chart or tell to a commander who was fond of bar charts.

I knew from experience that estimating is a hard kind of decision making. You have to use some criteria to discipline your individual decisions then crank in some tolerances. On previous projects, I'd learned that Mother Nature decides where the tolerances are needed and that you can't anticipate her moves. I'd also learned that any carefully planned, organized and supervised project could be done in less time than estimated. The key was not the planning phase; the key was the work phase. You had to keep Murphy in his cage and use good hands-on supervision to make sure that nothing went wrong, which stacks the tolerances in your favor every time. I have never failed to beat a well-planned estimate.

I knew the above was true at the time, but had never written it down or thought it out, so it never occurred to me to explain it to the repair officer. I doubt if launching into an explanation of management philosophy would have been a good idea under the circumstances anyway. We took an hour to go back through the whole project step by step. He pinned me down with pointed questions, but we came out with the same time frame. When we finished, he slumped in his chair, still holding a red felt-tipped pen. He turned toward me and asked, "Tell me, how long do you think it would really take?"

Now, that was a different question. Without hesitation or thought, I blurted, "About fourteen days."

He threw the pen in the air, leaped to his feet and yelled, "How the hell can you say that! Didn't we just spend all fucking day going through this shit and didn't you just give me your best estimates!?"

Choosing my words carefully, I said, "I've been doing this stuff for a long time and after a while you get a feel for it. Shit, we can do anything in ten days; don't worry, we'll get it done during the refit."

That probably wasn't much help when it came time to brief the captain and squadron commander, but by now I had established an ugly reputation. When it came to nuclear repair work, I was never wrong and they all knew it.

When the submarine came back in from patrol, we were ready. I stayed on the job day and night for four days until the new valve was in and the root pass was blessed by non-destructive testing. I wiped out four sets of khakis and catnapped a few hours at a time, but we finished all the welding in nine days and had the equipment reinstalled two days later.

Eleven days is less than fourteen days and one-third of the time predicted by the bar chart, so my record—and my reputation—remained intact. The submarine went to sea on time and about a year later I was awarded the Navy Commendation Medal for my contribution.

Sixty Fathoms

After my family arrived in Scotland, I stayed at home whenever I didn't have the duty. My routine was to leave home early in the morning, catch the boat out to the ship, eat breakfast in the wardroom and then begin the work day. Well, Murphy's law being what it is, the one morning there was a need for me to be a little early, I happened to be a little late and found two problems when I got there.

The first problem involved my Good Samaritan deed of picking up a warrant officer and driving him to the boat landing. He lived in an upstairs apartment in downtown Dunoon, which was the town near Holy Loch. When I got there, I had to parallel park my Volkswagen station wagon on the street. The VW was an American model with the steering wheel on the left and I was in Scotland where you drive on the left side of the road. Fortunately, there was a space right in front of his place; unfortunately, a lorry was double-parked in the street just beyond, where I had to pull up and then back in. Like a good citizen, I sat in my car and waited for the driver to return. When he came out and saw me waiting, he motioned for me to just drive around, so I rolled down my window, pointed and said, "I want to park there."

When he heard my American accent, he barked, "You damned Yanks think you own the whole street!"

I leaned out and announced to the whole world, "If we foreclosed on the fucking mortgage, we'd own the whole country!"

Without further conversation, the lorry moved. I picked up my buddy and we went out to the ship. As I headed into the wardroom for breakfast, Jack cornered me and said the executive officer wanted to see me, but that first he wanted me to eat and catch the next boat to the drydock; we had a problem.

The USS Abraham Lincoln SSBN-602 had been on its way in from patrol, running submerged at a base depth of three hundred and fifty feet while trying to slip past a Russian trawler, when she ran aground doing about nineteen knots. The ship bounced toward the surface and water started rushing into the torpedo room bilges. The men in the torpedo room shut the watertight door leading aft and hit the internal compartment salvage air, which pressurized the torpedo room and stopped the flooding.

They surfaced and came up the Firth of Clyde and into Holy Loch at night with the torpedo room pressurized then went directly into our floating drydock, which had the blocks set and was flooded down and waiting. Jack wanted me to assess the damage and see what we had to do.

When I got to the well deck of the drydock, I was confronted by a large canvas curtain rigged across the end to prevent anyone from seeing in. I walked behind it and stopped in my tracks. The submarine was sitting on blocks facing me with a big hole where the bottom half of the bow used to be. Electrical cables, sonar transducers and sections of anchor chain were hanging down from the cavity with pumpkin-sized rocks embedded in the crushed metal. It looked like a big black shark with an evil grin, except there was no jaw, no throat and no tongue.

That class of submarine had six torpedo tubes arranged in two vertical rows in the center of the cone-shaped bow. The two bottom torpedo tubes were gone. From the side, it looked like someone had made a clean cut with a big knife from the tip of the bow straight aft for about twenty feet, five inches below the four remaining torpedo tubes. Near the torpedo room bulkhead, which was the forward edge of the pressure hull, it became a jumbled mass of crushed metal and rocks.

I went inside the ship and down into the torpedo room. When I stood behind the torpedo tube breach doors and looked down in the bilges, I could see into the well deck of the drydock through a gash in the pressure hull that was about two feet long and three inches wide.

I learned they'd had war shots loaded in the torpedo tubes and the whole thing left me stunned and shaken, as it would any submarine sailor. The submarine had bounced toward the surface, so the collision hadn't expended all the kinetic energy. Had she been a few feet deeper and hit head-on, they might never have made it to the surface.

I reported back to Jack that we would have to do some pressure-hull welding, but that was about all I could tell and we would be ready as soon as we got the word. He said that was what he figured.

Next I went up to see an angry executive officer. It seems my shouting match with the lorry driver had now spread all over Scotland and everyone in the country, except the executive officer, thought it was funny. The Scots love a good comeback. He started in with, "We are guests here and you can't say things like that . . ." and it went downhill from there. How he could give me such a thorough ass-chewing without smiling is beyond me, but executive officers have to do some hard things now and then. Apparently, what made it so bad was that all the townspeople knew I was "that nuclear officer."

A board of inquiry was formed to investigate the grounding of the Abraham Lincoln, and a short time later I was designated by the board to get a group of technicians together and check out all the submarine's sensing devices for accuracy, such as depth gauges, dead reckoning analyzer, fathometer, etc., then report back with my findings.

Since the ship had run aground at a depth of about three hundred and fifty feet, it was assumed that they had run aground on the sixty-fathom curve, which is three hundred and sixty feet deep. All the other water along or around their track was deeper. But the ship had taken a star shot not long before the incident and was well away from the sixty-fathom curve, according to their navigational plot. The sensors all proved to be well within their tolerances, which eliminated several possible causes. A few days later, they discovered the real problem. The ship's navigation turned out to be right on and they were exactly where their chart indicated; unfortunately, their copy of the chart was wrong.

Navy charts have about the same quality-control standards as a twenty dollar bill and are subjected to a series of checks by dedicated federal civil servants, but this defective copy had managed to slip through with the lines of longitude printed in the wrong place.

When they plotted their position on the ship's copy of the chart, the collision point was about a thousand yards (one-half nautical mile) from the sixty-fathom curve. When they plotted the collision point on the same chart in the squadron office, they were right on the curve, which at that point in the world is a granite ledge firmly attached to the earth.

We welded up their pressure hull, installed a snowplow-type bow over the gaping grin and sent the ship back to the States on the surface. Then they told the media about it and all hell broke loose, especially with the antiwar crowd.

CHAPTER ELEVEN
San Diego

College 101

In December 1969, I got orders to the Navy Plant Representative Office, Lockheed Missile and Space Division, Sunnyvale, California, for duty. It was actually a weapons officer billet reserved for a submariner, but since I was the only one available, I got it. I just wanted to go home and would have taken anything on the West Coast.

We arrived in New York one hour later local time and eight hours later by our clock, which left just two hours for Angelina and the kids to catch another plane to San Francisco. I took a taxi over to a motel in Bayonne, New Jersey. The next day I had to pick up our Volkswagen station wagon at the docks and drive it to California by myself.

I stopped in Cortez to see Mother and Dad. It had been eight years and things were quite different. Dad was retired and spent a lot of time looking out the window at Mesa Verde. They brought me up to date on all my siblings and we had a good visit. Dad was very proud that I had become an officer in the Navy, but there was no mention of how long I had been gone. After visiting with everyone, I went on to Sacramento and picked up Angelina and the kids, who had been staying with my brothers, one of whom I hadn't seen for eleven years. We eventually got settled in a civilian house in San Jose, put the kids in school and I started my new duties.

The Navy Plant Representative Office in Sunnyvale had exactly the same function as the Naval Reactors Representative Office in Groton, Connecticut, to oversee the work being done by a civilian contractor, who, in this case, was Lockheed Missiles and Space Division. Although in theory the jobs were the same, in fact, they could not have been more different.

I was assigned to the section responsible for making changes to the technical manuals for various weapons systems, most of which were classified, so I was back in the technical library business. A highly trained civilian subcontractor sitting in my office acted as my technical advisor, so my job really boiled down to signing the letters of transmittal that went out with the changes. I was an official rubber stamper.

About eight navy officers were assigned to the office. The commanding officer was a captain, the executive officer was a commander, and the rest were lieutenant commanders and lieutenants and included about three mustangs. We wore dress uniforms. About three hundred federal civil service employees did all the work while the navy officers spent their time traveling around the country visiting weapons facilities. The senior civilians, many of whom had advanced college degrees, spent their time attending seminars and conferences. We had a huge training and travel budget. I got two pretty secretaries, one Chinese and the other Hawaiian. At first I thought I'd been transferred to the Air Force.

I dived into my new duties, looking for something to do or some problem to solve. The civil servants were suspicious of my intent and defensive that I might discover something wrong. One day I found a situation that an idiot could see was a problem. Copies of all the classified changes were going to an office with no possible "need to know." I traced the process to a female office manager and asked her why? "We have always done it that way," she said.

That is never the right answer and always a red flag to me, so I asked my boss about it when he returned from his next trip. He knew nothing, but gave me enough clues to determine that someone at that office had needed a publication for some legitimate one-time reason about five years ago, got on the distribution list and the rest was history. Nobody ever reviewed the distribution list.

Unable to ferret out any work or problems to solve, I decided to take some liberal arts courses at De Anza Junior College and maybe knock off a few more rough edges. During the next year and a half, I took several courses with a 101 behind them and managed to learn a lot.

In psychology, I learned about political science. In anthropology, I learned about political science. In political science, I learned about the history of the Chinese people in Santa Clara County, as my female professor was writing a book on the subject. My English professor told the class every sea story I'd heard during my twenty years in the Navy and they all had happened to him personally; he was really down on the military. I laughed at his sea stories and got an A in the course, but I still can't diagram a sentence. In philosophy, I learned where those big words come from; you know, words like existentialism. I also learned that if you let the professor know you're a navy officer and a conservative, you'll get a B in the course instead of an A, no matter how good your weekly grades are. It was quite an experience.

Before long I was becoming a problem at work. I wouldn't travel because I didn't know anything about missiles or nuclear warheads and had already overdosed on science and technology in nuclear power. Worst of all, I was not spending my share of the travel money. I told them I wasn't interested in nuclear weapons or the horse they rode in on. They tried everything. One day they took me into a highly classified room and showed me to-scale models of reentry vehicles. I was invited to conferences, which were always smooth presentations with printed brochures, coffee and pastries. I thought about the conditions in the shipyards and wanted to puke.

One day they had a conference for my benefit. The presentation was made by a group of impressive young engineers who were in the process of making up a concept package for presentation to the Navy. The concept involved possible methods for rescuing men from a sunken submarine and they thought it would be right down my alley.

Soon after they started, it was obvious to me that none of them had ever seen the ocean or talked to anyone who had. Apparently they had seen a photograph of a submarine tender with its service booms rigged out and several submarines tied up alongside. There were lines going from the service booms down to the submarines and they concluded that the submarines were moored to the service booms. . . . *wild horses couldn't drag me out of here . . .*

The concept included things like anchoring a submarine tender over a sunken submarine and then using the service booms to lift the submarine off the ocean floor and raise it near the surface or lower rescue bells down to get the men a few at a time. They were very full of themselves and just wanted to know if I could see any problems they had missed.

I didn't know where to begin. First of all, anchoring any ship in deep water is a neat trick if you can swing it. Then, I didn't want to ruin their day by telling them the lines coming down from the service booms were shore power cables, so I said, "It looks good to me," and forced myself not to describe where their concept would wind up if it ran into an admiral wearing dolphins. I am not qualified to judge how well Lockheed built ballistic missiles, but I can guarantee one thing: they sure knew how to spend taxpayer money.

Not long after that, I called the submarine officer detailer and told him he had to get me out of there; I was going crazy; send me to sea; anything. He came through with orders to the USS Dixon AS-37, a new submarine tender about to go in commission in Norfolk, Virginia, and slated to be homeported in San Diego, California.

I finally used some of the excess travel money, took a government-sponsored "business trip" to San Diego and bought a new house on Cabaret Street in the San Carlos area about a quarter mile from Patrick Henry High School. It was the first home I'd ever owned and I was determined to plant my family and never move them again.

Leadership

I reported to the Dixon a couple of weeks before it was commissioned. I was back in familiar territory now and loving it, until the executive officer explained to me that I was going to be the first lieutenant while the ship traveled around through the Panama Canal and went through underway training in San Diego. After we got settled in San Diego, I would go to the repair department, become planning officer, and set up the same system I had designed for the Simon Lake.

"I can't even spell first lieutenant," I grumbled.

It didn't work; that star on my sleeve had done it again. The captain wanted a full lieutenant who was a qualified officer of the deck underway to be the first lieutenant and I fit the bill. I already knew the captain, a four striper who had been the skipper of the Abraham Lincoln when she ran aground on the sixty-fathom curve while I was in Scotland. By the time my meeting with the executive officer was over and he had said, "Welcome aboard," I knew I liked him.

The first lieutenant was the deck department head and also the gunnery officer. The ship had single five-inch gun mounts fore and aft, a mark-56 fire control system, an A1 shore bombardment computer, battleship anchors, many small boats, traveling cranes, a 645-foot hull to keep painted and a helo deck on the fantail that the captain wanted to get certified, so we could land helicopters on it. . . . *ok* . . .

I stowed my gear in my nice, new, private stateroom, changed into wash khakis and went down to the deck department office. I told the yeoman I wanted to see all officers and petty officers, first class and above, and they quickly assembled in the spacious department head office.

I took some time to look the group over. There were two chief warrant officers, both former submarine quartermasters, who wouldn't know much about this kind of operation, but there were several chief and first class boatswain's mates and gunner's mates plus a first class fire controlman, so it looked like I had plenty of help.

I began by saying that I would be their department head for three months, until we got settled in San Diego. I gave them a brief description of my background, which didn't, I pointed out, include time on the deck force. "If you play your cards right," I said, "you can run this department; just point me in the right direction, tell me what to say, and try to keep us out of trouble."

I told them I wanted discipline handled at the lowest possible level and expected every man to do his job the way he had been trained. I then excused everyone but the division officers and leading petty officers, whom I told to use their own judgment in running their divisions and to keep me informed. They, in turn, briefed me on current problems, which were numerous but not very serious. Most had to do with preparations for the trip to San Diego. I also learned that we had one more sea trial item to complete, which required test firing the forward gun.

A few days later I attended captain's mast for several men in the deck department who had committed various offenses before my arrival. It was now standard practice for the division officer and department head to accompany their men to mast, in case the captain wanted more information. Disciplinary problems were fairly rare in the submarine force, so I had little experience at mast in any capacity, and this was a learning experience for me.

The nature of the offenses and the way the men, their division officers, and the captain related to each other at mast gave me a lot to think about. My experience was that most of the first lieutenant's problems would be with personnel because the deck force was the repository for most new men and a classic hotbed of discontent, but we were also living in Admiral Zumwalt's "new navy," which operated under a set of rules considerably different from those I'd grown to respect during my twenty years in the Navy.

Admiral Zumwalt, who was the Chief of Naval Operations, had liberalized the Navy, which was not necessarily a bad thing, but in the process he stripped away two hundred years of tradition and replaced it with nothing. Tradition had been the glue that held the Navy together and made it an exciting and adventuresome life where the rules were as tough as the men and nothing was gained unless you earned it.

Now, all hands went into six-section duty and liberty was a right, not a privilege. Petty officers could no longer punish their men; they could only put them "on report" and the captain punished. Disciplinary problems festered until they became a captain's mast or court-martial, so all the shit floated to the surface and became a real mess. In effect, the enlisted ranks were now treated like trade union members with rights but no responsibilities and the only rules that applied were those that coddled them. And the yeoman and disbursing clerk problem, like everything else, just got worse.

The captain and executive officer spent the majority of their time dealing with personnel instead of management problems. Division officers and petty officers spent time holding hands and explaining why their men had screwed up, time they should have spent doing their jobs. We were buried in a sea of sensitivity training, leadership seminars, career counselors and similar programs.

Meanwhile, I had a big job that I couldn't do if I spent all my time at captain's mast, so I went for a long walk around the decks and did some thinking. John Paul Jones, one of the Navy's founders, once said, "Enlisted men are sly, cunning and bear watching." I'd been an enlisted man and knew firsthand that John Paul was right. The deck department needed a good dose of old-fashioned leadership and I was going to give it to them. *. . . Zumwalt can go to hell . . . I'll have my job done before he knows what happened . . .*

I decided I had something to say that probably none in the deck force had heard before, so the next morning I mustered the men on the forecastle and gave them my speech on leadership.

I didn't plan it that way, but before I spoke I noticed that from their vantage point, they would be looking at a lieutenant wearing silver dolphins, with the backdrop of a five-inch gun mount, the Jack[27] fluttering in the breeze and, beyond that, the harbor of Norfolk, which was full of navy as far as the eye could see. My speech went something like this.

"Good morning. I have called you together to introduce myself and say a few things about my philosophy for running the department. My name is Hansen and I will be the first lieutenant until the ship gets settled in San Diego and we start repairing submarines, then I will go to the repair department

"Yesterday I attended my first captain's mast as your department head. The men who went to mast all committed their offenses before I arrived. What happened at mast made me realize that some things need to be explained to the men in this department, so I ask you to listen carefully.

"Leadership is a two-way street. You men owe the Navy a day's work for a day's pay. The Navy owes you the wherewithal to do your job. The division officer's job is to tell you what to do. The petty officer's job is to show you how to do it. I am responsible for getting the work done and looking out for your welfare. The captain has the same job for the whole ship. That is how the Navy is supposed to work. I don't care what you think or what you have been told; that is the only way it can work.

---

[27] A flag consisting of just the blue field and stars in the U.S. Flag.

"Now, let me explain it another way. If you are a petty officer, it is your job to insure that the men working for you have the knowledge, skills, tools, time, material, and instructions necessary to do their jobs; otherwise, no man can do the job right. You don't tell a man what to do; your job is to show him how to do it. You don't tell a man to go somewhere and do something if you are not sure he knows how. If there is any doubt in your mind, your job is to take him there and make sure he knows how. When a man comes to you and tells you he has a problem, he is really saying that you have a problem. If he had a problem, it would already be solved.

"You men doing the work only have one thing to do: exactly what you are told, the way you were trained, and you do it right now, not later, not tomorrow, but now. If you don't know how to do a job, then say so. I learned long ago that there is no such thing as a dumb question and ignorance is not a crime.

"Everyone in this department will be treated equally; everyone will follow the same rules and be judged by the same standard. Any hint of unequal treatment for any reason will really upset me.

"If anyone in this department gets in trouble and I can determine there is a connection between the problem and lack of leadership, I will personally put his immediate supervisor on report and do everything within my power to bust him down to a job he can handle. If a petty officer gets in trouble and his chief is involved in the same way, I will do the same thing. If anyone gets in trouble and it's their own fault, I promise that I will treat them firmly and fairly.

"I want you to accept your responsibilities, do your job the way you have been trained and make it work the way it is supposed to. I want the problems solved at the lowest possible level. Petty officers are supposed to solve the petty problems and most should be solved at the third-class level; only a few should make it to the first class or chief. The only problems the division officers and I should see are those that require our attention for some legitimate reason.

"I have served in every enlisted rank from seaman recruit to chief petty officer and every officer rank from ensign to lieutenant and I will tell you from personal experience, the lower down the chain of command disciplinary problems are solved, the better the solution, and the farther up they go, the worse the solution. The last thing you want to do is go to captain's mast. No, let me correct that; the last thing you want is to let me fix a problem because you haven't. I guarantee that you will not like my solution.

"Now, let's wipe the slate clean and go to work. You will all be judged by what you do from now on. That's all."

For the first couple of weeks, my officers and petty officers were feeling me out and I was doing the same, but eventually everyone relaxed and things started going along smoothly and I was feeling pretty full of myself. Then I got one of those reminders that I was still in the submarine force.

It happened during a captain's personnel inspection, which was either in preparation for or part of the commissioning ceremony. Everyone was in full dress blues with medals and the officers were wearing their swords.

The captain, who was known as Mad Dog Boyd by his Naval Academy shipmates, was walking along the ranks inspecting one of my divisions, with the division officer and me close behind. He stopped, looked down at a man's shoes and motioned me over. I walked over and looked down. Both shoes were new, but the leather on one was thin and slightly wrinkled while the other was thicker and smoother. The captain asked if I could explain the man's shoes.

He was a second class petty officer wearing an immaculate uniform otherwise and my first thought was that he was too smart to try something stupid. I assumed it was an honest mistake of some sort and searched for a logical explanation. Unfortunately, I found one.

Being a country boy, I told the captain that one shoe was probably made of cowhide from the back of a cow and the other was likely cowhide from the belly of the cow. He pondered my explanation for a moment then asked the man, "Are those shoes a pair?"

"No, Sir."

I could have killed the little bastard and my phrase "belly of the cow" spread far and wide, to the complete delight of my officers and petty officers.

The Wardroom

Before we got underway for San Diego, we had to load our initial issue of five-inch ammunition and it was a navy tradition for ammo loading to be an all-hands evolution. That meant everyone including officers worked. The Dixon's crew numbered almost a thousand men, so I did some mental calculations then headed up to see the executive officer. Rather than call away an all-hands working party, I said, we should call away a working party of all nonrated men not on watch. I explained that there were about three hundred nonrated men onboard, so each man would only have to make two trips and this might be the last time in their naval careers they would get their hands on a live five-inch round. "They can write to their mothers about it," I concluded.

He nodded, "Make it so."

They passed the word, the men assembled and we started. The rounds arrived at the pier on pallets that our traveling cranes lifted up to the boat deck, where the men broke out the rounds and carried them to the magazines fore and aft. I was standing on the boat deck watching everything go smoothly when I noticed something odd. Although we had at least a hundred black nonrated men on board, there wasn't a single one in the working party; they couldn't all be on watch. About that time, the executive officer strolled by and I mentioned it to him. We looked at each other for a long moment without a word, then he walked off. It made me feel sad.

Finally we got underway from Norfolk, made a liberty call in San Juan, Puerto Rico, then headed across the Gulf of Mexico and through the Panama Canal. We tied up in Rodman on the west side for a day's liberty.

When I first reported to the Dixon, I'd gone down and introduced myself to the repair officer, a young commander, and the assistant repair officer, a mustang lieutenant commander, who shall remain nameless. They knew that I would eventually be in the department and the repair officer seemed glad to see me and eager to discuss the details of the planning office, to which no men had yet been assigned. The assistant repair officer's reception, while nice enough, was icy compared to my meeting with Jack Sousa on the Simon Lake, but I dismissed it at the time as a difference in personalities.

I was glad to be back in the West Coast navy, which I'd always considered "my navy" and the real first team, but after a few weeks aboard the Dixon, I began to see that it was a place with a lot of problems. The men suffered from an acute lack of leadership; the officers were consumed with turf battles with zero-sum rules; knowledge was hoarded; people played cards close to the chest; and no one helped anyone else do anything.

I thought back to an occasion on the Simon Lake when a half dozen officers were sitting around the wardroom table after the evening meal. A young ensign from supply came in and slumped in a chair with a sigh. Someone said, "What's wrong, Dave? No pony for Christmas?"

"One of my men has a bad problem," he said.

The command duty officer leaned forward. "Tell us about it."

He told the story and it was a real bear. It had everything: the wife, the kid, the car, the Navy and, best of all, no obvious solutions. The assembled officers, all mustangs representing over a hundred years of navy experience, swung around in their seats like a battery of big sixteen-inch guns and brought some power to bear on the problem.

We started out slowly. Someone asked a question and Dave answered it. We listened, then someone else asked a follow-up question. It was a very precise and effective method. We gradually walked the rounds in to the target. Within a half hour, Dave knew exactly how to solve the problem, what actions to take and a lot more about problem solving than he had when he walked in. That was the kind of thing that was missing on the Dixon.

The executive officer was the president of the wardroom mess and sat at the head of the table. The captain ate in the flag mess. The stewards always arranged the officers' napkin rings from side to side down the table by seniority. By now, I was a fairly senior lieutenant, but there were usually two or three officers sitting between me and the executive officer.

During the meal, the officers typically remained silent unless the executive officer spoke to them. At times you could have measured the tension across the wardroom table with a voltmeter. Well, I wasn't used to that crap and talked whenever I wanted. I was an open, happy person and enjoyed wardroom conversation, which could be about anything except religion, sex or politics and that left a lot of territory. I wasn't afraid of being in trouble with the executive officer; I'd spent half of my navy career in that condition.

Our operations were such that engineering, navigation, operations and deck were the only departments doing anything and deck was the most visible. The zero-sum game, which depended on making someone look bad in order to make yourself look good, was intensified by the fact that in the military the best way to stand out is in combat. At the time, the first lieutenant was, in a non-wartime sense, in combat all the time and looking good, so all they could do was watch and hope that I stumbled. Many of the officers in this watching category were in the repair department, which would eventually be my home, so by doing a good job I was creating enemies among officers whom I would need as friends later. I guess competition among officers doesn't have to make sense.

Meanwhile, the deck department was doing fun and exciting things every day. We got underway, tied up and anchored, held man-overboard drills, went through the Panama Canal, fired the guns and so on. To make matters worse, my division officers and petty officers had used their hammers and it had started to pay off. The deck department began to bloom like a sego lily in the sagebrush. We had zero disciplinary problems, or at least none that made it to the surface. During my time as first lieutenant, I don't remember going to another captain's mast. Men from other departments were putting in request chits for transfer to the deck department (I swear) which was probably the first time in naval history that ever happened. I wish I had saved some of those chits and could have dropped them on Zumwalt's desk.

The executive officer watched me carefully, asked odd questions, but never figured out how I did it, or if he did, he never said anything. The captain spent less time at mast and I was having a ball being just a plain first lieutenant. I helped people whenever I could. If one of my men came up with a good idea, I made sure he got the credit. I refused to play the zero-sum game, which got me some enemies, but also made me some friends.

Shellback

We got underway from Rodman and steamed southwest toward the Galapagos Islands to cross the equator, then turn around and head north for San Diego. We ran the fathometer all the time, to chart the bottom under our track for the record, and the trace showed a lot of sea mounts sticking up from the ocean floor like vicious spikes. It was one of the strangest trips to sea I ever made. We were on the equator, yet the weather was cold and stormy and it felt like I was on a big and lonely ocean. The radar scope was empty and the horizon looked farther away than usual through billowy clouds that appeared to be moving across the water in an odd way. I guess it actually was a strange new ocean for me. The last time I'd sailed on a surface craft in the Pacific was coming back from the Philippines, a long time ago.

I qualified as officer of the deck underway just before we reached the equator, and although I was a mustang lieutenant and had been in the Navy for twenty years, I'd never crossed the equator. That meant I was still a pollywog and so was Mad Dog Boyd. The executive officer was a shellback, signifying that he had crossed the equator, and he now acted like King Neptune, whose part he would play in the upcoming festivities.

The Navy has a tradition of initiating all pollywogs when they cross the equator, which usually involved some creative forms of torture. Since I was a rather visible first lieutenant with a devil-may-care attitude, I was a juicy target. Admiral Zumwalt's new girl scout rules should have precluded any serious forms of hazing, but this was the submarine force. I was going to catch hell and knew it, so I decided to go down fighting.

As we approached the equator, I rattled the executive officer's chain at every opportunity. It was all in jest, so he just smiled and, of course, kept score. One night some masked men, reportedly from the deck force, grabbed him and hauled him back to the fantail, where they put tar and feathers on him. That action would normally be a court-martial offense, but in the Navy, especially the submarine force, it was equivalent to throwing the president in the swimming pool at the company picnic. It took him half the night to clean up. I didn't hear about it until the next day and swear by all that is holy that I had nothing to do with it and never found out who did, but the executive officer will go to his grave believing otherwise.

I had the 0800 to 1200 watch as officer of the deck when we crossed the line, so the assistant repair officer, who was a shellback, relieved me, handed me a diaper and told me to report to the chief petty officers' mess for mess-cooking duties. *. . . they finally got me . . .*

I changed into the diaper and reported to the chief's mess, where I found the senior dental officer, a commander, dressed in similar attire. We hand washed dishes in the scullery for a while then were served breakfast, a big bowl of damp, cold, azure-blue noodles with yellow spots.

After breakfast we were escorted to the forecastle and joined a large group of pollywogs. They hosed us down with cold seawater then forced us to run a gauntlet, modeled after those of the Mohawks, which ran all the way to the fantail. I got hit so many times and so hard that I lost track. When I reached the fantail, the executive officer, who was dressed as King Neptune, personally cut off half my hair. Then I crawled through a trough of garbage while holding a thing in my mouth that looked exactly like a used tampon and tasted like I always imagined they would. Finally, I kissed the greased belly of a big black gunner's mate and was welcomed into the realm of King Neptune. The first lieutenant became a shellback the old-fashioned way.

I staggered up to my stateroom, threw the remnants of my diaper away, took a hot shower, put my uniform on and went up to relieve the officer of the deck.

A short time later, the senior watch officer, a shellback, requested permission to pass some word on the 1MC, which was, in effect, a warning for any men hiding out to give up peacefully and make it easy on themselves. I had the word passed and the sound had barely died down when the captain came running into the pilot house and asked what the hell I was doing. "Don't ever do something like that again!" he barked. I was shocked and didn't know what to make of it until I learned that we had a problem.

About twenty black guys had barricaded themselves in the emergency diesel generator room. They didn't think much of our little initiation ceremony and weren't about to participate. The situation was ugly. I realized the captain had just been venting, so I relaxed. The captain gave the black guys his word that they wouldn't be initiated if they came out, so the problem was resolved peacefully.

The admin officer told me later that the ship hadn't awarded them a certificate for crossing the equator. Of course, in the new navy all they had to do was write to the Bureau of Naval Personnel, prove they were on the ship when it crossed the equator and BuPers would probably have sent them a framed certificate via their congressperson with a cover letter from the Chief of Naval Operations apologizing for the Navy's mistake.

Anchors Aweigh

On our way north, we anchored in the harbor in Acapulco, Mexico, for some liberty. The deck department ran liberty boats back and forth and after all three duty sections had gotten one night of liberty, we started getting underway for our next port, home in San Diego.

Whenever they set the special sea and anchor detail, I was stationed on the forecastle. This time we had dropped the port anchor and when it came time for anchors aweigh, we started raising it. Our anchors, anchor chains, windlasses and the hydraulic motors that operated them had been taken from a battleship and were massive; each link weighed about ninety pounds.

When the port anchor got clear of the water and about halfway up to the hawsepipe[28], the hydraulic system jammed

---

[28] The opening in the bow of a ship where the anchor chain and stock are pulled through.

and wouldn't budge in either direction. The first class boatswain's mate in charge of the forward anchor detail immediately began explaining how we could rig in the anchor. He was still briefing me when the captain sent word down to secure the anchor as best we could. I told him to secure the anchor until I could go talk to them, then stayed on the forecastle until we had stopped off[29] the port anchor chain. We steamed out of the harbor looking like a big bull elephant with an erection.

This situation gave the officers in waiting an opportunity to enter combat and be heros by telling the captain how to rig in the anchor. He obviously didn't know or he would have given me the order in the first place. I stayed on the forecastle until the port anchor chain was secured, then went up to the pilot house. When I arrived, the OD cut me off by announcing that they already had a plan for the anchor; I wasn't needed. I left without saying anything and headed down to the executive officer's stateroom. When I went in, he looked up, obviously anticipating a pitch from me, and said, "Don't worry, we already have a plan to bring in the anchor."

"Mind telling me what it is?" I said. "I have to do it."

In the heat of battle, everyone had forgotten that little detail. The executive officer's face got red and he quickly outlined the very plan my first class had suggested.

"Sounds good to me," I said and walked out.

We used the starboard anchor windlass to haul in the port anchor one bite at a time, which required disassembling and reassembling links in both chains and stopping them off several times. Finally, we reconnected everything and stopped off both anchors for sea in the normal way, so we could still use the starboard anchor. It took almost all day, in the hot tropical sun, and I was on the forecastle for all of it.

---

[29] A large clamp is connected to the anchor chain to secure the anchor to the ship.

The next night I had the duty as officer of the deck on the 2000 to 2400 watch. We were still in warm tropical waters and I was standing out on the port wing of the bridge gazing down at the bioluminescence sparkling in the bow wave. The junior officer of the deck had the conn[30] and things were quiet. I heard some loud voices, so I walked to the aft end of the port wing and looked down to see what the commotion was. The port motor whaleboat was stowed on davits located on the deck below and the duty lifeboat crew was sitting around under it. They had a lot of company. Many members of the crew had little to do while the ship was operating like this and were tired of sleeping, so a classic all-navy bullshit session was going on.

There were about sixty men, with all ranks from seaman to master chief petty officer well represented. The debate was going hot and heavy and the subject was also classic: Who is the best officer onboard? I could not resist the temptation to eavesdrop.

After a while only two candidates remained: the weapons repair officer and the first lieutenant. The weapons repair officer was a mustang lieutenant commander and the senior watch officer. He was a good officer and would probably have gotten my vote. The debate raged on with many points made and considered until a first class petty officer made the final, decisive argument that ended the debate with general agreement. He got up and said, "I vote for Mr. Hansen. If we had to go into a combat situation, he would get us through, one way or the other."

That was the greatest compliment I have ever received.

---

[30] The officer with the "conn" gives all orders to the engine and rudder. The OD still has the "deck" and is in charge overall.

Condition Yoke

As we came alongside the navy Pier in San Diego, I was standing on the forecastle. Bands were playing, flags were flying and my family was waving from the pier. We got a few days' liberty, then had to go through underway training, which is another way of saying hell month.

All new ships had to go through it. The ship reported to an underway training command that may even have given the captain a fitness report for the training period. A team of several officers and senior petty officers from this group came aboard to conduct and grade the exercises. They were an experienced and sadistic lot with no discernible sense of humor. They did tell the officers assembled in the wardroom that we could have our pick of their wives and first-born daughters if we could set condition yoke the first time, but that wasn't funny. It took us over a week to get it right.

All navy ships, except submarines, have three damage control conditions, one of which is set at all times. (Submarines have only two, rigged for surface or rigged for dive.) To prevent fires from spreading and to maintain watertight integrity, which means to keep any flooding from reaching adjacent compartments or decks, all openings between decks (hatches), between compartments (doors) and all fittings (ventilation flapper valves, etc.) bear a small plaque with one of three letters inscribed on it: X (x-ray), Y (yoke) or Z (zebra). Each of the three damage control conditions is named after the letters on all hatches, doors and fittings that must be shut to "set" that condition. Condition x-ray is set during normal working hours and shuts the fewest number of openings; condition yoke is set at night and on holidays; and condition zebra, which requires that almost everything be shut, is set during general quarters.

Underway training was designed to train all men on the ship to act as a qualified crew and is similar to army and marine war games that are conducted prior to sending units into combat. The training consisted of exercises (drills) during which we practiced every activity that a ship must be prepared in: firefighting, gunnery, anchoring, man overboard, navigation, communications, radiological control, damage control, engineering casualties, medical emergencies, atomic, biological and chemical warfare and so on.

It was a rough period, but in some ways a lot of fun. The training team told me that my gun crews were better than some destroyer crews. They didn't just hit the target; they cut the tow cable and knocked it down. On one firing exercise, the forward gun wasn't doing well, so the mount captain in the after mount requested a cease fire. The executive officer and I were standing on the open bridge and pretty soon here came the after mount captain, who was a black first class gunner's mate, on his way to the forward gun. As he passed, I asked him what was happening and he said, "I'm gonna 'splain somethin'," and walked on. The executive officer asked me what he meant and I said, "Don't ask."

He strode up to the forward mount and climbed inside. A lot of yelling and loud noises followed, then he came out and silently walked aft. We started shooting again and the forward mount started hitting the target. That was the closest the executive officer ever came to figuring out my methods and I started using the term, 'splain, which seemed so much more appropriate in some situations.

The top scores were: navigation, outstanding; deck, excellent. The deck department might have gotten an outstanding also had it not been for one incident.

One of my seaman apprentices in the first division was the classic fuck up. He wasn't a troublemaker, just a redneck from the deep south whom trouble followed like a black cloud. I wish I could remember his name because it fit him so well and gave the story real flavor.

Since the training team had set ideas about every member of the crew being proficient to a certain level, it was obvious to the deck force chain of command that special precautions would be needed to keep our man out of the spotlight. My ingenious and resourceful petty officers managed to do that for the entire training period, almost. Unfortunately, the training team was also composed of experienced and resourceful petty officers who had seen it all before.

The box lunch, which was the last graded exercise, was designed to test the ship's ability to feed the crew while at battle stations with condition zebra set. It involved every department and had several elements. The cooks and mess cooks had to make up the box lunches, which were graded for adequacy and flavor. The sailing list was used to determine how many men were on board, and the battle bills were used to tell where the battle stations were located and how many men were assigned to each. And there were rules. We had to break condition zebra in an efficient and organized way to deliver one box lunch to every man onboard, no more, no less.

Near the end of the exercise, two things happened. They found one box lunch left over, and the training team discovered a man down in the bowels of the ship who was hungry and wanted to know when he could have lunch. He told them that he was in the deck force, so they escorted him up to the open bridge and delivered him to me. Deck didn't get an outstanding because we were, after all, cheating. There is a lesson in there somewhere, too.

The deck department yeoman was a seaman named Payton, who worked directly for me in the office answering phones, making up watch bills and so on. He was an excellent worker of the self-starting type. He wore an immaculate uniform and was a good-looking young man with a bright, cheery smile, but he had one problem—the biggest and best Afro I've ever seen— and it drove the executive officer crazy. On several occasions he said, "Do something about Payton's hair." I looked over the situation and realized I was treading on dangerous ground. The Navy had its rules, which I revered, but the blacks had their pride and were going through a rough time right then, so I could see a no-win situation. Payton never wore his white hat anyway and I had more important things to do, so I procrastinated.

One day the executive officer came into my office with a foolproof, two-step plan to get Payton. My part was to give Payton a formal, direct order to get a haircut, in front of witnesses.

"XO,[31] I won't play that game," I said. "Do whatever you want, but I won't be part of it." He glared for a moment then turned and walked out. As far as I know, Payton never got a regulation haircut and I was probably not the first officer to refuse such an order. I found out a few years later, in a very personal way, that I was not the last.

Skunks

When my duties as first lieutenant were over, a chief warrant officer relieved me and I reported to the repair department. It was about three weeks before the Dixon was scheduled to hold its first submarine refit. By now I believed that I could work with the repair officer, if I could just get past the assistant repair officer, who was from the old school, didn't like the new management systems and wasn't nuclear trained. He'd already cherry picked the parts of my system he liked and would probably sabotage anything that didn't make life easy for him, so I decided to play it cool and ask how they wanted me to proceed.

On the first morning, the assistant repair officer and I sat down to discuss the planning office. He thought I could easily get things ready in time to support the first refit; we still had a couple of weeks before it started. His interest was in getting the major repair jobs planned so that day he'd assigned two petty officers to the planning office for that purpose and wanted

---

[31] Respectful and abbreviated way to address the executive officer.

me to get that area up and running right away. Nothing had been done yet about organizing nuclear systems work as there were no jobs pending, but that was an area where he had some ideas. He also had ideas on the submarine shipalt program, which was handled differently here. The system here was like the old system in Holy Loch, but without all the problems. . . . *I have got to see this . . .*

During our meeting, virtually everything he said revealed how little he knew about running a planning office, doing nuclear repair work or working with the new quality-control rules. To me, he was not qualified for his job and probably spent a lot of time and effort hiding that fact. This insight made his attitude toward me more understandable: the last thing you want when you're in over your head is an underling who knows more than you do. The repair officer was pretty squared away, but generally deferred to the assistant, something I never understood.

I told him that I should start by setting up the administration of the planning office. I'd need to integrate it with his office, quality control, non-destructive testing, the division officers and shops. I also said it would take some time to train my petty officers in the various planning tasks. He realized, of course, that we couldn't just start doing it. Finally, I told him that what I needed most was at least one good petty officer, preferably one that was nuclear trained. Pleased to have anticipated something, he smiled and said, "I'm going to give you Russ."

I was hoping for a good first class petty officer and he gave me Chief Warrant Officer Russell, my old neighbor from New London. I believe he thought he was giving me a loser, but I had trouble containing my joy. After the meeting, I tracked Russ down and told him that he would be working for me as the nuclear systems repair officer. After a lot of grins and backslapping we headed for our new office.

By the time our first submarine refit started, we had a skeleton planning operation up and running, but actual organization of the systems was barely started when we temporarily stopped refitting submarines and the Dixon got underway for the Naval Shipyard in Bremerton, Washington, for her post shakedown availability.

Whenever the Dixon got underway, I again became the first lieutenant. I didn't relieve the chief warrant officer who had relieved me; I just did the job. I think the captain liked having me around because I wasn't afraid of battleship anchors or five-inch guns. While marking time in Bremerton, we got the planning office ready to rock and roll as soon as we got back to San Diego. The thing I remember most about our stay in Bremerton, though, was a camping trip.

One weekend, two chief warrant officers and I checked out some camping gear from special services and went up on Mount Rainier. We camped a couple of nights, caught some trout, sat around the campfire and had a nice, relaxing time. We were driving back along a mountainous forest service road when a black bear with two cubs crossed the road in front of us. They stopped in the brush about fifty yards off the left side of the road and we stopped to watch. We were in a small pickup and I was in the outside passenger seat. I opened the door to get out and both guys grabbed my arm and said, "Stay here; that's a female with cubs; she'll attack." I looked over at them and said calmly, "I'm not afraid of bears."

I got out, walked to the back of the pickup and stood quietly. The bears were looking at us, we were looking at the bears, and nobody moved. Reminiscent of my classroom yelp in the fourth grade, I let out a blood-curdling rebel yell and rushed over the shoulder of the road straight toward the bears. The momma huffed and ran off about thirty yards. The cubs headed for the tops of two nearby trees which, as a student of nature, I had expected. When the action stopped, though, I did a rapid triangulation and realized that I was now between a momma bear and her cubs, so I slowly, but deliberately, worked my way back to the pickup and got in, calculating all the way whether I could make it if she decided to charge. Back on the ship, the guys told that story over and over and it got better with each telling. It ended up putting a new wrinkle in my reputation: "Even bears are afraid of him."

When we got back to San Diego and put my planning organization in operation, it got mixed reviews. The shops liked the major job-planning packages, but didn't like supplying first class petty officers to act as nuclear work coordinators, doing freeze seals or working around radiation. Some men even had the attitude that the Navy couldn't make them work around radiation if they didn't want to, so there was quite a collision of cultures.

They especially disliked the new quality-control and work-order management rules and wanted to get the work requests as soon as possible. Under the old system, when a submarine came in for refit, the leading petty officers in the shops had gone down to the ship and found out which jobs were going to be requested, then ordered the material. That way, they had the job half-done by the time they got the work request through channels and totally done midway through the refit, which left lots of time for the golf course. The new rules prevented them from doing anything until they actually received the work request through channels and the "side trip" to the planning office on all controlled jobs was extending the waiting time. Tee times were missed and morale plummeted.

The new system was designed to prevent the kind of problems that abounded under the old system, where Murphy ran free and everything that could go wrong did. We were now operating under the new official intermediate maintenance management system, which was the law and supported by the repair officer and squadron engineer, so they had to accept it, but they didn't have to like it.

One day "they" became a skunk that sprayed all over my planning office. I never actually learned all the details, and can't remember now all that I knew then, but I do recall that the situation had three elements.

Element one involved several chief petty officers who had served with the assistant repair officer for years in the San Diego area and were all good friends. This group was especially unhappy with my new planning organization, but didn't let on publicly, so I wasn't aware of that fact or their relationship until later.

The second element involved an ongoing battle between the welding and radcon shops over glove boxes, a classic problem area and one I'd dealt with so many times that I had my own pet name for a glove box: magpie nest. The nest of the black-billed magpie is usually located about thirty feet up in a deciduous tree. It is made from a bunch of jumbled sticks about three feet in diameter and can be seen from a mile away. The opening is always camouflaged and even if you manage to find it, you can't get your hand in or see the egg chamber.

On a typical nuclear valve replacement job, the radcon shop installed a glove box around the work area to contain any radioactive material generated. At the same time, the weld shop established an inert gas purge through the line and terminated the purge inside the glove box through a series of filters. The purge gas pressure was very low and any back pressure could cause the molten weld metal to blow out like a miniature volcano, in which case the welders had to grind out the joint and start over. The glove boxes could be installed perfectly from a radcon standpoint but be unsuitable for terminating the purge and vice-versa. The two shops had to work together to satisfy both criteria and they were not sharing well.

I was on the side of the welders, which should have put me on the side of the assistant repair officer's men in the welding shop. The radcon officer was only concerned about doing his job perfectly and didn't give a damn if we did nuclear welding or not. The repair officer was not nuclear trained and was afraid of radioactive contamination, so he didn't know who to believe, the radcon officer or me.

The third element was our new system for routing work requests. One day a work request for a major repair job that was also a controlled job got back to the shop, apparently without having been planned. The shop had started doing it improperly, screwed up and all hell broke loose.

The assistant repair officer called me in, showed me the original copy of the work request he'd obtained from the shop and asked me to explain it. I recognized the job; it had clearly been routed to the planning office, but there was no planning information on it. It didn't make any sense, so I couldn't explain it. Our records showed that it had been logged in and out, but that's all we could tell. My men swore they had planned the job, but we couldn't prove it.

The assistant repair officer milked it for all it was worth. My fancy system wasn't working; my men were lazy and incompetent; I was not doing my job. I got a bad fitness report, which Captain Boyd let me read. I handed it back without a word.

A few weeks later, one of my men found a copy of the problem work request. It had represented a new kind of job, so he'd made a photostatic copy and put it in a file with some other sample jobs, then forgotten about it. I'd thrown the copy given to me in my desk drawer, so I dug it out and we compared the two. Both were written by the same person and were identical in every way, except two. The original copy the assistant repair officer had given me had no planning marks on it, but the photostatic copy had a full planning markup and a different date.

I called Russ and my men together, showed them what we had and told them to keep their eyes open, but not to say anything to anybody. Then we went on full alert and waited. Sooner or later the culprits would rush into Murphy's waiting arms.

A short time later, some of the assistant's buddies were busted for some kind of corruption by the criminal investigative division (CID) and some of his chief petty officer friends suddenly left the ship, permanently. On the same weekend, a nuclear weld job went sour and the argument with the radcon officer was settled in my favor, plus another duplicate work request was discovered. The whole mess reminded everyone of the first "unplanned" work request problem, and the captain ordered an investigation.

The investigation results were kept secret, but according to the grapevine, the original duplicate work request had exposed the corruption in some way and the culprits had diverted attention to the planning office to cover up their operation. I never found out what the corruption involved or how it worked, but I could understand their desire to kill two birds with one stone. A work request was similar to a purchase order and things could be charged against it, so it's not hard to imagine several ways to game the system, but apparently the checks and balances got them.

After the dust settled, the captain called me into his office and talked to me for quite a while about several areas in the repair department and finally asked, "Why didn't you say something when you saw your fitness report?"

"Captain, I couldn't prove anything then," I said.

The admin officer told me later that the captain had submitted a revised fitness report on me, which is a rare event in the Navy.

The admin officer was a junior mustang lieutenant and a good friend, who followed my escapades with glee. He relished my country sayings, but had a particular favorite. Whenever someone proposed an idea that I knew wouldn't work, I'd say, "It won't work."

"Why not?"

"You can't get there from here."

"Why not?"

"They haven't built the fucking road yet."

One day he walked into my office with his arms hanging down at his sides and a piece of paper in his right hand. "Well, they built the road."

"What road?"

"You made lieutenant commander and you're the only mustang in San Diego who did."

CHAPTER TWELVE
Portland

River City

When an officer is promoted to lieutenant commander, the Navy transfers him to a new duty station. I was aware of that, but had not called the detailer to request duty preferences. My family was settled and there was no way I could move them. Anna was on the dean's list at San Diego State; Teresa and Susan were in high school; and Brian and Gary were in junior high. My standing request was West Coast duty, so I took no action.

One day the repair officer told me that the repair officer on the USS Sperry AS-12, which was tied up at the next pier over, wanted to see me. She was the tender for Submarine Squadron Three, the squadron I'd been in when I was stationed on the Ronquil, so it was an old home.

I went over for a visit with the Sperry's repair officer, a lieutenant commander who, according to the grapevine, had been passed over once for commander, but still had one more chance to make it. He said the Sperry was going into the shipyard shortly for a major overhaul and would then start repairing nuclear submarines. He needed help setting up the repair department with the new management systems, and because of my experience in that area, he wanted me to relieve his assistant repair officer, who was being retired when they reached the yard. By the time the ship returned to San Diego, he wanted me to have in place the same kind of management system the Dixon had. It sounded like a good deal to me, so I told him to tell the detailer.

The Sperry was an old ship. She had been anchored off the coast guard station in San Diego harbor when I joined the Navy. I could remember looking longingly across the bay at her and the submarines alongside when I was in boot camp. Her keel had been laid three days after they bombed Pearl Harbor and on the same day they had bombed Sangley Point. Her main deck was covered with teak planking, like a battleship's, and the pilot house bulkheads were armor plated. During World War II, while stationed in the South Pacific, she had set a submarine refit record that will stand for all time. She was a proud old lady.

During the upcoming overhaul, they were going to remove the teak planking, install sanitary holding tanks and strip the wardroom and crew's mess down to bare metal and start over. The five-inch guns had already been removed and a nice big conference room would replace the forward mount. They were going to leave the propulsion system as it was.

The Sperry was propelled by a diesel-electric plant similar to the World War II type submarines she tended. She had two shafts connected to DC electric motors and a total of eight diesel engines that ran DC generators arranged in two engine rooms. She was given that type of propulsion system, instead of the normal steam plant, to insure that there would always be spare parts for the submarines she tended. Each shaft on the Sperry was propelled by exactly the same system found on one World War II fleet boat submarine.

The Sperry would be going into the naval shipyard at Bremerton, Washington, about the first of July, the same date I was to be promoted to lieutenant commander. I decided to take leave and report back to the Dixon in time to be promoted. By then I would have orders and would meet the Sperry in Bremerton. When I reported back to the Dixon, I learned that the Sperry was now going to be overhauled by Northwest Marine Iron Works at Swan Island in Portland, Oregon.

I drove my new Datsun pickup up Interstate-5 from San Diego to Portland. The ship had arrived a couple of days earlier and everything was still in a state of chaos. I met the executive officer and liked him instantly. He was a commander and an intelligence-type, who was chomping at the bit to get back to Washington and into the spook business again. I had already met the repair officer, but the captain was a four striper I had never heard of.

The executive officer told me that I would also take over the duties of senior watch officer and that he was going to dispense with the requirement for me to qualify as officer of the deck underway, because he felt I could handle it, and I would start standing duties as command duty officer right away. The captain gave me no greeting of any kind and I don't remember the first time I spoke to him.

When I met the men in the repair department, I got several first impressions. The repair officer was desperate, as I had anticipated, and afraid of the captain, who would be writing his fitness reports. The repair officers, petty officers and men were the greatest group of people I have ever known. I had finally found them, the West Coast sailors that I knew were there, somewhere; they simply had to be.

After relieving the outgoing assistant repair officer, I told the division officers to use their own judgment, to keep me informed and to get their yard work done as soon as possible. It was mandatory that we set aside about six weeks during the last part of the overhaul to train everyone on the new management system. I explained that fixing nuclear submarines under the new rules was a completely different world from fixing diesel-electric submarines under the old rules and that they had a lot to learn. I told them to send their men on leave now and get their work done because nothing was going to interfere with the training later. They headed out and accomplished everything I told them to do.

In addition to my other duties, the repair officer and I were to act as liaison between the ship and the shipyard for all the overhaul work, so I was going to be a ship super again. The Supervisor of Shipbuilding responsible for the work was in Seattle, at the headquarters of the Thirteenth Naval District, but since we had a lot of trained repair officers onboard, they decided we could do the job for them, which made sense to me. The ship super job only required one person, so after a few meetings with the shipyard, the repair officer took over the job by himself, which was fine with me. He needed to make points with the captain to make commander.

Almost immediately the River City Games began. The second day I was onboard, the Red Cross called and wanted blood. We wanted to make a good first impression on Portland, so a whole contingent of us volunteered. While I was lying on the couch with the needle inserted and doing my best to fill the container, a good-looking nurse came by and I don't know if it was my uniform, my dolphins or my good looks, but while professing never to have done this kind of thing before, she gave me her telephone number and asked me to call. My wedding ring didn't seem to phase her.

By contrast, one day I went into a local bank to cash a check. The female teller wanted to see a photo ID, so I put my navy ID card on the counter. She picked it up, threw it back at me and said, "We don't recognize those here." It had my photograph on it, was issued by the federal government and could be used in lieu of a passport, but it wasn't good enough for her. I asked to see the manager. By then, I knew that Oregonians hate California, so when the manager came over I explained the situation and said, "It's this or a California driver's license; which do you prefer?"

The manager was more sophisticated and knew the teller had made a mistake, so he apologized and cashed my check, which probably ruined her whole day. She was the exception, though. Most young things in Portland regarded sailors as exciting opportunities. Their mothers, on the other hand, likened them to "salmon, up the river to spawn."

About the third day, an official from the Oregon Department of Environmental Quality came onboard and wanted to give the captain a ticket and fine the ship for dumping raw sewage into the Willamette River and screwing up the salmon habitat. The captain politely told the official to give the ticket to the Commander of the Thirteenth Naval District in Seattle because the Sperry had no control over the matter.

Most people living in Portland were socialistic, anti-everything Democrats, with a lot of contempt for the U.S. armed forces so we were, first and foremost, something to protest against. We got roughly three bomb threats a week and it was soon obvious to everyone, except the captain, that the threats were phony and just a way to jerk the Navy around, stop the work, drag the job out, cost the taxpayers more money and make the overhaul last all winter.

There were some good things about duty in Portland. On North Interstate Avenue not far from Swan Island was a nice cocktail lounge and restaurant called the Alibi, which soon became the unofficial officers' club, although a few senior chiefs came in as well. The Alibi had some big, old-fashioned pool tables, good food, a cocktail waitress named Bonnie and a bartender named Walt, who was an ex-navy chief radioman.

I took my pickup to the Oregon coast and around the area on weekends, but during the week, I typically went up to the Alibi, had a few drinks, played pool and relaxed. I was never much of a drinker and had long since quit smoking which led to the discovery that scotch doesn't taste like swamp water. I had it on the rocks when I drank the hard stuff, but usually stuck to draft beer or a rum and coke.

One Friday I took off early and was sitting at the bar in the Alibi drinking a beer when a small pizza was delivered to the bartender and he gave me a piece. It was good, so I asked him where it came from and he said, "Luigi's, straight up Interstate, on the right."

It was early, so I decided to check it out; one small piece of pizza was never enough for me. I drove up interstate and found Luigi's, walked in and became a member of the third family I'd belonged to thus far in my life.

The bartender was an attractive dishwater blonde with nice legs named Velda. I strolled into the bar, gave her a bad time and she came right back so we became instant friends. She had a bossy demeanor, didn't drink liquor, used fuck in casual conversation and had a great laugh.

Luigi's was owned and operated by a consortium that consisted of Perry, Vivian and Sharon. Perry was also part owner of a business that made sawmill equipment in Salem and he was a long-haul truck driver transporting sawmill equipment all over the country. He was short, heavyset and sang Irish songs like a bird. He was one of the best men I've ever met.

Perry and Vivian were lovers. Vivian was a buxom redhead with a heart of gold and a tough disposition to compensate. She was the best bartender and waitress in Oregon, which had to make her the best there is. She ran the bar and restaurant and had a Rottweiler's attitude toward her three female bartenders, Peggy, Sally and Velda. Peggy was a tall blonde who looked and sounded like May West. Sally was another pretty blonde and a sweet lady. Finally, there was Velda, whom you have already met.

Sharon, who was the chef and ran the kitchen, was part of a two-sister act. Her sister was a special-education teacher with an American Indian boyfriend, whom Sharon referred to as the white girl and the Indian. Their mother was a good Irish Catholic and a sweet little old lady. She was the housekeeper for a Catholic priest and loved a drink of good whiskey, so everyone called her Whiskey Mary. One time her priest either died or got transferred, so I volunteered to move Whiskey Mary across town in my pickup. When I moved her, she wouldn't let me take the freeway. We had to take Burnside Street because that was the route she knew to get there.

One of the waiters was gay and a world-class actor who had the part of The Manager down cold. One time a young lumberjack trying to impress his date complained that there wasn't enough garlic on the garlic bread. This was no problem for The Manager who promptly ordered more garlic bread, but that didn't have enough garlic either. Eagle-eyed Vivian got the garlic shaker, went to the table, poured a pile on the bread, put her hands on her hips and growled, "Eat it or leave."

Luigi's was in a tough neighborhood and was a popular hangout for longshoremen, but I never saw a fight there. One night someone asked about it and Sally explained that whenever two guys started a fight, Vivian got between them, which meant they could no longer see each other, and nobody was dumb enough to hit Vivian.

The overhaul soon settled into a routine. A new lieutenant commander senior to me came aboard and relieved me as senior watch officer. By now, the repair officer was handling all the ship super duties, so I had a relatively light workload. The repair department was a delight, but we were surrounded by bad apples and the problems that did come up usually had no connection to us. The engineer officer, a mustang lieutenant, and his leading petty officers spent all their time chasing women, so nobody was watching that store. The first lieutenant was an arrogant chief warrant officer who desperately needed to have his ass kicked. Most of the supply, weapons repair, medical and dental departments had stayed behind in San Diego. The captain was religious, stayed in his stateroom most of the time, never got his hands dirty and I had the impression he'd rather be anywhere else. The executive officer came close to being my drinking buddy, but always maintained proper distance.

When I was the command duty officer, I toured the ship and noted that work progress in the engineering and deck areas was essentially a flat line. Other departments were obviously not going to get their work done in time, either, which meant that repair would probably have to do it and use up my training time in the process. I complained to the executive officer a few times, but it put a strain on our relationship, and, in any case, no action was taken, so I gave it up.

JAG Investigation

I returned from liberty one evening about 2230 and went to my stateroom on the living barge. My head had barely hit the pillow when the word was passed of a fire onboard the ship. I got up, ran over to the ship and found the command duty officer, who was the engineer officer. He said the situation was under control as far as the fire was concerned, but that a civilian yard worker might be missing.

The fire had been amidship on the starboard side, below a storeroom off the crew's mess. A welder had been cutting a hole in the deck for access into a void when the heavy paint lining in the void caught fire and produced a lot of dense, black smoke. When I arrived, everyone was looking for a missing yard worker and trying to determine for sure if he was gone.

Sometime later the Portland fire department arrived and a fireman equipped with a small breathing apparatus crawled down into the void through a manway located in the forward starboard corner of the storeroom. He found the man, dead, in the bilges straight down below the manway. He was the welder's fire watch, who had apparently gone down into the void in an attempt to extinguish the fire. They hauled his body out and the situation got very grim. He was a young married man and a daddy.

One of my men had been electrocuted accidently when I was on the Simon Lake, so I had been down this road before. I knew two things: there would be a JAG investigation and the accident scene should be preserved like a crime scene. I also assumed that with a ship full of officers on the scene, one of us would be assigned to do the investigation and that I was a likely candidate. I crossed my fingers; it was a job no one wants.

Early the next morning, people came down from the Thirteenth Naval District and a lot of high-level decision making went on. Everyone took a look-see in the void and the fire scene was hopelessly polluted. Finally, the captain had a meeting of all officers in the wardroom. He told us not to get involved in any way. The Portland fire department was responsible for fighting the fire and Commander, Thirteenth Naval District, was the responsible naval authority. We worked for Commander, Submarine Flotilla One in San Diego, and were out of it, so don't worry, he said; just go back to work and tell your men to stay clear of the area.

Well, Commander, Thirteenth Naval District, was a rear admiral, whereas Commander, Submarine Flotilla One, was a navy captain, who was called commodore. Stuff rolls downhill, so after the accident scene was thoroughly fouled and everyone involved had talked to everyone involved, the ship got the word: The Sperry would do the JAG investigation and Lieutenant Commander Hansen had been assigned the task.

My investigation was based on instructions from the Manual of the Judge Advocate General, but was basically an investigation by a single officer looking into the matter and gathering the facts. There were rules to follow and the end product was a report that usually contained three sections: Findings of Fact, Opinions and Recommendations. My specific marching orders asked for findings of fact only.

I donned my coveralls, got a flashlight and took a long, hard look at the scene. It was a typical void about twenty feet long, ten feet deep and six feet wide. It had a series of stiffeners running athwartship with limber holes in them, which means it was an enclosed rectangular space with bulkheads running across the short dimension that had a series of holes cut in them for access between bays. The void was preserved with a heavy coating of plastic paint that obviously burned easily. Vertical ladder rungs leading down to the bilge in the first bay were welded to the forward bulkhead under a manway in the deck above. The manway had a bolted flange cover and was located in the forward starboard corner of the storeroom. Using a cutting torch, the welder had cut about one hundred and fifty degrees of an eighteen-inch-diameter circle in the deck in the after starboard corner of the storeroom.

I contacted each of the navy witnesses and told them to write down in their own words what had happened and give me it to me. I told them not to talk to the other witnesses, exchange stories or try to correct anything, just to put down what they thought they saw and let me sort it out.

Since the navy crewmen were not yet ready to be interviewed and the civilian welder was, I started with him. He was the only witness from the shipyard and when I questioned him, he had his attorney present.

The welder told me . . . while he was cutting the access hole, he started getting smoke in his eyes and couldn't see, so he took off his welder's helmet and looked around. He didn't see anyone; the room was filling with smoke, so he ran out and yelled, "Fire!" He didn't realize until later that the fire watch, who happened to be one of his best friends, was still somewhere in the area.

Next I interviewed the navy witnesses, about six men in the duty damage control party who had been the first men on the scene. I read their stories, made some notes and called them in one at a time for questioning. On my second or third interview, I questioned a man who had been wearing an OBA[32] when he arrived at the scene. His story was very brief, not well written and gave almost no details, so I started walking him through it. I told him to relax, take his time and just tell me

---

[32] Oxygen breathing apparatus.

everything that happened, no matter how insignificant he thought it might be. He got with the program and we started going through it.

He told me . . . when they arrived, the storeroom was full of dense, black smoke that was also billowing out into the mess hall. Somebody said there might be a man trapped inside, so he got down on his hands and knees and started crawling into the storeroom. He crawled through the door and then to the starboard side, then forward along the starboard side. When he got to the forward bulkhead, he turned left . . .

I stopped him. "Was there anything on the deck?"
"Nothing but a manway"
"What did you do when you got to the manway"
"It was shut, so I moved on."
"How do you know it was shut?"
"I ran my hands around it and the cover was on."
. . . *oh oh* . . .

I now envisioned a slightly different scenario . . . the welder started getting smoke in his eyes, lifted his helmet, saw smoke billowing up from his cut and the manway and seeing no one around, he ran over and replaced the manway cover to stop the smoke and smother the fire, which would have been the commonsense thing to do.

I asked for another interview with the welder. I got it and he again had his attorney present. When I asked the question, "When you saw smoke coming into the storeroom, did you replace the manway cover?" he leapt from his seat and halfway across the room toward me in an apparent rage.

Now I had a problem. The welder's response to my question about the manway cover had been odd and excessive. By any scenario, his conscience was probably bothering him, but I couldn't see where he'd done anything wrong and thought it might help him personally if the truth came out and he realized that he'd done the logical thing. But then, why was he being advised by an attorney? Was I missing something?

I began reviewing the logic of the information. The first indication of a fire must have been an abnormal amount of smoke around the cut and possibly smoke coming out of the manway. If I assumed that the fire watch was standing in the storeroom behind the welder, then I also had to assume that he purposely went into the void after he knew there was a fire in it. I have yet to meet a man dumb enough to do that. The only other possibility was that the fire watch was already in the void when the fire started.

Then I began reviewing my shipyard experience. Since a welder's vision was limited by his helmet, he needed another set of eyes during cutting operations. For that reason, it was common practice to station a fire watch on the other side of the bulkhead being cut into. The sparks from the cutting torch always flew out the other side. If a welder was cutting into the deck, the "other side" would be the deck below or, in this case, inside the void. If they had followed standard practice, the fire watch would have been stationed inside the void before the cutting started. An argument can be made that most men would not go into a void and crawl through limber holes then trap themselves in a place where a fire might start, but I have seen untrained men do some strange things.

The body of the fire watch was found in the bilge at the bottom of the first bay under the manway. The autopsy report showed that he died of smoke inhalation and gave no evidence that he had fallen, which indicated that he had crawled down on purpose, probably to escape the smoke. If he was inside the void when the fire started, then he was almost out and still functioning when he got to the first bay. He hadn't come out of the manway and had crawled down instead, which indicates the manway cover had already been replaced by then.

The manway cover was now a bigger question. It must have been replaced between the time the fire watch went into the void and before the navy OBA man found it shut, which left limited opportunities. Either someone else was in the area and replaced it, or the welder replaced it before he ran out. Common sense says the welder would not have replaced the cover knowing the fire watch was in the void and he did testify that he last saw the fire watch standing in the storeroom behind him. He also testified that there was no one else around.

I didn't know how to deal with the implications of the welder's action, which might have trapped the fire watch, when he "should have known" that his fire watch was in the void, so I went to the executive officer for advice. He told me to read my orders. The captain wanted a report that contained just the facts that I could establish.

Although I couldn't include it in my report because it amounted to my opinion, I was personally more interested in the role of the various institutions involved. Once I had my crosshairs on that bunch, I ran into political obstructions of all kinds. The main problem area was an almost total lack of any regulated system for repairing ships at the Port of Portland shipyard at Swan Island, which may explain why it took political pressure to get the Navy to send the Sperry there in the first place. The Supervisor of Shipbuilding sat up in Seattle and essentially washed his hands of the whole deal. Northwest Marine Iron Works, the private contractor, usually worked on civilian ships and routinely enforced only union rules, whereas most occupational, safety and health (OSHA) rules were ignored, especially by the union workers. The commanding officer of the Sperry was caught between a rock and a hard place, but even then he didn't exercise what little authority he did have. There was plenty of unmet responsibility to go around.

Northwest Marine probably had the most failings and should have had the greatest exposure, but as I understood it, they were protected by the workers' compensation system in Oregon. They were required to pay into the compensation system, but after the deceased man's family got a flat ten thousand dollars, Northwest Marine was protected from further liability, no matter what.

Northwest Marine, however, had not exercised proper control over the welder, who should not have been cutting into that void in the first place. Nor had they properly trained the fire watch not to enter a void or tank unless it had been checked. Entering a void or tank was a big deal in the ship repair business and could only be done under strict rules and after the void's atmosphere had been checked and certified to be capable of sustaining life and not dangerous. The void might have contained explosive gases that the cutting torch could ignite, causing an explosion and potentially killing a lot of people. Any void with a heavy plastic paint lining would never have been certified for cutting due to the obvious fire hazard. The welder did not have a burning permit which was designed to prevent this kind of problem in the first place. These cardinal rules were known well by all shipyards, military and civilian.

The Port of Portland shipyard didn't have an effective burning permit system. The captain had the authority and should have insisted that someone set one up, but didn't. As I remember, Northwest Marine did start getting burning permits after the fire watch was killed, but I don't know how the system worked or who ran it.

Rules designed to protect the firefighters union allowed only the Portland fire department to fight fires within the city limits. The Sperry crew, which included men highly trained in fighting shipboard fires, was only allowed to fight fires on the ship under limited circumstances, which was a deal I never understood or agreed with. In any case, the Portland fire department's ability to fight shipboard fires was not tested in this case because the fire was out before they were even called.

The fire alarm system, which had been approved by the repair officer in his role as ship super, was a joke. The shipyard had rigged a telephone line from the Sperry quarterdeck to the guard shack at the main gate, which, as I understood it, included two circuits: one circuit sounded a buzzer in the guard shack and the second was a phone line for talking to the guard. When a fire occurred, the officer of the deck was supposed to ring the buzzer then tell the guard where the fire was. The guard would then call the fire department. Unfortunately, when our fire occurred, the line had been disconnected, so the fire department wasn't called until the guard learned of the fire through the grapevine. The officer of the deck had not been briefed properly and thought all he had to do was sound the buzzer, which he'd done.

Why it had taken so long to find the fire watch was an easy question to answer. The navy damage control party didn't look in the void because it was full of dense, black smoke and no one could survive in it without a breathing apparatus. The standard navy OBAs worn by the navy crewmen were too bulky to go through the manway opening. The Portland fireman who eventually found the man was equipped with a breathing apparatus similar to a scuba diver's air bottle. He took the bottle off his back, passed it through the manway opening then went through himself. One thing was sure, the Portland firefighters were better equipped to rescue people.

I took a personal interest in this case. The lack of burning permits, phony fire alarm and who-fights-the-fire procedures had all been approved by the ship super. Training of the officer of the deck, who was not properly briefed, was the responsibility of the senior watch officer. Originally I had held both jobs, but those two fangs had been pulled by officers who were senior to me and a young daddy had died. That bothered me, yet there was nothing I could do.

In the weeks following the incident, the Portland fire department invited the repair department for a visit. A couple of division officers, some senior chiefs and I went over, but I don't recall the repair officer being there. During the visit, we discussed the incident with some officials and they recognized their need for shipboard firefighter training and asked for our help. We gladly arranged training sessions for their men.

My JAG investigation report contained only the requested findings of fact, which were very few. The rest, including the above, is just my opinion. My recommendations would have been numerous and although most would now be moot, one remains applicable: all JAG investigation reports should be classified confidential (because they could result in a court-martial) and go directly from the reporting officer to the Judge Advocate General. They should also all contain findings of fact, opinions and recommendations. In other words, if you want to know what's going on, listen to the troops.

Thank You

The Sperry overhaul package included new living and working areas on the ship. By early spring, work had progressed to the point where the crew moved back aboard ship, which now had a new multicolored crew's mess, a new crew's lounge, refurbished berthing areas, plus a fancy new wardroom with the best ambience of any I have been in.

When the repair department work was done and I was ready to start training, a lot of ship's work remained unfinished, especially in deck and engineering, so the repair officer came up with the idea of doing a refit on ourselves. Each department would submit work requests to the repair department; we would assign a ship super and do it up right. He told me he thought I could manage the training somehow.

Then, when the refit started, the repair officer went on a month's leave and I became the acting department head, so he got credit for the refit and I did the work. The troops in the repair department were good, so we managed to get some training done despite the added workload.

As acting repair officer, I had to be at any captain's mast involving repair department personnel and the next Friday I attended mast. The accused man was a second class petty officer in the radcon shop, whom I knew and liked. He was a good man who had recently married a lovely little redhead.

The master at arms force had found part of a marijuana joint on the deck behind his locker. That was the extent of the government's case. The man claimed he knew nothing about the matter and there was absolutely no evidence to the contrary. The man testified earnestly and frankly on his own behalf and his wife even came and testified that he never touched drugs. When it came time for my comments, I told the captain that he was a good man and that we had never had problems with him. The captain found him guilty and gave him two weeks' restriction with extra duty. I was dumbfounded. . . . *how do I get out of this chickenshit outfit? . . .*

The next weekend I was the command duty officer. It was a Sunday afternoon. The executive officer was on the beach, the captain was in San Diego, and visiting hours were in progress. I had been doing paperwork in the repair office and decided to stretch my legs. I walked out to the quarterdeck, checked in with the OD and nothing was happening, so I decided to make a tour of the ship. When I went by the new enlisted men's lounge, I poked my head in. Two sailors were sitting in easy chairs reading books, and on the couch, looking longingly at each other, were my restricted man and his new redheaded wife.

I motioned the restricted man out into the passageway. "I'm only going to say this once," I said. "My stateroom is number 314; it locks from the inside and I will be touring the ship for hours." His face lit up and he said, "Yes, Sir!"

I toured the ship, got involved with something in one of the repair shops, ate dinner in the wardroom, took the 8 o'clock reports and then, after visiting hours were long over, I went up to my stateroom. I found some crumpled-up tissue paper in my waste basket (shit-can) and on my desk a thank-you note, handwritten and signed by the little redheaded wife. It was one of the sweetest things I have ever read, just precious. While reading it, I got a satisfying feeling that a goal post was back where it belonged.

Chinese Fire Drill

Every evening, except Sundays and holidays, we held a fire drill for the duty section. It was a surprise, but it always came shortly after the evening meal and early enough to be over before the movie started in the crew's mess, which was about a thirty-minute window. The drills were timed from the moment the word of a fire was received at the quarterdeck until it was under attack by two fire hoses rigged to the scene. All Sperry fire drills went off like clockwork; the fire was attacked by two fire hoses in about four minutes flat, every time.

I remembered that the same fire drills on the Simon Lake had taken about eleven minutes and one in nine was exceptional. I knew the crew on the Sperry was good, but they couldn't be that much better than the men at site one, so I decided to check it out.

I soon found the reason; instead of opening the valve on the fire main and charging the fire hoses, they were simply rigging empty hoses to the scene. Something told me that was wrong. I had just finished a JAG investigation of a fire that killed a young daddy and had read the autopsy report. Then, too, I could feel Murphy's presence.

The next time I had the duty, I told the duty engineer officer, a senior chief petty officer who I knew had been an instructor at Firefighting School, that I wanted charged fire hoses on the drill that night. I detected a slight grin when I told him. That evening, it took the duty damage control party sixteen minutes to rig two charged fire hoses to the scene and they got water all over the place, so I had to hold up the movie until they cleaned it up.

My realistic fire drill accomplished three things. It put a black mark on our training records; it upset the damage control party and their leaders, the engineer officer and the damage control assistant (DCA); and I wound up on the executive officer's carpet. By now he was telling me the truth. "You can't do things like that; this is the new navy; you can't disrupt the movie; it upsets the men too much and the captain doesn't want us to make waves." . . . *do nothing, make no mistakes* . . . *boy is Murphy loving this* . . .

A short while later, our departure day arrived and we headed down the Willamette, into the Columbia and out to sea. As we passed under the St. John's Bridge, a contingent from Luigi's was waving and shouting at us and the captain thought it was an antiwar demonstration. I knew better, but didn't want to ruin his day. By the next day, we had crossed the Columbia bar and were about a hundred miles off the Oregon coast headed south. I was sitting in the repair office just after lunch when the DCA, a warrant officer, came in and asked, "Where do you want it?"

"Give me a clue."

"The fire drill"

"What about the fucking fire drill?"

He was upset, could see I was getting that way, calmed down and said, "The XO told me we're going to hold a fire drill your way, and wants to know where you want the fire."

I loved navy traditions, so there was only one answer, "the paint locker." The paint locker was a likely place for a fire to start, the classic location for a fire drill and a longstanding navy tradition. It would also appear that I was rolling over, although some might even interpret it as an insult: "Let's see if you can do an easy one." But I was in no mood to play games; and I really do love navy traditions.

They passed the word, "All hands man your battle stations," and rang the alarm for general quarters. A few minutes later they passed the word, "Fire in the paint locker! Fire in the paint locker!" and that was the part I was looking forward to. I just loved to hear traditional word passed on the 1MC and "Fire in the paint locker" was almost as good as "Now! Hear this . . .".

My battle station was officer-in-charge in the secondary damage control center, but we were just the backup. The firefighting was being managed by the DCA in damage control central. We would take over only if they were knocked out by enemy action, and since this was a drill, we simply monitored the situation.

We had sound-powered phone operators monitoring all the circuits and after a few minutes, we began overhearing reports from the other stations. Something was wrong. The paint locker was located on the boat deck aft of the pilot house, and when they opened the valve on an adjacent fire plug, there was no water pressure. . . . *now you know why I wanted charged fire hoses . . .*

Four minutes passed, sixteen minutes came and went and still there was no water on the fire. More time passed; people began to look at their watches and still nothing. I was surprised. No problem with the fire main system should be that hard to solve. It was a simple piping system consisting of some pumps that took a suction on the sea and discharged into fire mains routed throughout the ship. The fire pumps supplied the water pressure. There were valves at each fire plug and a few damage control valves located around the system, but that was about it. It was designed to be simple, accessible and resistant to battle damage.

The reports were baffling. They could find nothing wrong, yet after half an hour there was still no water on the fire and I started to get worried. We were on a ship that was over a hundred miles at sea and everyone knew that fire is the worst thing that can happen to a ship at sea and now we had no way to fight one. If this had been a real fire, men would be dying and everyone onboard knew it, so it was no longer amusing.

After an embarrassing forty-five minutes, they passed the word, "Secure from general quarters. Secure from fire drill." Apparently they had given up. I returned to the repair office and somehow managed to keep a straight face when I asked the repair officer what was wrong. "Stay out of it," he growled.

"They don't need your advice." . . . *they need help from somebody . . .*

The situation was worse than I imagined. According to the grapevine, the captain was livid, the executive officer was grim, and the engineer officer and DCA were bouncing around trying to find a problem with the fire main system. This meant they had effectively stopped fighting the fire as soon as they opened the valve on the fire main and got no water pressure and that they were not troubleshooting in a logical way or they would have found the problem already. They were obviously making emotional decisions.

Since my infamous fire drill in Portland was fresh in their minds, I guessed they might be thinking I had done something to the fire main system to cause this problem and had fixated on that. The repair officer's attitude indicated that I was at least under suspicion.

Virtually everyone on the ship knew the fire drill was for my benefit, which meant the DCA and his troops in the damage control party intended to put me in my place by attacking the fire in four minutes flat. But they failed miserably and the ship's crew was now acting like the cheering section in the Colosseum as Christians were thrown to the lions. To say the least, emotions were running high.

Time passed and more word began to filter out. They'd done a double valve lineup on the fire main the night before we left Swan Island, so they decided that nothing could be wrong there. They had four fire pumps running, so there had to be plenty of water pressure. They concluded that something really complicated had to be wrong.

On the other hand, the problem looked simple to me, but I had the advantage of thinking logically instead of emotionally. You always check the simple things first. A damage control valve was probably shut somewhere—there were only a few of them—so why didn't they just check them? Had it been a real fire, I would have spoken out come hell or high water, but under the circumstances, I watched silently as the drama continued hour after hour and the crew members, who had suddenly discovered they were Christians, kept score.

Three and a half hours later, when the ship would have been a burned-out hulk, they found the problem. A damage control valve that isolated the upper forward section of the fire main was shut. The valve was a rising-stem gate valve located in the disbursing office. When open, the rising stem interfered with the carriage return on a disbursing clerk's typewriter. He had shut the valve the morning we got underway from Swan Island and used the typewriter to fill out a request chit to take a plane to San Diego instead of riding the ship. His excuse? He was in a hurry and just forgot to reopen it.

Although shutting the valve was a court-martial offense which put the lives of every man onboard in jeopardy, the disbursing clerk didn't even go to captain's mast. This was the new navy and the captain didn't want to make waves. He wanted to make admiral.

InSurv Board

The day after the big fire drill fiasco, we got more bad news. Rivulets of oil were seen coming out of the stack and running down its side and it was soon determined that all eight main engines were affected. Apparently, during the overhaul the wrong-sized parts were installed or something was adjusted incorrectly or both. In any case, the symptom was oil out the exhaust.

I knew how to repair nuclear reactor plants and submarine auxiliary systems, but had no experience repairing big diesel engines. At the time the engines were overhauled, the repair officer was handling all the ship super duties so I was not familiar with the overhaul details which in retrospect was a big mistake on everyone's part, including mine. I later learned that there was a dispute about whether or not the engineering department had given the correct plans to the shipyard. Northwest Marine claimed they'd done everything in accordance with the plans they had received.

I knew that no one had been in charge in the engineering department during the yard period, so I was doubtful that they had checked anything. On the other hand, Northwest Marine made a living repairing civilian merchant ships, most of which have big diesel engines, so my bet was that engineering had dropped the ball. Of course, no one asked my opinion, so I decided to get under my desk; Murphy was running free, kicking ass and taking names.

We limped into San Diego and went into the nuclear submarine repair business. I was soon immersed in a new set of problems involving everything from work management to personnel. Our submarines had been without a mother for months and were crying for attention. They had long since run out of ship's plaques and all their stainless steel lockers were full, so they desperately needed more. It was a hectic time, most of which I spent going from one crisis to another. I never got to my in-basket until after liberty went down. The individual problems that I remember most were associated with the new men we were getting. They had all been introduced to the Navy under Admiral Zumwalt's new sensitive rules and they were quite a bunch.

One night when I was command duty officer, I got a call from the duty yeoman asking to get a temporary ID card signed so a man could go on liberty. It was 0200 and I had been asleep, so I told him to come up to my stateroom. By the time I had gotten up and put on my pants, there was a knock at my door. I opened it and a first class yeoman came in with some papers. A man was with him, so I motioned him in as well.

Before signing the ID, card I asked the yeoman, "Why does he need to go on liberty at this time of night? Can't this wait until morning?" Well, that was a mistake.

The man was a third class petty officer who had been in the Navy all of seven months. He had gone to nine weeks of boot camp in San Diego, then taken two weeks' boot leave. After his leave, he had returned to the Naval Training Center for a sixteen-week school. He graduated in the top ten percent of his class and was promptly promoted to third class petty officer. After graduating, he took another two weeks' leave, which left him with zero on the books. While on that leave, his baby had gotten sick, so he sent a telegram to the ship saying he was taking another two weeks' leave, which he didn't have. The ship fired back a telegram ordering him to report to the ship immediately, which he ignored, thinking the ship hadn't received his telegram.

About an hour before our meeting, the shore patrol had found him in the alley behind the YMCA in downtown San Diego talking to a known homosexual. They checked his ID card, which had been altered to show that he was over twenty-one and could drink, and destroyed it on the spot. They then brought him back to the ship.

Now, although he was two weeks absent without leave (AWOL), we couldn't hold him because he hadn't been to captain's mast yet and he wanted to go on liberty to be with his wife and child, right now.

The yeoman sensed my rising anger and whispered, "You've got to let him go; we don't have any choice."

I didn't say anything. I was flooded with memories of all I'd endured before I made third class petty officer, but the thing that kept me from losing it and breaking him into little bitty fucking pieces was the certain knowledge that he could never walk in my shoes. . . . *if it doesn't cost anything; it ain't worth anything* . . .

I signed the ID card, handed it to the man and asked, "What department are you going into?"

"Repair."

"Do you know who I am?"

"No."

"I'm the assistant repair officer."

He blanched, took his ID card and left. I never heard from him again, but when I checked with his division officer later, he said he was a good man. . . . *by what standard?* . . .

Shortly after we arrived in San Diego, the Navy Board of Inspection and Survey came aboard to investigate the problems with our main engines. It was going to cost a bundle of taxpayer money to repair them and the Navy was upset. The "InSurv Board," which was somewhat like the National Transportation Safety Board (NTSB) that investigates airplane crashes, was a group of highly qualified officers, who reported directly to the Chief of Naval Operations and had a lot of power. They were onboard to examine the main engines and talk to witnesses. The ship's list of witnesses did not include me because I was in repair, not engineering, and had nothing to do with the main engines. Besides, the last thing the captain wanted was me talking to the InSurv Board about our overhaul in Portland.

I was in the repair office going through my in-basket late one evening after liberty had gone down when a mustang lieutenant commander, whom I recognized as a member of the Insurv Board, walked in, poured a cup of coffee and sat down as if he owned the place. I looked up and realized that I was looking in the mirror. We were alone, but neither of us said a word. He sipped his coffee, leaned back in his chair and said, "You were here, Jerry; tell me what happened."

We had never been introduced, but the bastard had my number and knew it. I couldn't help smiling and didn't bother asking what he was talking about. I also had his number. I poured my own cup of coffee, organized my thoughts, then told him the whole story, chapter, verse, and line. After a few follow-up questions, he thanked me and left. We never formally introduced ourselves and to this day I don't know his name, but one thing was certain: the InSurv Board now knew which closet door to open and that's all you ever need.

I never said anything and am positive the grapevine didn't make a sound, but by now the captain had no doubt noticed that I wasn't helping advance his agenda and might even be standing in his way. My complaints about engineering while we were in the shipyard, the fire drills fiasco, the main engine failures and now the beans I'd spilled to the Insurv Board, which would create another mess for him, were becoming a pattern he couldn't ignore. All this negative publicity was shining an embarrassing light on him and making one thing crystal clear: if he was ever going to make admiral, he had to neuter Lieutenant Commander Hansen.

Snake Pit

Shortly after we got back to San Diego, my situation began to deteriorate rapidly. I was now confronted with a slightly different version of the problem I'd encountered on the Dixon, which I hadn't seen then, and, now that I was older and more experienced, still couldn't see. My division officers supported me one hundred percent and the repair department started doing good work right away, so repairing submarines wasn't the problem.

The problem—my problem—was the repair officer and the captain. The repair officer constantly wanted me to do things that wouldn't work or would hamper our ability to manage the department properly. Frankly, I don't know whether these ideas came from him or the captain. The captain's clear purpose in life was to make admiral and he was willing to expend any resource and have others pay any price to do it. He viewed me and the repair department as so much money in the bank to be spent on anything the squadron asked for: don't try to manage it, just do it. I knew the repair department was a finite resource and that the final destination of that path would be some serious problems.

Neither one had a clue how to repair nuclear submarines and should have let me manage the department workload and make them heros. But I was part of the problem, too. I didn't suffer fools easily. I probably should have learned by now to look the other way occasionally, but I was still operating the old-fashioned way; I was hell-bent on preventing problems in the first place, not fixing them after they broke.

On a more personal note, my marriage was on the rocks and taking its toll emotionally plus I was sinking into an unhealthy contempt for the new Zumwalt navy, along with many of my contemporaries at the time. The Navy had changed radically and it just wasn't the same great adventure anymore.

One afternoon I was getting last-minute reports from my division officers when the medical officer came in and asked to have a word. We were about finished, so I said, "Sure," and we walked out on the main deck and leaned against the rail. He asked me how things were going and if I was having any problems. His odd question put me on full alert and I asked, "What do you mean?"

He was a little hesitant at first then realized the conversation would go nowhere until he put his cards on the table. He told me never to repeat what he was about to say and, if asked, he would swear our conversation never took place. I said gravely, "Go on."

"There are some powerful people out to get you, Jerry. They wanted me to help but I refused . . . I wouldn't be part of it. They're going to set you up some way, get you angry, then send you to the psycho ward and bust you out of the Navy with a medical discharge." He added that he thought I was a good officer and would do what he could to help, then warned me to be on the alert for anything out of the ordinary. "Whatever you do, maintain your cool." I swallowed hard and thanked him. . . . *Jesus* . . .

Nothing out of the ordinary happened for about ten days. The repair officer hardly talked to me and things seemed to be going smoothly. Then late one afternoon, as I was about to leave for home, the repair officer popped into the office and said the executive officer wanted to see me. I went up to his stateroom, where both the new executive officer, who had just recently reported aboard, and the captain were waiting. My friend, the old executive officer, had by now been relieved and was back in Washington in the spook business and probably thanking his lucky stars.

The captain spoke up and told me he was going to give me an unofficial letter of reprimand.[33] He handed me the letter and told me to read it. I did. It was a series of untrue and unprovable accusations by unnamed individuals that was well designed to make anyone angry.

Because I had been forewarned and had dealt with real man-eating sharks before, I maintained my cool and zeroed in on their weakness. "Who are my accusers?" I asked. "The Constitution says I have a right to confront them."

They obviously had not anticipated that response because they got visibly angry, so I decided not to push it. "Is that all?" I asked.

It was and I left. I had dodged that bullet, but they clearly had a plan and were moving, so more would be coming. I felt vulnerable—no, it was worse than that—I was at nine on the panic scale. There would be something I couldn't deal with. I thought about getting a lawyer or carrying a tape recorder and a lot of other things went through my mind during a long, sleepless night.

The next morning, as I was walking up the gangway, the medical officer rushed down to meet me and said, "Listen, and don't ask questions. Go back to your car, go to Balboa, see this commander and do whatever he says." He handed me a slip of paper and hurried back up the gangway.

I went back down the gangway and up the pier to my car then drove straight to Balboa Naval Hospital. I located the building and commander on my note and introduced myself. I

---

[33] A black mark on your record that the captain doesn't need to prove is true and to which you have no recourse.

could see from the title on his door that he was in charge of the psychiatric ward. We sat down and he said, "Tell me what happened; start at the beginning."

I started with my first conversation with the medical officer and went on from there. He asked a few questions then said he wanted to put me in the ward for three days of evaluation. He explained that the Navy could do two things, prove I was crazy or prove I wasn't, and that I had to volunteer to take the test. I asked for his advice. He smiled, leaned forward and said, "Go to the ward."

The plan was to prove I was emotionally stable before the captain could take his shot at proving otherwise, and we were going to use the same judge. The only difference, and it was a big one, was that the test was now my idea and not the captain's.

They escorted me to the enlisted men's ward where I changed into blue pajamas. I knew it was against navy regulations to place officers in the same medical ward as enlisted men, but this was a test and apparently they were going at me from every direction.

It was a nice big airy ward with a single row of hospital beds down each side and a big aisle in the center with a corpsman station about halfway down, which included a room with reinforced glass all around it. There must have been twenty patients in the ward, mostly guys about nineteen, some walking around acting normally and some walking around like zombies with a freeze seal on their brain.

I noticed that the corpsmen spent their time talking to the men and the men who were better were doing the same thing. It appeared to be the custom or routine, so I started going around talking to the guys. You could be talking normally to a man one minute and a few minutes later they were putting him in a straight jacket or strapping him to his bunk. It was a very intense place and no unstable person could have handled it for three days and nights without going off the deep end, so it was an effective and brutal test.

Later that evening the corpsmen had a shift change or something—corpsmen always stand weird duties—and a lieutenant nurse came by. She talked to the corpsmen, looked over at me, then walked over and said, "Commander, what are you doing here? You shouldn't be here." . . . *part of the test* . . .

"You better check my chart."

She looked at my chart, then came back with a sweet smile and said, "We may discharge all these patients this weekend, but your ass is going to be here 'til Monday."

When she left, I went back to work: the corpsmen wanted me to help three patients go to the mess hall for dinner.

Taps was at 2200, so I went to bed. The day's stress had taken its toll and I was asleep almost immediately, but was awakened an hour later by the sound of a man screaming hysterically. Three big corpsmen were trying to control him. The significance of where I was suddenly hit me like a big flood of misery. Eventually my heart stopped pounding and I calmed down, but a jumble of thoughts kept me awake until about 0300. I lay there in the dimly lit ward. . . . *so Hansen . . . what now? . . .*

I wasn't worried about making it through the weekend; what bothered me was being there in the first place. Sappy as it sounds, I had always believed that I was doing something good for my country, but my devotion to duty had helped ruin my marriage, damage my children and caused me to miss a lot of sun and fun. The way I was looking at it, my navy, and by extension my country, had turned on me and this was the thanks I got. I was shaken and bitter and couldn't remember how long it had been since I'd walked out through the sagebrush and seen an Indian paint brush. I could handle any job and clean up any mess, but being forced to spend a weekend in a snake pit to keep from being thrown out of the Navy was where I drew the line.

Late Sunday afternoon a first class hospital corpsman came to the ward and asked me to come into the office. He shut the door, smiled and said, "Well, you're not crazy and we can prove it. Now, my job is to write up your evaluation; would you like to help?" I could tell by his demeanor that I was dealing with one of my own kind, so I said, "You're the expert; I'd like you to do it." When I read my evaluation, I did notice that he got one thing wrong. He said I wasn't even a little bit crazy, but it was a given that I had to be at least thirteen percent crazy to get in the submarine force.

They discharged patients in the morning, so I was in uniform and ready to go early Monday morning. My old friend, the lieutenant nurse, came in and said, "Get out of here, Commander; you can still make breakfast in the wardroom." That was one of the nicest things a woman has ever said to me. I made it to the Sperry in time for breakfast and when I went into the wardroom, the repair officer happened to walk in just behind me. When he saw me, his face went white and he said, "What are you doing here?!!"

"I work here."

"Aren't you supposed to be in the hospital?"

"They kicked me out."

He turned on his heel and literally ran toward the captain's cabin. Whatever their plan was, my presence back on the ship was clearly unexpected. They didn't have me admitted to the hospital, so that option was now gone and I was on the loose. They had to assume that I knew they were out to get me and might even be contemplating legal action. They probably wouldn't give up now but would finish it somehow. I assumed they would lay low, working on an alternate plan, and would probably cover every possibility except one, which was what I was counting on. What they couldn't know was that my heart was broken and my fighting days were over.

My plan was simple and based on the belief that none of them would bother to check my service record, look at the calender or read *Navy Times*. I was eligible to retire right then, and to make matters worse for them, a new law required that I be retired before October 1, 1975, or lose about sixty dollars of retirement pay each month for the rest of my life.

I waited for my next duty day as command duty officer. Men who stood that duty were part of the personnel reliability program and had a pink cover over their service records, which required that any hint of abnormal behavior on the man's part be reported to a responsible authority immediately. Men in that program had access to the nuclear weapons and were not supposed to be unstable in any way. I wanted to stand that duty one more time for my own benefit. And, in a way, I was challenging my commanding officer to do something about it.

The morning after I finished my CDO duties and was relieved, I went to the ship's office and gave the admin officer a letter addressed to the Secretary of the Navy requesting that I be retired from the Navy. As they say, I put my papers in.

The admin officer confided to me later that when he gave my letter to the executive officer, he read it, crumpled it up and threw it in the shit-can without saying a word. He told me that he had retrieved the letter, smoothed it out on the desk and said, "XO, you have to let him go; they changed the law and he must be retired before 1 October and since he's an officer, we have to retire him by 1 September."

It was almost the middle of July and they were in a vise. My sudden departure couldn't be hidden from the squadron commander; none of the division officers were qualified to do my job, and it would take the detailer until January to get a relief.

I kept counting. On August 1, I went up to the executive officer and told him I wanted to be relieved of all military duties for my last month onboard, in accordance with Sperry tradition.

"I'll tell the senior watch officer," he said.

A few days later, the repair officer asked me when I would like the ship to hold my retirement party.

"You bastards tried to feed me to the sharks and now you want to give me a fucking party?! Tell your captain to shove it up his ass! I won't go if they have one!"

There was no retirement party, but I signed and dated my letter to the Secretary of the Navy on July 14, 1975, and the copy in my service record is unsigned and dated July 24, 1975, so they were busy doing something for ten days.

On September 1, 1975, I signed the paperwork, walked back to the quarterdeck, saluted the Colors and they passed the word, "Lieutenant Commander Hansen departing."

My navy career was over.

EPILOGUE

A few months after I retired, I got a letter from the officer who had eventually taken my job as assistant repair officer on the Sperry, a mustang lieutenant, an ex-naval reactors rep and a personal friend. He thanked me for the management system I'd set up and said he'd spread the word far and wide that it was the best system he'd ever seen and wouldn't change a thing. According to the grapevine, the captain who tried to feed me to the sharks didn't make admiral, so I was generally pleased with myself and the status of my reputation.

About ten years later, the Dixon came into Portland for a liberty call. When she arrived, I went down to the dock, told the officer of the deck that I was a plank owner and asked to see the repair officer. I wanted to see how the nuclear submarine repair business was making out.

The repair officer, a commander, met me at the quarterdeck and escorted me up to see the captain, a four striper. I was surprised to learn that my reputation had preceded me. They knew who I was and sat me down and picked my brain for two solid hours. Most of my management system had survived, but parts had fallen by the wayside and by now no one knew why I did this or that. I filled them in and they took notes, mostly in the area of organizing nuclear repair work. Afterward, the repair officer and I toured the repair spaces, looked over the physical plant and discussed it in some detail. Finally, we spent a couple of hours in the repair office discussing things then ate dinner in the wardroom.

While I was visiting the ship, they were still looking for the duty driver, so not much had changed. They did have a two hundred more sailors (female) in the repair department, but averaged the same number of submarines in refit and production man-hours per day, so the taxpayers were now paying a third more for the same work, but I guess social engineering is almost as important as sensitivity training. Other than that, I have had very little contact with the Navy.

My first civilian job was as a senior planner at FMC Corporation in Portland, Oregon, where they were building some medium-sized oil tankers for Chevron. When I started work, they had one ship about ready for sea trails and two more under construction and the situation was similar to the one on the Simon Lake when I became the planning officer: they had engineering and production departments, but were just now setting up a planning department. Had I learned about the job a few days earlier, I would have been hired as the planning officer.

My first task was to write division operating instructions on such things as a work-order system, material-identification system and a sea trial manual. When I turned them in to the planning manager, he asked what I thought of the operation. I told him the system and instructions would work, but that their tanker project wouldn't work out. He looked startled and asked why. I told him they were already in trouble and asked, "Who was the dumb bastard who thought you could build ships without a planning department?"

"The big guy."

I next worked for two different firms in Portland as a marine surveyor, a job associated with marine insurance. The first firm, which did classification surveying, always represented the steamship company. The second firm, which specialized in cargo surveys, always worked for the cargo interests.

Classification surveying involved the details of ship construction and repair and certifying a ship's seaworthiness. Cargo surveying was heavily involved with the gory details of marine insurance and settling claims.

Finally, I hung out my own shingle and started doing cargo surveys for various steamship companies, which hired me as an independent third party to determine the cause and extent of damage to marine cargo after a casualty. I loved the job: the pay was good and all I had to do was go from one crowd-pleasing disaster to another examining things, taking photographs and measurements, obtaining samples and then writing a report outlining my findings, which was used by an adjustor to settle the claims.

Angelina and I got divorced a year or so after I retired and not long after that I went on an emotional roller coaster for several years. Among other things, I learned that you can never actually divorce your children's mother. I went through two short marriages, a few long-term relationships and spent some time in singles bars. I saw a lot and learned a lot, but won't bore you with any of it.

When the dust settled, I was retired, single and living on my navy retirement pay. I was farming two-thirds of an acre on the bank of the Alsea River, sixteen miles up Highway 34 from Waldport on the Oregon coast. I was trying to sell the place and then move back to Portland. One Friday night I happened to stop in the lounge at the Bayshore Inn in Waldport. My friends Mac and Judy were there with a guest.

Her name was Marleeta but everyone called her Marty. She and Judy had been cheerleaders together in high school, where she and Mac had been voted "the two most talkative students" in their class of thirty-three students. Marty had spent time working in the foreign service at various posts including the American Embassy in Saigon during the Tet Offensive, and had recently returned from a tour at our embassy in Beijing, China. She had moved up from the San Francisco Bay area a month before and was now living in Waldport and writing a mystery novel set in China. She was forty-nine years old and had never been married nor had children. She was a natural redhead with a degree from Stanford who had once ridden an East German motorcycle through Yugoslavia by herself so she could write a magazine article about it. . . . *strange stuff . . .*

Judy called me over and introduced us. I sat down and we engaged in small talk. Before the night was over, we had danced several times and I had discovered that she liked Scotch, tolerated country music and was deeply interested when I told her that I could dazzle the average housewife with my cooking. I also got her phone number, but she told me not to call before the next Thursday at the earliest, because she was very busy with her book. . . . *lucky if I call by next Friday . . .*

I met Marty on a Friday night before the Sunday that was my fifty-ninth birthday, which I expected to spend alone. Well, about nine o'clock Sunday morning, she called and said that her cat had gone out looking for her on Friday night and had been run over and killed. She had spent all day Saturday crying and burying him and needed some company. . . . *that's better than the dog ate my homework . . .*

I suggested that we go to the Adobe in Yachats, sit in the lounge, watch the breakers, have a couple of drinks, stay for dinner and get her mind off things.

"And, you can tell me how a nuclear reactor works," she said. And, that's what we did. It turned out that Marty is a devoted cat person and her all-time favorite cat, Normie, really had been run over and it really had devastated her.

We started dating, which was more like a collision with lots of sparks and loud noises, but things progressed rapidly. We started living together, paid off the place with her savings, landed a new double-wide mobile home and set up housekeeping—to the complete dismay of all our friends, who were making hard-money bets that our relationship wouldn't last three weeks, tops.

I am Marty's mountain man, although she won't give me the satisfaction of calling me that. She said that what appealed most about me was that when I started a job, I also finished it, cleaned up the area and put my tools away. Her previous boyfriends had to have at least a master's degree, but apparently they couldn't do things. She claims that what really landed her was my clean pickup, blue denim jacket, meticulous garden and chickens.

Marty is my soul mate and with her I found real happiness. She is pure gold inside and the first person I ever trusted completely. She is a farm girl at heart and a true earth muffin who bakes whole wheat bread from her own freshly milled flour and even published a book on the subject called *Flour Power*. We have now been married thirteen years and my kids just love her, especially my Susan, who now has a buffer when dealing with me. Marty says I am "high maintenance," but that I filled a big empty place in her, all the way to the brim. I will say the same thing about her.

Shortly after Marty and I started living together, the stake president of the local Mormon Church called and asked how I was doing. Had I sold my place yet? I told him that I had met a new lady and was going to stay and probably continue to be a black mark on his attendance records. (I had not attended church since boot camp.) A few days later, he called again and said he wanted to talk to me about that woman I was living with.

"I don't think so," I said and slammed the phone down.

A few days later two men in dark suits hand delivered a letter ordering me to the church for a disciplinary hearing. I tore the letter into little bitty pieces and threw it in the shit-can. I had no doubt done things in my life to warrant that action, but nothing Marty and I had done was illegal, immoral or offended God in any way. A couple of weeks later I got a certified letter informing me that I had been excommunicated from the Church of Jesus Christ of Latter Day Saints.

My navy career left scars that I didn't recognize for many years. On a recent visit to my son, Brian, in San Diego, we went to the navy commissary and behind us in the checkout line was a retired master chief petty officer and his wife. We got to chatting and comparing notes and the chief's wife said that the only thing she didn't like about retirement was her husband's nightmares. One thing led to another and we discovered that the chief and I were having the same nightmare. In the dreams we found ourselves back on active duty in the Navy with some kind of uniform problem. I'd be back as planning officer with only a first class radioman uniform to wear or one of a hundred variations with the same theme. Both wives were waking us up to stop our jerking and apparently frightening moans. The chief's wife said she had looked into the matter and learned that it was post traumatic stress syndrome. I don't know about him, but I'm still having those dreams.

Finally, I want to speak directly to my grandchildren, for whom I originally started writing down the stories in this book. If you ever want to get a sense of who your grandfather really was, go to San Juan County sometime in the early spring. Walk out through the sagebrush and look for an Indian paint brush. You will surely find one, and if you are lucky, you will see a mountain bluebird.

Then you will know me.

ORDER FORM

YES, I want ___ copy[ies] of **Bears, Skunks & Wildcats,** by **Gerald P. Hansen (ISBN 0970540124) at $16.95.**

My check or money order payable to *Jermar Press* for $_____ is enclosed.

Name _____

Organization/Company (if applicable)

_____

Address_____

City/State/Zip_____

Phone/e-mail (optional) _____

Please return to:
Jermar Press
1790 N. W. Grandview Dr.
Albany, OR 97321-9695 USA

JERMAR
❖ PRESS

http://www.jermarpress.com